BIODIVERSITY CONSERVATION AND WILDLIFE TOURISM

BIODIVERSITY CONSERVATION AND WILDLIFE TOURISM

By
Taj Rawat
M.A. (Sociology)
PG Diploma (Information Management & Public Relations)
President
Mountain Research Foundation
Dehradun (Uttaranchal)
(India)

DPH
DISCOVERY PUBLISHING HOUSE PVT. LTD.
NEW DELHI-110 002

Published by:
Tilak Wasan

DISCOVERY PUBLISHING HOUSE PVT. LTD.
4383/4A, Ansari Road, Darya Ganj
New Delhi-110 002 (India)
Phone : +91-11-23279245, 43596064-65
Fax : +91-11-23253475
E-mail : parul.wasan@gmail.com
discoverypublishinghouse@gmail.com
web : www.discoverypublishinggroup.com

***First Edition:* 2012**
ISBN: 978-81-8356-754-1

Biodiversity Conservation and Wildlife Tourism

Printed at:
Shree Balaji Art Press
Delhi

Preface

The forests and the wildlands of the world are disappearing at an alarming rate. It is estimated that two third of the original forests of the world have been lost in the past one century. Once covering 14 per cent area of the earth's land surface now they are left to 6 per cent which will disappear in next 40 years.

It is estimated that 137 plants, animals and insects species are lost every day due to the loss of rain forests. This is equal to 50,000 species every year. At present, 121 important drugs sold worldwide come from the rain forests. The Amazonia contains two third of the world's rain forests covering an area of 3.5 million km^2. This includes the countries Brazil, Colombia, Peru, Venezuela, Equador, Bolivia, Guyana, French Guyana and Surinam. All the above countries are facing continuous deforestation and two third of the forests there have been cleared in the last sixty years. Deforestation in Brazilian Amazon is increasing sharply as 27 per cent forests were cleared in 1978 (16,800 square km.). Since 1972, 5,32068 square km. 13.3 per cent of the entire Amazon region has been lost. These figures may lack some square kilometers as 6 hectares of land do not appear within the range of satellite camera. It also misses 10,000 to 15,000 square kilometers forest land destroyed by the vehicles and saw machines of logging crew. It is estimated that by now 20 per cent of the rainforests of Amazonia has been cleared for timber, agriculture, road and housing, for grazing land, ranches, and farm houses. In 1987, 204,000 square km. rainforest were burnt to clear for agriculture. In 1988, 1,21,000 square km. was burnt for agriculture of which 48,000 square km. was virgin rainforests.

The wildlife is badly disturbed by the continuous felling of rainforests of Brazil. There were more than 3000 woolly spider monkeys in the rainforests of Brazil but only100 are left now. Several species of anteater, two species of sloths, two species of armadillos, 13 species of primates, Emperor tamar, woolly monkey, Jaguar, ocelot, bush dog, and North Andean Huemul, 1500 species of birds, Andean condor, harpy eagle and hoatzin are found in the Amazonia and will become almost endangered. The black caiman and spectacled caiman and bear also found in Amazon wilderness. One fifth of the bird species of the world are found in the Amazon forests.

The rain forests of Congo, Gabon, Cameroon and Zaire are disappearing sharply. The mountain Gorillas are found in Congo, Rwanda and Uganda rainforests but these are being cleared for agriculture and timber. The Pigmy chimpanzees in Congo, Orangutan in Sumatra rainforests have become an endangered species now as this is the last generation of the monkeys without tails. The people visit these places just to see these amazing animals. The National Parks in these countries are doing well in wildlife tourism. But the rain forests in South East Asia are not safe at all. Borneo, Java, Sumatra, Papua New Guinea have lost their primary rain forests and rest are on the verge of destruction.

The mountain forests are a great storehouse of wildfruits, nuts, berries and seeds. The Caucasus, Caparthians and a few other parts of Southern Europe have some of the species of wild fruits and nuts. Among them are wild pears, apples, plums, pistachio, pomegranate, fig, wild wheat and other food plants that no longer survive in the plains. The Sierra de Manantlan (9,449 feet) in Mexico have some wild species of Maize.

Once the juniper (Archa) forests that covered the Tien Shan and Pamir Alai in Kyrgyzstan and Kazakshstan have been wiped out. Of the 20,000 km^2 forests in Soviet Central Asia, there are only 4,600 km^2 juniper forests now.

Since the 1952, the Mount Everest, more than 500 expeditions have scaled the mountain. Each time 5-10 tonnes of equipment is needed of which one third is left behind while coming down. This has made Mount Everest a dumping ground of pollution. The other peaks are also facing a dump of garbage. There is a great need to clean the garbage and protect the mountains from over trekking and pollution.

Some countries have done well on wildlife tourism in the world. Among them are: British Columbia (Canada), Amazonia (Colombia, Peru and Brazil), The Andes mountains, Virunga National Park, Garamba National Park (Congo), Hornbill Sanctuary Park, (Thailand) Orangutan Sanctuary (Sumatra), Java, Borneo, Papua New Guinea and Hornbill Sanctuary in Philippines are among the best wildlife Parks in the world.

The Kruger National Park in South Africa is drawing maximum tourists from all parts of the world. There are several wild animals in this park i.e. lions, elephants, ziraffe, zebra, bears, deers, stagdeers, impala deers, rhinos, buffalows, wildebeests, bisons, leopards, tigers and several species of primates and wildboars. A large number of small mammals are also found in the park. The reptiles, wild birds and orthopoda spineless animals are found in large numbers. The tourists, explorers and Safari Park lovers come to enjoy life in the National Kruger Park in South Africa.

At present, there are 30 new bio-diversity hotspots in the world which are on the verge of extinction. There are some 60 old bio-diversity hotspots in the world which are not maintained properly by the concerned governments and park authorities. These parks and protected bio-diversity hotspots are drawing millions of tourists every year but their maintenance is not good in proportion to their income. This is a very sad experience.

Some poor countries are killing and trading the remains of wild animals. Extreme poverty, unemployment, illiteracy and crime has led them to the smuggling of elephant bones, leopard skins and bones, rhino's horns and skins and several skins of monkeys as these item fetch them 1,00,000 US$ in the international market. It is estimated that every year 45,000 elephants are killed in African continent for the tusks which have a large demand in China, Japan and Western Market. The Rhinos are killed for their horns and skin. As 2000-3060 rhinos are killed every year from Africa and Asia. 70,0000 wildbirds, including 5,00,000 parrots all over the world, 20 percent among them come from South East Asia. Several millions of butterflies and insects from SouthEast Asia are illegally smuggled to other parts of the world. Besides this 50000 spotted cats from South America and Central Africa are exported illegally to other parts of the world including western countries. The monkeys and Apes are also being exported to some wealthy countries and rich business houses. 60,000 Apes from Central Africa and South East Asia are exported every year to some countries. Such illegal activities have badly ruined wildlife all over the world.

In India the Kings and British Army Officers killed tigers. In1939, there were 20,000 to 30,000 Tigers in Indian forests. In 1972, there were only 1,827 tigers in the country. Maharaja of Sarguja had a record of killing 1,150 tigers in his lifetime. In 1981, there were 4,80,000 elephants in East Africa and the number has been reduced to 100,000 because of illegal ivory trade.

The Oceans are facing scarcity of sea animals in different parts of the globe. In1933, 30,000 whales were killed for food in USA and other countries. In 1960's the number rose to higher and higher. In 1962, 67000 whales were killed and by 1972, 40,000 whales were killed every year. According to a scientific estimation 1000 blue whales, 4000 hump back whales remain in Atlantic waters. Before whaling begin, there were 250000 blue whales, 30000 hump back and 300000 fin whales in the oceans. Now, the number of fin whales is 4,000. Some oceans are now without whales.

The bio-diversity hotspots in the world can be converted into the largest wilderness or National Parks just to protect the precious species there. The rich-biodiversity hotspots have been explained there in the book. Besides, the bio-diversity and wildlife tourism, national parks and wildlife management, wilderness tourism in the world, wildlife tourism in India, extinction of bio-diversity in some parts of the world is a matter of concern to all. The bio-diversity all over the world should be protected by providing modern methods of surveillance. This has been effective in most of the national parks of the world.

The bio-diversity should be protected and utilized for the human recreation in the form of wildlife parks just to encourage tourism in developing countries where wildlife is still in an excellent state.

The book is a master piece in "Bio-diversity Conservation and Wildlife Tourism and has given a comprehensive account on the subject explaining the extinction of wildlife in various parts of the world.

In this book the bio-diversity of the world has been studied from every angle and has been made conducive to the needs of students of environment and wildlife tourism. The most important thing is that the emphasis has been given on nature and bio-diversity conservation and its positive utilization for wildlife tourism the world over.

The book is written for the students of environmental studies and wildlife tourism with international perspectives. The book is useful to writers, journalists, environmentalists, volunteers, wild life personnels and students of environment, ecology, nature tourism and tourism. The author has done a marvellous job by writing this book on bio-diversity and tourism presenting all the information in a nutshell. The book is a milestone in wildlife tourism in itself.

• **Dr. J.M.S. Negi**
Professor
Tourism Management,
National Advisor, Vasant Kunj,
New Delhi-110 067

Author's Write ....

Protection of wildlife and using it for the purpose of tourism is an excellent idea and some of the countries of the world are making a great advantage of it. The countries which are making huge profits in wildlife tourism, wilderness tourism and nature tourism are British Columbia (Canada), Manu Naional Park (Peru), the Amazon National Park (Brazil), Amazonia Wilderness (Brazil, Columbia, Equador, Peru, Venezuela, Guyana, Surinam, French Guyana and Bolivia), and some of the Central African countries which are bio-diversity hotspots are doing well in wildlife tourism. South Africa is the leader of National Parks which earns maximum revenue from its national parks, mainly from the Kruger National Park which is spread upto 25,000 square kilometers. This park is called tourists paradise where more than 5 million tourists visit every year.

British Columbia is a world leader in Wilderness Tourism. The State earns US$9.1 billion every year and provides direct employment to1,17,000 citizens. Also 20,000 indirect jobs. In Australia, the Great Barrier Coral Reef has become a great source of income and is earning more than 5 billion Australian dollars every year.

Spain is making huge profits through its wild lands, islands and natural areas. A country with 40 million population attracts 50 millions tourists from far and near every year.

In South East Asia, India has achieved a lot from Rajaji National Park, Kaziranga National Park, Ranthambhaur Tiger Sanctuary, the Great Himalayan National Park, Kullu and several other national parks in the country which are getting more than 6 million foreign tourists every year. This number could reach to 12million if there were proper stay points near the boundary of the national parks.

Thailand's Hornbill Park, Gunug Leuser National Park, Indonesia are receiving an excellent number of tourists from the foreign countries.

Swiss Alps National Park, Switzerland is the best managed and maintained park in the world. The park draws millions of tourists every year. Reason to draw the maximum tourists is that there are hotels, restaurants, stay points and libraries at the boundary gates of the park. The tourists are rich and royal and stay in the two beautiful hotels near the park. This provides better relaxation facilities for the excellent income group tourists and for some days, they stay in the hotels and observe the beauty and the beast of the swiss Alps. Some western countries have constructed hotels, restaurants near the wildlife parks just to attract more tourists in the country This has matched the needs and requirement of the tourists visiting the parks and wildlife sanctuaries.

In South African National Parks, there are hotels, restaurants and recreation clubs inside the wilderness and wildlife parks. The Kruger National Park is such well equipped park in the world which collects a maximum numbers of tourists. This park has become economic backbone of South Africa besides other industries.

There are fifteen chapters in the book explained systematically. 1. What is Bio-diverty! 2. Reasons of Extinction of Biodiversity, 3. Bio-diversity of India, 4. Bio-diversity of the World, 5. Bio-diversity of the Oceans, 6. Bio-diversity of the Rain Forests, 7. Conservation of Bio-diversity, 8. Bio-diversity and Wildlife Tourism, 9. Bio-diversity Hotspots in the World, 10. National Parks and Wildlife Management, 11. Wildlife Tourism in the World, 12. Wilderness Tourism in the World, 13. Importance of Wildlife Tourism, 14. Wildlife Tourism in India, (15) Wild Birds and Tourism. Every chapter contains the facts and figures related to the state of wildlife, tourism and conservation efforts by the concerned governments. At the end of the book there are some indexes explaining the tourism vocabulary, proper observation mentioned in the book and references related to ecology, environment, bio-diversity conservation, nature tourism, national parks and their proper management to encourage wildlife tourism in the country has been explained with comprehensive reports.

The book has been written for the students of higher education in ecology and wildlife tourism in the country. The textual material is given studying various angles of environment, wildlife and tourism which provides all the information regarding the most beautiful parks of the world which have established a record in wild life tourism.

I think the book itself is a milestone in bio-diversity conservation and wildlife tourism. All the suggestions to improve the quality and standard of the book are always welcomed.

• **Taj Rawat**
Mountain Research Foundation,
Dehradun, Uttaranchal

Contents

1

What is Bio-diversity?

The Importance of Bio-diversity : Biological diversity is known as bio-diversity. A large number of different species of animals, trees and plants which make a balanced environment in the nature is known as bio-diversity. There are several bio-diversity hotspots in the world known for their rich wildlife and plant species. Bio-diversity plays an important role in our life as it indicates the balance of our environment to a great extent. The presence of living animals and plant species in a region is known as the bio-diversity of that region. The biodiversity includes all living animals and plants including the water animals in that area. The whole eco-system contains a rich bio-diversity in that region.

There is always some geo-physical and climatic change over this planet. Besides, some natural calamities or destructive changes occur on the planet like earth quakes, volcanoes, landslides, floods and the events of cloud bursts. The great reptiles like Dinosaurs, Tripanosaurs and several other species both herbivores and carnivores have disappeared from the earth. The carnivores (flesh eaters) were the most dangerous and on some occasion killed the herbivoures in the forests. That was the most fearsome age of the wild animals on this planet. There were always some changes in the nature of wild animals and plants after a long period.

In the same way in the past four billion years, there were several climatic and environmental changes over this earth. During this process of change several species of wild animals and plants were completely vanished away. Among these are the large mammoth elephants, horses, wild bulls, buffalos, birds, giant ferntrees are not alive now. They all have disappeared because of global warming and sudden consequent changes in the environment. Some 40 million years ago a meteorite from the outer space fell over the earth in South America and this created a lot of energy and dust clouds over the earth. This had caused the global warming forming hot fuming, dusty clouds, covering the sky into darkness.

This made the earth more hotter. This hot temperature was not tolerable to most of the animal' and plant species including dinosaurs and ferns. As a result they died instantly. This was the major reason for the death of dinosaurs over this earth just after the explosion of meteorite. It is estimated that the size of meteorite which exploded over the earth was around ten kilometers square. The whole environment was full of hot clouds of dust and gases. The plants, animals, insects and reptiles of that age vanished away after the heat produced through the striking of meteorite over the earth.

After two billion years, the earth went through several changes. Like rise in temperature, the oceans became hotter and after sometime, there was cold age (Ice Age) on the earth. The animals and plants which were not capable to adjust the climate also died instantly. In this process of warming and cooling of the earth several species of plants and animals died and disappeared away forever. This was a great ecological change.

In the early stages the oceans were warmer. In some parts of the oceans, there was no life at all as the temperature rose up to 60°C. The huge animals died instantly including the bacteria's and coral polyps. In the later 20,000 to 8,000 years the temperature of the oceans decreased gradually and the oceans once again became full of life.

The coral reefs of Australia came into existence 20,000 years ago. Although the coral reef creation process continues, in the warmer tropical ocean. But there are some coral reefs which came into existence more than 20,000 years ago.

It is estimated that 4.5 billion years ago when this earth came into existence, several unicellular animals and plants came into existence. Once there was a vast kingdom of huge trees, plants and animals over this earth. Some of them vanished away because of sudden climatic change, warming of the earth and ocean and sudden initiation of Ice Age.

These four billion years of the creation of earth : several animals and plants came into existence and most of them disappeared because of geo-physical changes and the environment of the earth.

It is estimated that one third of the bio-diversity was lost in every one billion years of the existence of this earth. As a result there was a lot of imbalance between wild life and the plant kingdom.

The increasing global warming, sudden climatic changes, rise in the water level of oceans is a symbol of destruction of the ecosystems and the bio-diversity.

There is a great change in the climatic and ecological patterns of this planet in every one lakh years. Due to different geo-physical changes there was a sudden climatic change over this earth in every one million years.

After the formation of earth, there were some devastating changes on the surface of earth. These changes were into the forms of volcanoes, earthquakes, Tsunamis, and tectonic changes between various plates under the earth. Besides these there are some climatic and environmental changes over the earth.

Since 1800, there was continuous deforestation all over the world. In some countries two third of the forests were completely vanished away. This has reduced the green cover over the earth. As a result there was continuous drought, flood, soil erosion, landslide, lapses of water sources in the first quarters of 20th century. Some 30 percent forests were cleared up for agriculture, urbanization, construction of roads and housing for the rural poors.

In the 1940s some of the original forests were completely disappeared from the industrialised countries. The global warming began only when a large percentage of forests were completely destroyed from this earth. Nearly, 40 percent of rain forests have been destroyed in various countries. This has badly changed the environment of the world and this process has given way to the global warming which has resulted into the extinction of a part of bio-diversity from this earth.

Despite educational and social awareness, some of the contractors and timber merchants were mercilessly felling the trees from the forests which once were very much useful to environmental sustenance and the very basis of the survival for several forest communities in India as well as abroad.

The tropical rain forests are still being exploited by some timber companies of the world. These forests shall be continuously exploited in the name of "Bio-diversity and Business" a slogan given by some handful countries which alone want to exploit all the forest wealth of developing countries through their timber trade. Quick money through quick destruction of the forests and bio-diversity.

There were some valuable plants and animals species over this earth which have been disappeared before we could establish some research work on them.

The question arises that how much bio-diversity is safe in this planet as a large portion of it has already been disappeared without knowing their specific qualities. This has been a biggest challenge to the biologists who had been engaged into their systematic studies. Some plants have been disappeared without knowing their proper classification, identification and medicinal values.

The global warming has destroyed the mountain top vegetation from the green mountains of the world. The plants and herbs have been disappeared at the mountain tops and the plants from lower heights have come up to take their place. This has shown in whole Himalayan region, Alps in Europe, Kenia highland mountains and Rockies in USA and Andes in South America. The sudden changes in the environment has shown clear indications that 30 percent of plants and animal species have been vanished away from the earth.

The real phase of global warming began in 1970s when there was no sufficient rain in the Indian Himalayan region and most of the part of the earth remained rainless. This was a big setback to our forests, agriculture and water sources. Particularly, the mountain region of the Himalayas had to remain under the shadow of dry rain. This was a big set back to our farmers whose agricultural land was depend on the monsoon rain.

The migration from the rural regions of the mountains continues to the metropolis and small towns as most of their agricultural land remained high and dry.

The crops in the fields dried up and the production almost remained nill. This was enough to stir the sentiments of the farmers who were emotionally attached to their agriculture. The agriculture provided them full confidence, year round employment and attachment to their culture and tradition.

The water sources also dried up. The water levels in the rivers reduced to one tenth. This had hurt most of the mountain dwellers and they finally decided to settle down in the metropolitans or small towns. A large number of them settled down is Delhi, Bombay, Rishikesh, Dehradun,

Ghaziabad and Faridabad. Only 10 percent of people old and resourceless remained back in the villages.

In this way, the real migration began in the 1970s and 1980s when there was no rain at all and the temperature rose higher than before.

If there is no water, no food, then who would like to stay back in the villages. In comparison cities provide better employment and educational facilities for the young aspirants. Technical and engineering education provide better opportunities, for jobs to younger generation.

Migration is more painful : When the farmers leave their traditional land behind and settle down in other parts of the country the migration process is quite painful. The people all the time remember their traditional agricultural land, village forests, rural setting and other natural lands where their forefathers had lived for centuries. And in the houses they had played up and grown up in the lap of mother nature. The streams, rivulets and water falls are the witness of their great affection to their motherland.

The river valleys agricultural lands are quite fertile and always produced the foodgrains and vegetables of their expectation. The water level in the rivers reduced gradually and in the years ahead the crop did not rose according to their expectations. The highland agriculture almost dried up while the river valley crop was depend on river water and it was always in good state. There was no rainfall at the proper time and the moisture of the mountain agriculture dried up quickly. It was very difficult to grow main crops and vegetables in the mountains. They were emotionally attached to their houses, agricultural lands, orchards, rivers, mountains and valleys. They migrated to the plains of Dehradun to educate their children and make their career well in engineering, medical, teaching and forestry. After spending more than 25 years in Dehradun and other parts of the country, they never forget to visit their homeland twice in a year on the occasion of Pooja celebration, Holi, Diwali, Raksha Bandhan, Shivratri, Navratri, and worshipping their Gods and Goddesses. Some of the families could not forget their homeland. Some of them stayed back in villages. Some of them did not come back, but always remained in touch with their Kith and Kin in the villages.

Loss of cultural identity : After settling down in plains of Terai from their mountain ancerstral lands, they did not feel good in the plains of Terai, although the land was fertile and gave them an excellent crop. The ancestral agricultural lands, orchards and houses were much more lovable to them rather than newly bought land in the Terai regions. The people from different cultural background lived there and at the first instance it was quite difficult to cop-up with them. The mountain people remained, honest and sincere in their attempts and established their empires through their hard and sustaining work. To protect their mountain identity was prime motive for the mountain people.

The best qualities they displayed was to establish honesty, sincerety, and faithfulness among various communities and exhibit communal harmony and goodwill among various groups working in the different field of life.

There are people from various cultural backgrounds which live in peace and harmony. Among them are Sikhs, Punjabis, Nepalis and people from Uttar Pradesh and Terai. The Bogsha and Mahara are the original people of the Terais but the people from other communities snatched away their land and they were thrown to the margin. The Bogsha's and Mahara's are the most backward people of the terai and live a nomadic life. They survive on basket weaving, carpentry, box making, and masonry work. They are the poorest, aborigines and ancient tribes of the Terai region who once had largest chunks of lands. The life of Bogsha is full of misery and are almost secluded in modern society. They have not seen progress or development.

Impact on Culture

When some people from a community migrates to a new place, there is loss of culture. The other dominant communities who have already dominated the area for several decades have played a major role in influencing the people from other cultural backgrounds. In this way, the newly migrated community is easily influenced by the religions entities of other people and are attracted in large numbers. In this process they forget their own cultural identities and places of worships. Their cultural idenfity is marginalised and sometime they completely forget or lose their own cultural identities. In the language of sociology, this is a wrong and harmful process for the communities who lose there cultural, social values and religious identity. They are easily influenced by the cultural and religious values of other communities.

In this process, it is necessary to protect their cultural and religious values for a longer period. The cultural values provide them peace, self satisfaction and natural environment for their survival. Their own religious and cultural values inspire them to survive for a longer period. A borrowed culture is always harmful and unnatural for the rise and growth of a society. Every religion and culture has its own characteristics and importance. The good ethics and values should be restored for a longer period maintaining peace and harmony within different ethnic and religions groups. This creates social harmony and goodwill among various communities and support is gained through various social groups while displaying their ethnic and cultural values.

It is certain that the some violent groups, and religions which harbour fundamentalism in the world are a threat to a civilized society. This is the age of liberalism and modernity and international rules of social and religious harmony should be followed by every community.

Native Tribals and New Invading Groups

In Himalayan Terai, the people are facing environmental, social and economic change. But these changes are not for the well being of people as these are leading to the extinction of human culture and environment.

The growing population in the world have encouraged people to encroach over the wildlands for housing, roads and other developmental work. This has badly damaged the greenery of forests, disturbed the environment and polluted the fresh water lakes and springs for ever.

The natural areas have been invaded by the illegal encroachment by the farm house owners, road constructions and the land mafias at a larger scale. This has reduced a forest cover to an unexpected limit and thus damaging the ancient forests, bio-diversity and turning some animal species into rare one.

In the past one century, the wetlands, have been reduced upto 40 percent. The major drinking water sources in the world are on the verge of disappearance, because of growing population, agricultural expansion, pollution and global warming. It is estmited that 3.9 million hactares of mangroves in the world have been destroyed completely.

The above destruction of fresh water sources and mangroves have destroyed a large number of bio-diversity in the region. Among those species are pandas, musk dears, water fowls, several species of frogs, crabs, fishes, water birds and insects.

Besides this moths, butterflies, buzzfly, snails, grasshoppers, mantic and several other animals and insects have been vanished away because of the destruction of wetlands and natural areas.

The other animal species like turtles, water snakes, lizards, mouse, marsh rabbits, otters, salamanders, water bottom animals also were disappeared in such circumstances. The global warming, increasing pollution and developmental work have destroyed several ecological zones. The effected ecosystems include (1) The Alpine Wetland Ecosystems (2) Tropical Wetland Ecosystems and (3) Semi-temperate Ecosystems in the world.

When an ancient forest land is destroyed, an ecosystem is destroyed and when an ecosystem is destroyed a whole world of animals, micro animals and plants is destroyed. Such events encourages us to learn more things about an eco-system and its importance to human life.

The forest and its bio-diversity creates a suitable environment for the survival of human being over this planet for a longer period. If the bio-diversity is lost and the standing forest land is lost, the future ground for the survival of humans and wild animals is lost. This has witnessed in the form of a long spell of climatic changes over the earth. To study awetland is just like to study the environment and ecosystem of the oceans.

In this way, we have a great sense to learn that the conservation of Bio-diversity is quite important to human being.

The Ecological Variations

There are several ecological zones over this planet and these varies from cold climatic regions to tropical regions. The ecological variation is because of different geographical formations of our planet.

Ecology

A particular environment whether it is cold climate, tropical desert, the plant and animal species have adapted themselves according to the ecology of that region. This adaptation has taken place since millions of years of evolution and naturalisation of the fauna and flora in that region.

Ecology is called "the science of environment". Now we can say at the Ecology of the Himalayan region is quite different from that of tropical regions or a desert region. The mountains are the symbol of colder climates while the tropical regions are known for warmer climate. Over this planet the ecology varies from place to place.

1. The Mountain Ecology

The cold climate environment, alpine plants and wild animals have developed a mode of life to live and exist in the colder climates of the mountains like the Alps and the Himalayas. The Ecology of Mountains is quite different from that of warmer regions. In the same way the ecosystem of a lake in colder climate is quite different from the lake of warmer countries.

2. The Desert Ecology

The environment of the deserts is quite different from that of greener regions. In the deserts thorny bushes, trees, plants and the thick skinned animals like camel, wild ass, the dears and bighorns are found in the surrounding. For example the Sahara desert, the Govi desert, the Thar desert of Rajasthan and some deserts in USA have different species of plants, animals and bushes. In this way the ecology of the deserts is quite different from that of other greener regions. For example Atacama and Patagonia deserts in South America have quite different vegetation and wild life. The deserts of Sahara is quite different in flora and fauna from that of the deserts of USA.

The Ecology of Tropical regions

The tropical regions are warmer places where evengreen rainforests grow abundantly. The tropical forests like Amazonia, western Africa, Thailand, Cambodia, Sumatra and North Eastern Australia are some of the best examples of rain forests. The ecology and climate in tropical areas varies from place to place, although, these forests are situated at a particular distance from both sides of the equator. The ecology of rain forests of Amazon (Brazil) is quite different from that of Congo, Cameroon and Ghana in Aftican continent.

These regions are known as the "Bio diversity Hot spots" of the world as they are rich in fauna and flora and most of the species found there are endemic.

The most violent mammals, reptiles, bird fauna, amphibians, butterflies, moths, insects (orthopoda) and various plant species are found in the great wilderness of Amazonia.

The Amazonia wilderness have largest cover of rain forests in the world; almost two third rain forests are found here. The one fifth of bird fauna of the world is found here. The total areas of these rain forests is spread in five million kilometers square. The Amazonia is a rich bio-diverstiy hotspot.

The deforestation of Amazon forests can effect us anywhere in the world, even at the place we are sitting and talking just now. These rain forests are the lungs of the earth as they release a large volume of oxygen in the atmosphere and absorb the CO_2 from the environemnt. In this way, this process helps in the balancing the quantity of CO_2 in the environment.

About one third of the rain forests of the Amazonia have been cleared for timber, agriculture, housing, ranching and for the construction of roads for transportation.

The rain forests all over the world are known for their rich bio-diversity. But, these forests are being felled at an alarming state.

The forest fire, logging crew and cattles also reduce the forest cover. The Rain Forests Clubs, conservation bodies and NGOS have initiated a campaign to stop the clearing of rain forests from Amazon, Africa, South East Asia and Australia.

There is a great need to protect and conserve all the plants and animal species in the world. There are some useful instructions adopted by the world citizens to protect the original forests and wildlife.

1. **Reforestation campaign :** The native plants and trees should be planted at a larger scale. Two new plants should be erected in place of one felled tree.

2. **The invading plants or foreign species** should not be encouraged to grow in the original forests. The native tree species should be allowed to grow there. These are the most suitable species to grow in their natural environment. It is believed that 30 percent wild animals and 40 percent plant species have been vanished way from this planet.
3. **Mass Awareness Campaign :** The mass awareness campaign should be initiated with the help of local communities to protect the ancient and new forests and their biodiversity.
4. **Create Natural Habitats :** For birds, monkies and mammals (lion, tiger and bear) new natural habitats should be created for their survival. The felling of ancient forests and habitat loss has dwindled the population of several wild animals.
5. **Encourage Nature Tourism :** To protect the pristine natural lands and forests, we should encourage nature tourism on sustainable basis. Also, avoid the impact of tourism.
6. **Wild Life Toursim :** In Amazonia, several tours and travel companies from Canada, USA and Brazil are introducing wild life tours. Tourism camps are organised every year and earn a large bunch of foreign exchange.
7. The people of the world should be encouraged to protect the ancient forests in their countries.

2

Reasons of Extinction of Bio-diversity

Once the earth was full of forests, green plants and wild animals but sudden rise and fall in temperature vanished away everything including small plants. A large number of the species of fauna and flora found there also vanished away. It is believed that in the initial stage, the bio-diversity was in fragile and evolutionary state. Bio-diversity means biological diversity. It includes various species of plants, trees, herbs, mammals, reptiles, orthopoda, birds and other marine species in the ocean. These are considered a part of thriving bio-diversity. There is a great difference in forest bio-diversity and marine bio-diversity.

Four and half billion years ago when this earth came into existence, it was hot in the initial stage. Life originated after 3.5 billion years. There was a little bio-diversity on the earth and ocean as it took millions of years to develop life. The unicellular animals and plants came into existence first. The unicellular plants came fist into existence into the sea. It was a big change in the planet. First of all, it is necessary to study the origin of life on earth and the sea.

According to the eperts of earth science there was no life when the earth came into existence. It was a sphere of hot mud. The scientific estimation of the earth's coming into existence is considered 4500 million years ago. At the initial stage the earth was young and various changes occurred on it. Due to various geological changes it went through several hotter and cooler stages. The life began to develop in it only when it became cool and suitable for the evolution of life. After millions of years of natural changes the animals and plants came into existence through evolution.

The earth had air, water and minerals. It got energy from the sun. Air was full of gases which included carbon, hydrogen, oxygen and nitrogen (CHON), these were the essential elements to develop life on the earth. First of all, life originated in water. Once, a unicellular animal came into existence it began multiplying by itself, giving rise to more and more life on sea and earth. Early life was simple and fragile in structure. One reason was that it was unicellular like amoeba or bacteria. It was a big change when the life developed on earth and sea. The plants had chlorophyll which made food in the presence of light. Chlorophyll is a green substance in the leaves which makes foods for plants. in presence of sunlight. With the formation of chlorophyll, algae and several other multi cellular organism came into existence and they got widespread in sea water.

On land, life came into existence at a very later stage. This was an important change on earth. Life on earth evolved into the forms of mosses, ferns and the flowering plants on the one side and the amphibian reptiles, avies and mammals on the other side. It is believed that man came into existence only recently.

Time period of life on Earth	
1. Earth formed very early	4500 million years ago
2. Life originated probably	3500 million years ago
3. Earliest known life is	350 million years ago
4. Birds and mammals came later	60 million years ago
5. The trees and forests came	50 million years ago
6. Man probably came only	0.5 million years ago

The Eearth and its Resources

Air, water, soil and mineral are the major resources for life upon the earth. The earth receives the right amount of life and heat (energy) from the sun. Green plants synthesise food with the help of water, CO_2, minerals and sunlight into the form of energy. The food is made available to all the living organisms.

Surprisingly, there is multiplicities of trees and plants and animals over this earth. Food was synthesised by the plants as much more than what is being consumed. Over a period of millions of years, the earth became a great reservoir of animals and plant bodies, dead and living. Every animal and plant species has its own life cycle of existence over this earth.

On earth, there are several species of wild animals, plants and forests which we name the fauna and flora of a particular region. This we call bio-diversity or biological-diversity. Bio-diversity also includes micro organisms, tiny plants. They also contain the genes and ecosystems and help in building a living environment.

The bio-diversity we see on earth and ocean today is the end result of four billions years of the evolution of life. Since the creation of earth and till today several plants and animals came into existence and died after completing their life cycle. Some of the plants and animals died young as they faced drought or global warming in this period. It means we have lost a great portion of bio-diversity from this earth.

How much bio-diversity is there! Our combined knowledge is limited in support of this question : we have knowledge about some ecosystems on the earth. Because we described and invented them. We know a very small fraction about the total bio-diversity on the this planet.

We know this planet is a vast kingdom of wild animals and plant life. It is estimated that there are one crore to 8 crore plants and animal species on this earth and among them 14 million species are known to scientists.

We know very little about the genetic variability within species. We can save a few hundred species of plants and animals of commercial or scientific importance. When we destroy our natural areas or forest land, we can preserve these species for a longer period.

We Destroy bio-diversity

The bio-diversity includes, plants, herbs, insects, butterflies, grasshoppers, mantis, wild birds, rabbits, foxes, tigers, bears, snakes, lizards and several other herbs and animals useful to man and its environment. Our life is dependent on it.

Bio-diversity provides ecosystem stability, biological production (everything we eat) hence economic stability, medicines, housing material : woods, clothing and fuel. Bio-diversity is also the basis for religions, cultures and aesthetic values of various communities over this planet.

Sometime, we condemn other species to extinction either through neglect or because they stand into our way! We have wiped out them from the planet for our vested interests.

The freshwater ecosystem is also in danger! The main reason of the loss of the bio-diversity is the expansion of human population. The end result of almost all human activity sooner or later affects a fresh water ecosystem e.g. a brook, riverpond or lake. The impact can either be diverted in the form of habitat destruction, or indirect, via the air or water precipitation. The type of threat differs from the site, but may be divided into four broad categories.

1. Habitat degradation
2. Water quality degradation
3. Introduction of exotic species
4. Over fishing or over exploitation of the resources.

The first two factors are the principal sourses of loss of bio-diversity in aquatic ecosystems.

The most important causes of the loss of the bio-diversity are loss of habitat or destruction from clearing and burning of forests, draining and filling of wetlands, lakes and streams, and converting natural ecosystems for agriculture industry and human settlement in the larger scale.

Loss of Habitats : The main reason of the loss of the bio-diversity is the loss of ancient trees, forests and dwarf, bush-which an ideal habitats for the wild animals i.e. mammals, birds, reptiles and orthopoda (insects, caterpillar, grasshopper, mantis, butterflies and crawling centipedes) etc.

For example : We have lost a fine cover of ancient forests from the earth. These forests were the habitats of several wild animals and small plants and trees. We have lost a part of rain forests of Amazonia. These forests are being cleared at a greater speed. At present, 4 million kilometers square forest area is in danger as 16 lakh kilometer square forest land have already been destroyed by the timber companies. The expansion of agriculture, urbanisation, and the forest settlers have destroyed a large part of the forests in Amazonia wilderness of Brazil.

One fifth of the world's amazing bird species are found here in the rain forests. Among the most impressive birds are waterbirds, : red parrots, and pigeons. The most beautiful song birds are found is the deep forests of Amazon.

According to a report published in conservation news letter, the rain forests in Amazonia are continuously on the verge of decrease. By 1990, 27 percent of the forests equal to 16,800 square kilometers were cleared for various purposes. Since 1972, about 13.3 percent of entire Amazon forests (532068 sq. kilometers) has been lost. These figures could be underestimated as 15,000 square kilometers land is destroyed every year by the logging staff's vehicles and other heavy machines. The satellite cameras from space do not catch less than 6 hectares of land. In this way, most of the areas of the cleared forests remain unaccounted.

It is estimated that by now 20 lakh square kilometers of rain forests of Amazonia have been cleared by some timber companies or government agencies for agricultural development or settlement of the population at a larger scale.

Mexico's Forest fire : The Loss of Bio-diversity

There are regular reports of Mexico forests catching fire in the month of September. Every year there are some sensitive forest areas which catch fire and cause a lot of damage to the trees, plants and various species of wild animals.

In 1998, in the first six months, the fire burnt approximately zero square kilometers of forests in mexico in rich forest areas. Most of the fire is caught to have been caused by farming preparatory practices, including slash-and-burn agriculture.

In some cases, fires were deliberately set to provide changes in land use. The plan identifies 85 priority forests, covering a total of 1880 square kilometers in 21 and 32 Mexican states. These forests have been described as the sites of "Ecological Restoration" and will be subject to a legal status that brings change in land use and enables the Ministry of Environment to develop and implement forest recovery plan for each other.

Save Mexican Turtles : A Sensitive Eco System

The conservationists around the world are protesting against the Governments plan to sell the most beautiful beach Quintana Roo to develop the beach for personal purpose.

This beach is a haven for Green turtle chelsnia mydas and loggerhead turtle caretta ceretta: nesting.

After an international outcry on the Quitana Roo state beach but this does not satisfy the concerns of conservationists. Green Peace filed a lawsuit against one of the buyers. Sol Melia, a Spanish hotel chain. During the building of Fences and paths, Sol Melia destroyed species protected by Mexican laws.

Such alertness and awareness shown by some NGOS the world over is gaining momentum among the scholars, intellectuals and masses.

Sensitive Bio-diversity of Madagaskar

Gentle Lemur : This is a peaceful noctunal monkey like animal found in the rain forests of Madagascar. This animal is known as Alaotran gentle lemur cimper lemur griseus alaotrensis. This is an important endemic animal of Madagascar forests whose population has fallen by 30 percent.

The Durell Wildlife Conservation Trust is tackling the problem through mass awareness programme among the various forest communities.

Protecting the Amazon Rain Forests

The rain forests in the world are on the verge of destruction. These forests are the largest wonderful wilderness in the world. The Amazonia inhabit the two third rain forests of the world. The rain forests in the world are a home for a large number of birds, mammals, reptiles and insects. One fifth of world's bird species live in the vast forests of Amazonia.

A large portion of these forests is being felled by the logging crew of timber companies of Brazil. Forest fire is also a big reason for the destruction of trees and wildlife of these forests.

Some species of wild animals are on the verge of extinction because of loss of rain forests. The destruction of habiats and loss of wetlands are the major reasons for the disappearance of wildlife. Four states of Brazil have published a list of endangered wild animals.

The list has mentioned 257 important species i.e. 3 Cnidaria (coelentrates), 7 molluscas, 13 crustaceans, 47 insects, 1 Diplopoda, 39 fresh water fishes, 9 marine fishes, 4 amphibians, 9 reptiles, 82 birds and 43 mammals.

The first state to draw up a list was Parana which prepared a list in February 1995. Followed by Mines Gerais in January 1996 and Sao Paulo in February 1998 and the last was Rio de Janeiro.

The Loss of Frogs

Medicine From Ecuadorian Frogs : Some wild animals are beings used as medicine by some advanced countries.

The population of poison dart frogs in the Andes mountains of Ecuador may get extinct if the frogs are continually exported to USA to extract medicine from them. This will automatically will lower the population of poison dart frogs (poison arrow). These frogs Dendrobates species found only in the foothills of the Ecuadorian Andes. Two Ecuadorian Environmental organizations explained that 750 poison dart frogs were taken into USA in 1996 without any permission from Ecuadorian Government. This is against the international wild life rules. Such illegal smuggling of frogs will endanger the dart frog species in the Andes.

The US based pharmaceutical company Abbot Laboratory is responsible for this illegal import of Dart frogs from the Andes. This laboratory has developed a painkiller from the dart frogs. This pain killer has no side effects, whose active ingradients is derived from the poison secrated by the poison-dart frogs.

The Ecuadorian authorities want to gain economic benefits from the Abbots Laboratory Project earnings from the new analgesic (ABT-594) have led Ecuador to seek benefit from Abbot's discovery but Ecuador has no legal means for this because the USA has not ratified international conventions dealing with biological resources.

This is one big reason for the extinction of wildlife from the Andes. The 750 dart frogs is a big population which took years to exist there. USA has been importing a large number of plants and wild animals from the South East Asian Nations also and has been exporting them for the purpose of economic benefits.

Export-Import of Wildlife

USA is the largest trader of reptiles : It has been proved by some international agencies like International Environmental

Agency, UK and Fauma and Flora International UK that USA is the largest trader of wild animals in the world.

There are vast pools, ranches, farm houses and private zoos in USA where some rich people breed and export some species of wild animals including some reptiles : A report below explains the reality of importing and exporting of the reptiles. The number of wild animals and reptiles have increased many fold. But a report of Traffic North America, September 1998 explains this fact more authentically. USA is the largest trader of live reptiles in the world.

Between 1983 and 1992, the US trade in live reptiles increased nearly twenty fold and jumped from 28 percent to 82 percent of the global market.

More than 2.5 million live reptiles were imported in 1995 and in 1996 the USA exported or re-exported 9.5 million reptiles, primarily to Europe and East Asian countries. The reptile trade principally supplies the pet industry as well as growing food market.

THE HABITATS OF WILD BIRDS

New bird from Andes of Peru

An strange bird: The black spectacled brush finch found in the Andes of central Peru has been seen after a long time. Earlier this bird was not seen in the wild of Andes. The bird Atlapetes melanops inhabits the humid shrubs on both sides of the deep canyon formed where the Rio mantaro intersects the eastern Andean ridge and probably has a very limited areas of inhabitation. Some birds like the humid scrubs and moisturous bushes which breed insects for the small birds.

Pale-headed brush finch : Some small and large birds have been spotted in some parts of the world after a long period of interval. Earlier, it was thought that some of the birds have been disappeared from the forests, heathlands and mountain valleys. But some of them still survive and have been spotted in the wild.

The pale-headed brush finch is a beautiful small bird from southern Ecuador patch forests. The brush finch Atlapetes pallidiceps which had not been recorded since 1969, has been rediscovered. The six individuals of them were seen in the ancient patch forests of southern Ecuador.

The Vanishing wild lands

The European wildlands and meadons are disappearing at an alarming rate. The wild grasses, flowering plants and herbs have been disappeared in the last three decades. The main reason is global warming and urbanisation process.

The population of butterflies is under constant threat. There are some 576 species which are under direct threat. Some 17 species are threatened at global level and 52 at European level. The main theat comes from agricultural changes and land development for farming or housing.

The Fragile Ecosystem of Chidderwala

Honey birds of Childderwala : Chidderwala is a beautiful village of Dehradun district situated in between Saung river and Toya river on National Highway Nepalifarm (Doiwala) Dehradun. The honey birds of the village are quite popular among the ornithologists and bird watchers. In the year 1984, there were some 200 pairs in the area but after 1999, the number began to decline to 20 paires (male female) ten times decline in the population. Global warming, habitat loss and growing human pollution have caused the bird population decrease in the valleys and forests of Raja Ji National Park and Saung River banks. Flowering bushes, long stalked flowers and spiralling plants with sweet honey flowers have been vanished away in the past three decades. The flowering bushes in Toya river marsh , Saung river and Bhambhak rivulet have disappeared in the area since 1971. The ornithologists and biologists say that the global warming is the main reason for the disappearance of the flowering bushes of Chidderwala, Doiwala and Raiwala. The flower honey is the main food of honey birds. In the past one decade, we have seen continuous decrease in the nests of honey birds in the gardens, agricultural fields and forests. The nests were located in the river banks only as there were some flowering bushes. The honey birds make their nests 100 meters way from the flowering bushes.

The Habitats of Tailor Birds

Tailor birds : The Terai region of Uttaranchal is full of amazing birds. The small birds mainly depend on insects, fruits and flower honey. One of the most important bird is Tailor bird which is an expert in weaving nests into a very beautiful way. It folds two leaves of a tree and sew it into a fine way to make a beautiful nest. Sometime other species make their nests on the sugarcane leaves or elephant grass leaves by weaving green threads of the leaves. The habitat loss have made them more vulnerable to survive.

The Red Crow

Pan Kauwa : The black-red crow is found in the sagurcane fields of Terai region. The voice of the crow is like wild fowl but its shape and size is like a common large crow found in the forests near wetlands.

This bird makes a large Bhadoo like nest in the river bank bushes and lays four eggs. After hatching the eggs within ten days, the baby birds fly away with the mother. This bird has become, a rare one in Teria areas.

The Long Tailed Birds

The Karaoon (Magpies) of Tharoch valley : The Karaoon is found in large numbers near the river banks and valleys. In Shimla district of Himachal Pradesh, there are some beautiful river valleys known for white paradise and large magpie birds. We can locate them near Tharoch and Bharmana valleys near Chaupal and Nerwa city. Karaoon and Saraoon are two species of magpie. One is blue magpie and the other is red brown magpie found in the warm valleys. These birds make their nests on the trees grown on the high rocks and remain safe from the prey birds. The birds have become rare because of disappearing bushes and trees.

Goathoo (wild Cat) : This wild Cat prey on birds, rabbits and other small animals in the forests. This wild cat, the mother of domestic cat is found in the forests of Dehradun, pine (pinus himalayensis) and oak forests in Himachal and Uttaranchal. This has been spoted in the forests of Chaupal (338 square kilometers), Tharoch and the Pastures of Taalraa.

Hataal (Ataal) River Valley : Hataal River valley between the border of Himachal and Uttaranchal is known for its rich bio-diversity. In the last three decades, several small mammals, reptiles, song birds, magpies, weasels, mongoose, wild cats and various other animals have been vanished away because of global warming and loss of moisture. The level of pollution in the rivers and streams has increased ten times. This has led to the disappearance of fresh water fishes, crabs and river bottom fauna in a large number.

Loss of Moisture Loving Plants

The moisture loving plants, fruit bushes and long stalked flowering plants have been disappeared from the river banks and mountain slopes. The Kainth and Khaina (ficus auriculata) bushes and trees have been vanished away in the last three decades.

Katra Siyaraa

The red brown wolf, black bear, mountain tigers and small (mammals have disappeared from the local areas. Among the magpies (Karaoon and Saraoon), water fowl, wild fowl, white paradise, black magpie : Dhainchoos are rarely found in this valley. But now very few birds remain there in the wild. The magpie birds are red brown Karaoon and white blue saraoon (the longtailed birds). The large ancient trees in the valleys have been completely vanished away. As a result, there are no epiphyte orchids on the trees now. Once the valley was thriving with the black magpie (Kaljeenth : Dhainchoo) of Katraa Siyaaraa Valley.

The Valleys of Wild Birds

The black bird with bifurcated tail lives near the river valleys in the mountains of Shivalik. After many years, two nests were located in the month of June 2008 in the Katara Siyaaraa valley. Although the bird was seen in the valley every year. Every nest was seen with two or three eggs and the presence of two baby birds after the hatching of eggs. This was a good starting of Dhainchoo after many years. In the month of June 2009, the bird Dhainchoo (black bird) was seen in the village of Childderwala with its nest in a mango tree in the garden near a sugarcane field. Two baby birds were seen in the nest. The bird almost seen near the houses in the Saung River. This was an interesting finding that the bird was seen with nest in the semitropical Terai region of Dehradun district. Primarily the bird is located in the Shivalik hills and valleys in Kumaun and Garhwal (Uttaranchal). Loss of ancient habitats, disppearence of caves, rocks and natural areas have reduced the population of wild song birds in the Shivalic hills. Dhainchoo is basically an inhabitant of Shivalik hills of Uttaranchal.

Goginee Valley : Goginee Valley is an important valley for the prey birds like eagles and vultures and are also visible on the high rocks. The high rocks of Goginee valley are the ancient habitats of eagles and vultures. Only a few prey birds live there now.

Godiyoon: The Black Bird (Dhainchoo), skylark, magpies, white paradise, blue bird, (Neelkanth), mouse bird (mush chiriya), bulbul (Chuphlya Galadar), suradi, tailorbirds and honey birds are found in this beautiful narrow valley. In the past three decades 90% species of wild birds have been vanished away. Only a few song birds are visible now as there are some good heathlands to protect them. Very few long trees and traditional habitats are visible now. The old habitat loss, global warming and increasing pollution is a great threat to them. Global warming has reduced the cold climate herbs. The invading herbs and plants have taken their place in the valleys. This has created a lot of imbalance in the presence of fauna and flora of Shivalik Hills. The river water of this valley has been reduced to one inch while three decades back the presence of water in the river was upto six inches. The gushing water of this valley now has turned into sweet memories of the past among the writers and jounalists who come to visit here during holidays.

There are several reasons of extinction of bio-diversity. The natural and manmade reasons are more. The global warming is the biggest enemy of bio-diversity loss over this earth. We, the aware citizens of the world should do our best to protect the whole bio-diversity of this living planet.

3

Bio-diversity of India

India is famous for its biological diversity in the world. It has five distinct bio-diversity zones which are known for their rich fauna and flora. In every zone the plants and animals have their distinct nature, ecological importance and a different way of inhabitation.

The bio-diversity of India is distributed in five zones seeing its varied ecological characteristics and geographical importance. It is certain that the plants and animals found in these regions might have taken millions of yers to adopt themselves according to the ecological system in those places.

1. The Himalayan Zone : The Himalayan region covers an area of about 3.4 million kilometers square (1.3 million square miles) It is divided into three separated longitudinal zones : Outer Himalaya : The line of foothills averaging to 1000-2000 meters. The Great Himalayas : This is the main range of lofty mountains spread upto 6,000 meters. North of the Great Himalaya (the Zaskar Range) is quite distinct from it.

2. Eastern Zone : The Eastern zone consists West Bengal, Sikkim, and North-Eastern states. In West Bengal, Sundarban,

Assam (Brahmputra river delta). Kaziranga National Park, Arunachal, Meghalaya, Manipur, Mezoram, Nagalnad, Tripura are among the beautiful places known for their rich and varied bio-diversity.

3. Western Zone : The western zones consists Rajasthan, Gujarat, (Gir forests and mangroves), some parts of Maharastra are included in it. The tigers, lions, sambhars and deers are included in it. The desert animals in Rajasthan are habitual to live in desert ecology. The plants and animals both are adapted to arid environment.

4. Central Zone : This part is known as Madhya Bharat or Madhya Pradesh which is known for its most beautiful animals both mammals and birds. The forests are densely populated and various species of animals, trees and plants are found in the forests and near the river banks. This includes Madhya Pradesh, Uttar Pradesh and some parts of Orissa.

5. Southern Zone : Kerala, Karnataka, Tamil Nadu and Andhra Pradesh. The Southern Zone constitutes a large part of mangroves and forests with distinguished bio-diversity : plants, animals and insects are the main features of these forests. The mangroves are continuously being destroyed by the farmers for farmlands, settlers for housing and mining and drilling activities by the private business houses. This has caused much more damage to the mangroves and forests of Southern Zone which is a hot-spot of bio-diversity. The trees, plants, mammals, reptiles, birds and insects are found in large numbers.

The Sandalwood forests : The sandilwood forests of South India are the most fragile now. The wood is being exploited to extract sandal wood oil and scents. The sandalwood forests from the south have been wiped out by the sandal wood smugglers. It is estimated that every year Rs. 400 crore sandal wood is being smuggled from the southern states. These forests are endemic and now only one third of the forests have remained standing in these states. The continuous felling of sandal woods, has eroded the ecosystem of the forests. The mammals, reptiles and birds in those states have become rare and most of them have been migrated to bordering forests.

Small Bushes of Katraa Siyaaraa (Uttarakhand)

Several species of trees and evergreen bushes which are endemic to this region are disappearing at an alarming rate. For example, Timul, Bedoo, Khaina (Ficus auricutata) and the small bushes and large trees are gradually disappearing. The Ringalee Ghass (the bamboo grass) the smallest Bamboo in the world has been disappeared from the large portion of this valley. The decreasing of moisture and increasing global warming have caused the disappearance of some plants and animals. The invading plants and trees are spreading in the forests.

Bio-diversity of the Himalayan Region : The immense mountain barrier of the Himalaya extends in a huge arc for more than 2500 Km (1500 miles) from Nanga Parvat (8,124 mts.) in Kashmir through Nepal, Sikkim, Bhutan and the North Eastern Frotnier Agency to Namcha Barrua (7,782 mts.) in extreme western China.

The Himalayan region covers an area of about 3.4 million kilometers square (1.3 million square miles).

The Himalaya is a huge mountain barrier and has a marked effect on the weather conditions by obstructing north ward movements of the monsoon. It brings extremely heavy rainfall to the foothills but very little to the Tibetan Plateau above, leaving it in a rain shadow. The variations can be compared Ladakh (Little Tibet), where an annual rainfall does not exceed 75 mm (3 inch), with the Eastern Himalayas which receivers the full force of the monsoon, and where normal rainfall is in excess of 2,000 mm (80 inch), though 5,000 mm (200 inch) is not unusual rainfall. Some places get considerably more rainfall in the world. On the other hands, the Himalayas protect the plains of India from the bitter cold that is a marked feature of the Tibetan Plateaus.

The Bio-diversity : The Study of bird fauna in the Himalayan region is of particular interest. The large birds : The pheasants of which there are 49 species, some of them with numerous sub species.

In 16 genera are especially well represented in the Himalaya Tibet-Sichuan region. These birds include Impejanus pheasant, resplendent, copper blood pheasant, decked in green and grey with black and white markings and dauped with crimson; satyr tragopan which is among the most beautiful pheasants, the monotype snow partridge; and red jungle fowl. This is the gamebird ancestor of the domestic fowl.

The Cheer Pheasant are among the rare birds which are found in lower Himalayan valleys and Arunachal forests.

The Western Himalayan Tragopan is found in the higher altitude of Western Himalayan forests. The Blyth's Tragopan is found in the Eastern Himalayas.

The Himalayan mountain' Quail, a bird of Western Himalayan foothills, has not been recorded since 1868, it is believed that it still exists.

Bio-diversity of National Parks

The best example of Himalayan Bio-diversity is Sagar Matha National Park in Nepal. This park is known for the high attitude fauna and flora. The Terai Forests of India are the best examples of wildlife and floral diversity. The semi-temperate forests are a rich source of timber, fuel and fodder for the tribals. The mammals include elephants, tigers, bears, wild pigs, stag deers, marsh deers, fox, rabbits, shahi (porcupine), monkeys, langoors etc. These forests and national parks are rich in bird fauna. Nanda Devi National Park, The Great Kallu National Park of Himachal, Rajaji National Park (Uttaranchal) and Western Himalayan Wild bird Sanctuary,

Sarahan in Himachal Pradesh are among the best examples of mountain flora and fauna.

Fauna and Flora of Sagar Matha

The Sagarmatha National Park is in the northeastern Nepal with an area of 1148 square kilometers. The park covers the upper catchment of Dudh Kosi river system, a distinct geographical entity enclosed by high mountain ranges. The park's northeastern boundry lies along the main divide of the Great Himalaya; coinciding with Tibetan border. The park's four main glaciers Chhukhung, Khumba, Gokyo and Nangpa La feed deeply incised valleys which drain into the Dudhkosi river and its tributaries, to form the part of the Ganges River system.

Wildlife

The park is a high-level breeding ground for wild birds. There are 162 recorded bird species in the park. Among them are blood pheasant, robin accentor, white throated red-start and grandala. Other important and beautiful birds are : Tibetan snowcock, snow partridge and Himalayan Monal (Lophorus impejanus) which are the inhabitants of high altitude mountains and colder climate.

Bio diversity of North Eastern States : The North Eastern States are amazingly beautiful and so is their wildlife. The lush green mountains, valleys, rivers, waterfalls and water springs all of them attract us amazingly.

The North Eastern states of India are full of forests and greenery. Some of the forests are standing crops from the very ancient time. The trees and plants species in these states are endemic and most of them are moistrous forests.

These forests are rain forests and are known for their evergreen nature. The ferns and orchids are amazingly beautiful plants and have several species in the wild. The large cover of forests of ferns and orchids indicates that despite the global warming, the forest still generate moisture for the plants like fern and orchids which thrive in the wild. The orchids are epiphytes which grow on the trees but have their own food. They are not parasites at all. The terrestrial orchids grow on decomposed biomass in the moisturous land. The saprophytic orchids grow on rotten biomass, leaves, wood and branches.

The North Eastern mountains and forests remain full of orchids, ferns and several species of lily. There are several varieties of plants and wild animals which are endemic to these forests and whose scientific studies still require a lot of survey and research work on their habitation, ancient origin (DNA study etc.) and ecological adaptation.

The deers, rabbits, porcupines, weasels, monkeys, tigers, bears and other mammals small and large are found in these forests. The lizards, snakes turtles; frogs, waterfowls, wild fowls, and species of monal are found here. The bird fauna is rich and beautifully described from the forests of North East. The Assam forests, Meghalaya, Arunachal, Nagaland, Manipur Tripura and Mezoram are the finest examples of bio-diversity. Both rain forests, and rangelands are covered with moisture loving plants. Some species of ferns, orchids and lilies are quite popular here.

Bio-diversity of Madhya Pradesh and Maharastra : The forests of Madhya Pradesh and Maharashtra are densely populated and rich in bio-diversity. Particularly, it is known for its National Parks and rich bio-diversity both mammals and avifauna.

The parks are known for different species of mammals, reptiles, amphibians, avifauna, orthopoda, river fishes and other wild animals which attract millions of tourists every year. The National Parks are the best examples of the conservation of bio-diversity. Some Parks are more dense, deep, explorable and suitable for regular safari tourism. Among the large mammals are lion, tigers, bears, leopards, cheetal and dears. The wildboars, monkeys, langoors porcupines, rabbits, mangoose are found in the National Parks of Madhya Pradesh.

The Avifauna is most spectacular and attractive in the dense forests of Madhya Pradesh. The birds with several species from hornbill to Milky hen which always impresses our heart and mind are found in the forests of Madhya Pradesh.

Kingfisher, woodpecker, wildfowls, waterfowls, magpies, koel, nocturnal birds etc. are also visible in the National Parks.

Attraction for wild birds : The wildlife in the forests of Madhya Pradesh is quite amazing. The wild animals are known for their cornivore and herbivore nature. Some of the mammals of Madhya Pradesh have unique features and characteristics in nature. Some species of tigers and lions are quite distinct in India.

The best thing in Madhya Pradesh forests is that of its rich bird fauna in the world. The varities of its wild birds, peacocks, multicolored wildfowls, waterfowls and the special large sized birds are quite impressive. The white fowls, red and dark red colour birds, dark yellow colour birds, large-red headed woodpecker, brown hornbills, kingfisher and some species of the laughing birds are the source of great entertainment. The bird watching in the camplife activities are the best recreation in the wild. The birds of heaven in extreme red colour and extreme white colour (the milky white) are quite popular among the bird watchers. Such special varieties of birds are not found in other parts of the world.

Forests have a large numbers of unique flora and fauna which should be protected by all means. Such tourist destinations should be protected and developed with modern amenities. This will encourage more tourists and more foreign visitors. There should be some well equipped stay points near the national parks to relax and enjoy holidays.

Bio-diversity of Bhutan, Manas River and Sunderbans : There are several bio-diversity hotspots over this earth. The best among them are 60 top forests and wildlife areas. At present some 30 new bio-diversity hotspots have been marked all over the world.

The Manas and Sankosh rivers in the borders of India and Bhutan are the habitats of wildbirds and golden langoors. There are several beautiful species of plants and trees. The wild animals are known among the tourists visiting these spots. The Golden langoor (Presbitis McGeei) and other species of primates are found here. The Golden langoor is a rare species and is found in only this region. The area of Golden langoor is spread up to borders of Assam : The rich bio-diversity between Manas and Sankosh rivers is known among the wildlife lovers of the world.

The mountain tiger, black bears, deers, foxes, rabbits, porcupines, weasels, mongoose etc-are found in the forests-of Manas and Sankosh rivers in Bhutan and Sundarbans in West Bengal. The Sundarban delta is known for its Sundari tree which is an evergreen plant widely spread in the delta. The wild boar is common in Sundarbans. The rabbits and wild fowls are also in good populations. The spotted deer (Axis axis) and wild boars (Sus coria) and tiger (Panther Tigris) are common sight in the bushes of Sunderban. The Sundarban is spread upto 10,000 kilometer square on Indian side and 26,000 sq. km. between India and Bangladesh. The two third part of it is in Bangla Desh.

In Assam, Kaziranga National Park and Manas National Park are among the most popular wildlife parks in our country. The parks attracts millions of people every year. In 2007, the Kaziranga National Park suffered the worst. From 1997 to 2006 some six Rhinos were killed each year. But in 2007 the number of poaching rose to 10 in the park. Located in Assam, the park is known for its single horned rhinos. This species is found in only in Assam. Manas National Park has a large population of rhinos but they were wiped out during the civil unrest in the late 1990. This is a global bio-diversity hotspot and World Heritage Site also which is in good state now.

Bio-diversity of Kerala, Karnataka and Tamil Nadu

The bio-diversity of the southern states of India z.e. Kerala. Karnataka and Tamil Nadu is quite different from that of Himalayan states of India. This is because of different ecological features and geological difference. In the Himalayas, the wildlife is adapted to colder climate. In the warm climate of the southern states, an amazing range of fauna and flora is found in the forests. Kerala have some moisturous forests and evergreen vegetation which have a range of beautiful mammals, reptiles, primates, tigers, wild boars, bears and several other small mammals which are endemic to these forests.

The evergreen natural vegetation of Kerala attracts the tourists from the foreign lands. The forests have a large number of herbs with great medicinal values. Some of them are life saving medicines and are useful to human being. There are numerous plants, herbs and tree species which are of immense medicinal value to the people. The endangered lion tailed macaque (Macaca silenus) of Western Ghats (Kerala, Karnataka and Tamil Nadu) is found is these states. The Western Ghats still harbour a high diversity of flora and fauna and is one of the bio-diversity hot spots. The diversity includes several species of Primates, notably, the endemic lion-tailed Macaque (Macaca selenus) and Neelgiri Langoor (Semnopithcus johnii). The range of occupancy of Lion tailed Macaque is 250 square kilometers. This is a small area for a Macaque who require a vast chunks of forests to roam here and there in search of food. The food includes mostly forest fruits and beries. In comparison, the above area is very small for the primates to move from one forest to another in search of food and inhabitation.

Bio-diversity of the Mangroves of Western and Eastern Ghats : The Western Ghats is considered one of the richest biodiversity hot spots in the world. The evergreen trees, moisturous bushes and grasslands are a heaven for wild animals to move and breed freely in the open natural environment.

The Sirsi Honnavara in Karnataka is the main bastion of lion tailed Macaque. There are more then 750 individuals and they are confined to unprotected areas of reserve forests. The forests are near the human population, agricultural lands and livestock reserves. The experts have requested the government to make it a long term conservation area just to protect this unique primate species.

Sirsi Honnavara is an ideal place for their habitation and these should be protected with the support of local citizens and forest authorities.

The liontailed monkey (Macaca silenus) and Nilgiri langoor's (Semnopithecus johnii) are rare species and this require peoples support to protect the primates.

The Silent Valley National Park, Sirsi Honnavara Areas, Kudrmukh National Park, Someshwara Wildlife Sanctuary are the main bastion of these primates.

Shararathy Valley Wildlife Sanctuary (431 km^2). The forests of Talekaveri and Pushpagiri Wildlife Sanctuaries are classified as medium forest type with Mesua ferea-Paloanium ellipticum vegetation. The population of lion-tailed monkey in the entire Western Ghats is estimated at 3,500 to 4000.

In Tamil Nadu Indira Gandhi Wildlife Sanctuary, Shendumey-kulathaparha Peppara-Neyger (Kerala state), Silent Valley National Park (Kerala), Kudremukh Someshara (Karnataka), Sirsi Honnavara (Karnataka) are the main attraction for wild life (mammals, reptiles, birds, butterflies, insects and river fauna.)

The Shivalik Hills

The small Shivalik Hills 4000′-7000′ are rich in bio-diversity. The birds, mammals, reptiles, insects and butterflies are found abundantly. There are some beautiful examples of fauna and flora of Pauri Hills in (Uttaranchal).

Seeku Dhaar Red Fox : The Shivalik Hills are the most beautiful manifestations of nature. The forests, bushes, rock caves, valleys and pasture slopes always impresses with their enchanting scenic beauty. Seeku Dhar is quite famous for its oak and deodar forests, small semi-temperate vegetation and bushes are a habitats of tigers, bears, rabbits, weasels and wild foxes. The red fox is found here in the caves in the valleys in dwarf forests. The wildland between Seeku Dhar, Ghandiyaal Khaal and Shrikot village is a heaven for such animals. The wild fowls, teater, chakore, kingfisher, black magpie (kaljeenth), tailorbird, surady, and in the warm valleys humming birds are seen here. The beautiful song birds like red finch, black finch, Turtle Dove, Kaffoo, Koel, Hilaansh and laughing bird is found in the oak forests.

As far as the wildlife survey and research work is concerned some research organisation can take the bad. The habitats of the Red fox can be spotted in the wildlands of SeeRu Dhaar. The systematic research work can be conducted on the habitats and roaming area of the animal. The whole wildland is spread upto 3-4 kilometers. There are small patches of forests and rest is open, barren grassland with beautiful natural views.

Dhainchoos of Goginee valley

The Gonginee is a most beautiful valley in the Pauri Hills of Uttaranchal. Dhainchoo is a 13 inch long prey bird found in the valleys of Shivalik hills. It is dark black bird known for its shrieks. It makes nests on the traditional trees and bushes above 10 or 15 feet heights. During a survey, the nests of the birds were found in Haidaa, Khinna, Khareek, Bheunl, Guava, Bamboo, Behadaa, Amlaa and Mango trees. Besides this, long thin trees of local origin are the best known for nests in the wild of Goginee valley.

Some 35 years ago, there were a larger numbers of birds in this valley as a very small fresh water river passes through the valley. During summer the quantity of water becomes quite small. The river water remains to 3-4 inches during summer. It it is a lifeline for the fruit eating birds of the area. The flowering bushes, fruit trees and berries are abundantly found in the valley. The birds of pPrey and wildfowls are also found in the valley. The small songbirds, bulbul, mouse bird, Huppoe, woodpecker, turtle dove, Koel, Kaffoo, Kingfisher, and hornbills are found in the local forests. The valley is a heaven, for wild birds and small animals.

The Tigers of Daaligand : Daaligaad is a small forestland with 4 square km area. This unique forest has a great variety of plants, trees, bushes and hebal medicines. The orchids, ferns, mosses, wild onion, tulsi, aquatic plants, sisau, paapadee, peppermint, blackpeppermint and other sweet smelling plants are found here in abundance. The biological diversity of Daaligaad is rich and inspiring.

At present, there are several species of floweirng plants. Some tuberous plants and herbs are found in the wild of Daaligaad. The tuberous plants, orchids, ferns and Ghanyaa (the wild vegetable), Asheen and Shakeens are some flowering bushes used as food vegetables by the villagers. The wildlife is rich and varied.

Among the mammals mountain tigers, bears, wild boars, fox, rabbits, weasels, primates (monkeys and langoors), porcupine and wild cats are found in the bushes amidst the forests. The area of tigers is spread upto Ghora Dhungee, Daaligaad, Naagarja Dhaundaa, Gaamaath, Maroda and Jaakhnee forests in a range of 4 square km. Mostly, they attack domestic animals and human beings.

Karaoon (magpies) of Godiyoon : The Karaoon, the true magpies in the hills are found in warm, forests and valleys of Garhwal and Kumaun (Uttaranchal). A small river generates from a very small water source here. Some bamboo and local trees from the very ancient time area favourite place for nesting. Karaoon mostly nests in bamboo, khareek and tall deodar trees in the forests. The places of their nests are near the river. Godiyoon Valley is a nature's pleaceful paradise. It is a mixture of agricultural fields, green lands and pastures. Nearby areas are like heathlands and wetlands provide a fertile environment for the nesting and breeding of karaoon and other small birds in the nature.

Skylarks of Haidee Dhaar : The Shivalik hills and pastures upto 3000-4500 ft. are a heaven for skylarks. The semi-temperate pastures, bushes and tallgrasses with slope walls are a favourite nesting areas for the skylarks. The nests are seen on the field walls or near the rock cavities surrounded by the wild grasses. The movements of skylarks is seen by telescope or by hiding under the bushes. The insects in such grass lands are found abundantly. The wild fruits, berries and land berryfruits are found abundantly. The green pastures have a nice growth of moths, fliess, grasshoppers and small insects. Global warming, increasing pollution and destruction of natural areas have made the population of skylarks vulnerable.

Teetars of Naagarja : The Naagarjaa is a mountain peak at 6000 ft. The Deodar forest patch with scarce growth of pine and oak trees have made it a most beautiful place for the trekkers and explorers. It is an ideal place for the inhabitation of wildbirds, teeter, chakore and wildfowls. Some beautiful species of small birds are found in the forests, buses and stone caves. Teetars are the best song birds which are very clever and always speak out during rainy season. They hide themselves under the bushes and at the same time call their mates from the nearby bushes to assemble near a rock or huge bush to hide.

The preparation for nests goes before 10-14 days of laying eggs. The simple clay ground or bare rock ground with four-five sticks of wood or grass in the name of nest. The eggs laid are 6, 8 or 10 in numbers. The eggs are as large as the eggs domestic fowls and pure white in colour. After 10-14 days the baby chiks come out and move with their mother.

Red finch and black finchs : Shilwanee : This is the best place for the breeding of wild birds. The land is best known as heathland and is full of thorny bushes with fruits. Some of the birds despite insectivorous are fruit eaters also. There are plenty of small song birds in the barrenland which make nests over the branches of bushes and some others on the walls of pastures and lay three to four eggs there. Some bird lay red eggs, some blue, some green and some brown with spots.

Sadkhet : Chakore : Sadkhet is a barrenland with the rubbles and agricultural fields. The area is dotted with large trees and small bushes which create a magnifiscent view from the far and near. It is foothill and moisturous valley and is known for insectivorous plants. The thorny bushes and long grass creates a good habitats for wild birds of this region. The birds like chakore, wildfowls, turtle dove, teetar, kingfisher, Karaoon both blue and red are found here. The small song birds are found in abundant numbers. The thorny bushes and berries remain full of fruits and small birds enjoy these during summer. Chakore gives about eight eggs in a simple nest under the bush. Sadkhet valley is popular for the habitats of chakore.

Mousebird : Dhaarkot, Bajarkhat : The mouse bird, bulbul, tailor bird, bushfinch, turtle dove, red finch, black finch are found in large numbers. The moisturous plants and thorny bushes make a good combination and make a ground for the insect breeding. The mouse birds, bulbul, turtle dove and wildfowls catch them in large numbers. The water fowls of the area have been vanished away because of drying up the water sources. This has created a big problem for the survival of wild birds and insects. The mouse birds are an amazing birds. The birds are always jumping up and down from the wild bushes. The small forests of the bushes and dwarf trees are a natural place for their breeding. The mouse birds and bulbuls aways make nests either in bush branches or on the wall cavities of the rocks.

The Beautiful Baheli forests : The Baheli oak and cedar forests are the oldest in this area. The pine forests also are of ancient time. The wild birds mammals, reptiles and primates are found in the forests. Baheli is 50% grassland and 50% forestland. The main species of the forest trees are Pinus himalayensis, deodara cedrus, myrica esculenta, rhododendron, Himlayan oak and several other plant species are found here in the wild. The pastures, valleys, forestland and grasslands are quite enjoyable during trekking. The natural areas and forests in Baheli remain most pleasant the year round.

Among the mammals are tigers, bears, wild boars, primates, foxes, rabbits, porcupines, weasels, wild cats and wild mouse are found in the forestland and grassland.

Bio-diversity of Daaligaad forests : The Daaligaad forests are quite amazing for varieties of plants and trees. The whole forestland is a mixed vegetation of dwarf plants and trees. Most of them are dwarf evergreen trees with green shining leaves and white stems.

1. **The Mountain Mahua Tree :** Useful in fodder and firewood. The poisonous parts of the leaves are used to intoxicate fishes and then catching them into the river water.
2. **Shakeen and Asheen :** The flowering bushes : These food vegetable bushes are found in the semi-temperate zones in Shivalik hills. The flowering buds are used in making breads, namkeens and vegetable and used in food items.
3. **Ferns and lingad :** A large number of mountain ferns are decorative plants. Some fern species are used in food vegetables from the very ancient times. The fern "lingad" are used as food vegetables. The paste of boiled lingads is mixed with flour to make breeds for food.
4. **Orchids :** Orchids are most beautiful flowers. They are found in Pauri Garwhal, Pithoragarh and almost

whole of Shivalik Range of Uttaranchal. Shivalik mountains are a haven for orchids. Two types of orchids epiphytes and terrestrial are found in Shivalik hills.

5. **Lilies :** Lilies are most impressive flowering plants i.e. Lily himalayensis, Lily tigris and Lily martagon.
6. **Jangli Piyaaj :** Urginea indica is a species of lily. It is a herbal medicine found in Pauri hills.
7. **Haida :** Haida is a fruit tree with sharp bitter taste is considened a medicine for cough, fever and other diseases.
8. **Amla :** Amla is a wild fruit rich in Vitamin C and is used in various medicines in India. It is also used in several food items as pickles.
9. **Timla :** It is a ficus family fruit rich in gum and Vitamins. It is said that skin diseases and cancer can be cured by this fruit.
10. **Khaina :** (Ficus auriculata) : Khaina is from ficus family and is known for its sweet fruits rich in vitamins also fight cancer and skin diseases.
11. **Tunga :** Tunga bushes have fruits during winter months and are used to clean stomach and skin deseases.
12. **Dhaula :** Dhaula are a sweet flowering bushes and its flowers are used in various pickles and medicines to cure various diseases. These flowering bushes are the native plants of Shivalik hills.
13. **Gadh Mahua :** Gadh Mahua is a dwarf, poisonous, dark green leaf tree used to kill fishes in the river. Although this green leafy tree is not used as fodder for cattles.
14. **Khinna :** The paste of Khinna leaves is also used to kill fishes in the rivers when it is mixed with River water into the form of a paste.

15. **Surai :** Surai is a cactus and used to poison fishes. It is also known as Sullu, Suru or Sulla.

Floral Diversity : Around 110 trees, plants and flowering bushes are found in the hills. These are useful for human being in the form of food vegetables, medicines and fruits. Some 14 tuberous roots, 10 orchid species, and lilies are found in the wild of Daaligaad, Uttaranchal.

Zoological Diversity : The mammals, reptiles, primates, rabbits, avifauna, porcupines, weasels and other small mammals are found in Daaligaad forest area.

The birds are : Teetar, chakore, wild fowls, turtle dove, Karaoon (magpie blue and red), red finch, black finch, mouse bird, bulbul, white paradise, waterfowls, blue bird, black magpie and several other beautiful birds are found in the wild of Daaligaad and surrounding small forests.

There are more than 2000 dense forest areas, scenic forests and grasslands, natural areas, some national parks in the hills of India and many more in other states of the country. All these should be protected in favour of wildlife and eco-tourism activities. Such efforts will protect our forests and also will generate foreign exchange through nature tourism, eco-tourism, and wildlife tourism in our country.

4

Bio-diversity of the World

Biodiversity : The bio-diversity of the world is found in different countries and islands of the world. It is mostly concentrated in the vastly expanded rain forests of the world. These forestlands are more enchanting, amazing and recreational. From floral to zoologial diversity, the whole world is a living laboratory of plants and wild animals where the experiments on various animals, their survival, food chains and survival of the fittest, laws of biological evolution are occurring with a systematic process on the planet. There are numerous plants and animals with their amazing nature and ecological importance. The bio-diversity is found in various habitats in the world. The whole process is an ecological occurrence managed by nature itself.

There are several reasons of vanishing away the wildlife of the world. Among them main reasons are: global warming, pollution, human population, deforestation for human settlement, agriculture, ranches and farm houses. The agricultural expansion and development work has led the maxium deforestation in the rain forests of the world. The bio-diversity of the world is badly suffered in various parts of the world. The bird fauna is the worst sufferer among them.

• **Himalayan Monal (Lophorus Impejanus):** It is an endangered bird of the Western Himalaya. The reason of its extinction is its hunting for its feathers, meat and Kalgi in Pakistan Himalayas. In the past sixty years, it was first spotted in 1980 in the pastures of Chanshal valley in Himachal Pradesh.

• **California Condors:** The California condors are now an endangered species. This is the largest bird of eagle species and is on the verge extinction. There are only 33 California condors in the wild now : Some 18 condors in California and 15 in northern Arizona. Every year, there are some efforts to breed them in captivity and release them in the wild. This process has made the population of condors capable to survive in the wild.

• **Sierra Bighorns in Peril :** Famous Sierra Bighorn sheep (ovis canadensis) population is declining every year because of continuous hunting. Now the population is limited to 100 individuals. The subspecies occurs only on the crest and the eastern slope of Sierra Navada Mountain Range in California, USA. One reason of decline in the population of the wild sheep (Bighorn) is considered the hunting and the disease. The domestic sheep are not allowed in the habitats of the wild sheep in the Sierra Navada mountain ranges in California. Some of them are killed by mountain tigers. These are the wonderful goats in the world.

• **Endangered Mexican Grey Wolf :** Mexican Grey wolf (canis lupus) were released in the Apache National Forest. Among the 11 wolves 5 were shot by the hunters. In Eastern Arizona, two of them were shot by the hunters. Three were taken back into captivity.

• **Rain forests of Amazonia :** These are the largest wilderness and rain forests in the world covering about 4 million square km forests in Amazon area. It is estimated that around 1.6 million forests of the rain forests in Amazonia have been destroyed by the timber companies, farming process and urbanization.

The Amazon is known for its amazing wildlife and bird fauna. The wild animals include elephants, bears, tigers, jaguars, stag deer, small deers, caiman, crocodiles, black crocodiles, Python and Boa tree snakes. Several other species of water snakes like Anaconda are found in the wilderness of Amazonia.

One fifth of the world's birds population is found in Amazon forests. There are most beautiful and amazing bird species in these forests.

• **Brazil's Atlantic Forests** : Once the Atlantic forests were spread to one million kilometers square but now are reduced to 2%. The Atlantic forests are famous in the world for their peculiar ecological existence. Now, there are only one third of the Atlantic forests existing in the Southern Brazil. On the 20th October 2005, Brazil's Ministry of Environment announced the creation of two protected areas in the state of Santa Catarina. The 12,481 hactare Araucarias National Park and the 6,563 hactare Mata Preta Ecological Station are of great importance to protect the Atlantic forests. The remnant forests of the Parana or Brazilian pine (Araucaria angustifolia). The Araucaria pine forests of Sorthern and South eastern Brazil, a distinctive formation of the Brazilian Atlantic forest, once covered more than 20 million hactare but devastated by the timber industry and for agricultural development has reduced to remnants covering a mere 20% of that area. The pine has been on the Brazilian threatened species.

Australia's Temperate Rainforests : The temperate rain forests of Australia have unique ecological existence in the world. These forests are located on the North Eastern Coastal strips of the continent. These are the most beautiful rain forests known for amazing wildlife.

Rich Biodiversity of Socotra Archipelago : These islands belong to Democratic Republic of Yamen in the Arabian ocean. The islands are known for more than 300 plant species, more than 60 butterflies and moths and 21 reptiles endemic to this archipelago. There are 24 bird ecosystems. The species are threatened because of the construction of roads and uncontrolled development. If the road is constructed through the islands, 19 bird species would be affected by current contructive activities.

The environmentalists and bird lovers have requested to Yamenese government to construct workable roads only and not the network of roads. They may pollute and drain these islands.

Fiordland: New Zealand : New Zealand government has porosed to create two giant island sanctuaries for wildlife in Fiorland. One of them is Secretary Island (8,140 ha) off Doubtful Sound and Resolution island (20,860 ha) off Dusky Sound will be transformed into safe havens for threatened wildlife. However, before all this can happen, pestcontrol measures will be undertaken to control or-eradicate the mice, deer, rats and stoats that have been recorded from one or other of the islands. It is hoped that the islands will become home to threatened species such as kakapo, mohua (yellow head) and rock wren. Resolution island may also be big enough to allow translocation of the threatened blue duck on to an Island Sanctuary for the first time. The Fiordland are the last standing forests in NewZealand.

The famous Grasslands of the world : There are some famous grasslands in the world known for their ecological existence. Some of them are found in colder places and some of them in tropical grasslands.

The Eurasian Steppe : The Eurasian steppes are in existence from the lce age. During the Ice Age the grass cover of steppes was quite different, distinct and small. The velvet or moss like grasses were in the existence at that time.

These are the large areas of land with grass and a few trees grow especially in South East Europe. The steppes of Russian Siberian grasslands are quite popular in the world. Once the mammoth elephants existed here.

The African Savannah : These are the plain, open, wide grasslands but with few trees. The trees are scattered and sometime are quite scarce.

Veld : The flat open land in South Africa, with grass and trees. The velds are the natural large pastures in South Africa and are a haven for birds, mammals and reptiles.

Pampas : These are the largest areas of lava that are covered with grass and have few trees. The pampas are the famous grasslands of South America.

The Australian Grasslands : The Australian grasslands have its distinguished characteristics. Some of the grasslands are within the wilderness like Kakadoo. The Kakadoo National Park, Australia and other wilderness Parks have some beautiful grass lands. Both wild and domestic animals benefit from them.

Downs : An area of open land with low hills, especially in Southern England, full of grass. The south downs are popular grasslands in England. The Downs are also found in Australia.

The Australian continent is the largest island nation which is surrounded by pacific ocean. It has largest grasslands in Australia. Australian wilderness like Kakadoo and Tasmania are the best examples of rich bio-diversity.

South American Savana: The South American Savannas are quite popular among the sheep and goat herders. These grasslands are a home for a large number of mammals, dears, wild birds and reptiles. The famous bird poto which resembles to the barks of a treestem is found in the wild of South America (Brazil).

North American Prairies : These are the famous grassland pastures of cold climate. These are the flat wide areas of land in Northern America and Cananda. The land is covered with many trees and originally covered with wild grasses.

The wild mammals, reptiles and birds are found here in the bushes and trees. The grassland is an ideal hiding place and habitat for the large birds of these grasslands.

The Ecology and Bio-diversity of wetlands : The wetlands all over the world have a distinct ecosystem and bio-diversity. There is some unique ecological system of the wetlands of the world. There is not similarity in the ecology and bio-diversity of the world. The wetlands are located in the different geographical areas and have their different ecosystems.

For example, the wetlands in the Himalayan region, and the wetlands in the tropical zones and the wetlands in the Arctic region have different ecosystems and ecological variations. All the wetlands have different ecosystem and bio-diversity.

The Wetland Bio-diversity : The wetland bio-diversity is known for its distinct flora and fauna (aquatic animals). The lakes usually are surrounded by moisture loving trees and aquatic plants. For examples aquatic, plants, water animals, amphibians, (Frogs, snakes and crocodiles) are some of the animals of the wetlands. Besides this fishes, bottom fauna and several other micro organisms are found in the wetlands.

The Wetlands are a lifeline to several mammals, amphibians, reptiles and birds as they take shelter in the wetland and get enogh food and water for their survival. There are amazing wetlands in the world. The wetlands in Amazon, Andes, Atacama and Patagonia have different ecological systems and environment. Each wetland has its own animal and plant kingdom with its characteristic of adaptation.

The Pantanal : Pantanal wetland is an amazing ecosystem in the world. It is among the largest wetlands of the world, covering an area of 210,000 kilometer square. The Pantanal is quite well known for its marsh deers which number 60,000. This population is around Uberaba lake and in the Flood Plains of Negro River in the South East of the Pantanal. There is no any evidence in the decline of the population of the marshdeers (Blastocerus dichotomus) in Pantanal wetlands since 1974.

1. Patanal is known for its animals (mammals), reptiles, birds and poisonous insects.
2. Several amazing species of birds are found in the Pantanal forests and wetlands. The strange bird Poto is found here. It has a colour of the tree barks and takes rest on trees in day time and flies in the night.
3. Several cranes and water birds are found in this amazing wetland.
4. Crabs, molluscs and snails are found in this wetland.
5. Several plant species of dwarf trees, tall trees, bushes and wild grasses are found in this wetland. There are hundreds of species of aquatic plants and moisture loving plants. The people from far and wide come to visit this wetland just in enjoy its bio-diversity. Due to its different landscapes it has become a tourist's paradise.

Kushiro Marsh : Kushiro Marsh is a water submerged marshland where water birds, fishes, water bottom animals are found abundantly. Several water plant species known for their characteristics are found here.

The wetland is a home to several aquatic plants and wild animals. The wetland grass, trees and bushes provide shelter to birds, cranes and insects. Marshland is a heaven for several amphibians also.

Yancheng Marshes : Yancheng marshes are famous for its wild vegetation, aquatic plants and wild life. The marshes are known among the botanists of the world. This is among the largest wetlands of the world and is known for its different plant species.

Mekong Delta : Lower Mekong Basin comprises parts of Laos, Thailand, Cambodia and Vietnam and covers an area of 6,20,000 sq. kms. The upper and lower Mekong basins cover more than this area. In this way, the Mekong Delta is the largest wetland in the world. The lower Mekong Basin is the home for 60 million people. About 80% of the population is predominantly rural and rely heavily on natural resourses for their livelihoods. Distribution of the population varies greatly across and within the riparian countries, the Mekong Delta, the Vietnamese Central Highlands, and the Khorat Plateau in Thailand are far more densely populated than large parts of Cambodia and Laos. Physiographic features include uplands with peaks up to 2900 m. in northern and northeastern Thailand.

There are several aquatic, marsh bottom plants in the Delta. The wildlife is varied and characteristic.

The Sundarbans : Sundar Bans are known for Sundari trees which are widespread in Ganga Brahmputra Delta in West Bengal and Bangla Desh. The two-third of this delta has moved toward Bangla Desh. There is only one third of Sundar Bans Delta in West Bengal. The ecology of Sundarban wetlands is tropical and the wild life is distinguished, different and diverse. The marsh deers, tigers, leopards, snakes, birds, green snakes, turtles, water birds are the main attractions of Sunderbans.

Longbeach Lagoon South Africa : It is a most important Wetland of South Africa which is a heaven for waders, waterbirds and water animals. The wetland is under threat from port expansions, pollution from sewage, urban development and town infrastructure development. According to Bird life South Africa, the lagoon which is a Ramsar site provides shelter 24,500 waders in the summer, of which 93% are Palaeartic migrants.

One of the most serious threats to the lagoon is the expansion of iron ore terminal which is set to double the capacity of exports. This expansion has been criticized by conservationists because of its expected impact on it. The hydrology sediments has effected bird life and shore line of lagoon. Damage to the lagoon caused by the original part development in the early 1970s is still in evidence on the eastern shores of the lagoon.

Garamba National Park : The number of Rhinos in Africa is declining day by day as the poachers are killing them for bones, skins and horns. The skin of Rhino is very costly and fetches up to 60,000 US dollars in international market. Most of the African people are poverty stricken and kill the wild animals for money. Garamba National Park is between the boundaries of Congo and Sudan. Now, there are fewer black Rhinos than they were 30 years ago. Once in the Parks of Zimbabwe, there were 67,000 Rhinos but now there are only 3000 Rhinos alive in Chabore Safari Park, Manapools National Park and Saiji National Park. The Unesco World Heritage and European Economic Commission have financed in thousand of dollars to save these Rhinos in the forests of Zimbabwe.

Latest estimates put Africa's total Rhino population at 14,720 of which 3,630 are black Rhinos, which have seen an increase of 500 (15%) in the past two years. There are currently 11,080 white Rhinos although as few as 20 are northern white Rhinos a race now reduced to a tiny population in Garamba National Park on the border of Democratic Republic of Congo and Sudan. There are still reckoned to be 90% fewer black Rhinos than there were 30 years ago.

Wadden Sea : The Wadden Sea is a small sea and there is a worldwide call to protect it from the oil pollution. The World Wide Fund for Nature has called for the protection of Wadden Sea which is surrounded by Germany, Denmark and the Govrnment of Netherlands. Twenty thousand sea birds were killed because of oil pollution.

World's Second largest Wetland, Congo : World's second largest wetland reserve has been designated in the Democratic Republican of Congo. This is the second largest wetland in the world after the Queen Mauda Gulf Migratory Bird Sanctury in Canada.

The 5,908,07 hactares makes up Congo's Grand Affluents Ramsar Wetland. There inhabit 300,000 people as well as many species of birds and is an important source of water. The four major tributaries of the Congo flow through the newly designated area and three rely on a transport network for local communities. The wetland reaserves designated at the same time as the Grand Affluents Wetland include areas on major tributaries of the Congo and two coastal wetland reserves. This wetland has a great importance to the people living there as well as the wild animals found in the periphery of the wetland.

Ningaloo Coral Reef : Ningaloo is among the most beautiful Coral Reefs of the world known for its rich marine biodiversity. This fragle coral reef is 300 km long along the remote coastline of Western Australia. It is one of the longest fringing coral Reefs in the world and hosts many threatened species of fish, turtles, dugongs, whales and whale sharks.

The Government of Western Australia recently took a decision to expand the areas and ban the fishing nets in Ningaloo Marine Reef Park. The area has been expanded from 10 to 34 percent.

The new projects are on the pipeline to all two third of the Parks recreational fishing and seeking one third for prosperities of the natural ecosystems.

This decision follows one by the Australian Government to increase the area protected in the Great Barrier Reef from 4.6 to 33.4% meaning that 11 million hectare of this world famous reef are now protected by a network of sanctuaries.

Ningaloo Coral Reef has become quite popular among the tourists and Marine Park explorers of the world. There are several varieties of fishes, crabs, mussels, sponges, clams and other bottom animals of human recreation.,

Galapagos Archipelago: The Galapagos island is quite popular among the tourists and biologists all over the world. A spotted bird which lives on the trees only is found here.

The Galapagos Islands are known for their rich bio-diversity. The Galapagos are known for Darwin Research Centre which was established by Charles Darwin during his exploration of these islands.

The Isabella island was completely devastated in the forest fires of 1985. The 25,000 acre land of Isabella was burnt into ashes in the same year and most of the plants, trees and wild animals died with the flames of fire. The island is 80 kilometers long and 60 km wide. The 25% part of the Island is evergreen and remaining is a dry and have burnt with the lava of volcanoes. This Lava melts from the fire of volcanoes of this Island. The population of Island is 1000 and 150 live in Santo Thomas isolated colony. Galapagos is the breeding centre of rare turtles of the world. The Elephantos turtles have become rare. It is said that only one male elephants turtle is surviving in the Galapagos and a search for female turtle is continue.

Madagascar : The island of Madagascar is known for its rich bio-diversity in the world. The famous forests and grasslands of Madagascar are being protected by Unesco World Heritage Department. In 1995, Germany also donated 30.5 lakh dollars for the protection of fauna and flora of Madagascar. The wetlands and forests of Madagascar are well known in the world. Several water birds, mammals, reptiles and fishes are found in the wetland, which create a habitat for rich bio-diversity of plants and animals.

The Meller's Duck (Anas melleri) : This rare duck is found in the wetlands of Eastern Slopes of the central highlands of Madagascar. But the Mallard Anas platy rhynchos is common and the other ducks are different species of ducks.

The genetic analysis indicate that the duck is distinct from Mallard species and from its nearest geographical contender, the yellow-billed duck Anas condulata, and may have evolved from a non-climorphic an ancestor of the African black duck, Anas sparsa.

The declining numbers of the Near Threatened Melleri duck highlights the need for adequate protection of its wetland habitat.

World's Largest Marine Reserve : An area of ocean equal to the size of California has been formally designated as a Marine Protection Area by the Pacific Island Nation of Kiribati. At 4,10,500 square kilometers the Phoenix Island, Protected Areas is the largest such reserves in the world and protects one of earth's last intact Coral Archipelago Ecosystems. Within the reserve's boundaries are eight coral atolls unsurveyed submerged reef systems, sea mounts, deep sea habitats and tuna spawning grounds. The largely uninhabited Phoenix Islands are located in the central Pacific, between Hawaiii and Fiji and form an archipelago stretching for several hundred kilometers.

Papua New Guinea: The rich bio-diversity is unique and amazing in the world. The larger red parrots, beautiful song birds, mammals, butterflies insects, plants and colourful fishes are exported to rich countries. The amazing flowering plants, bushes and various species of orchids are found here.

A vast areas of tropical forests have been wiped out for the plantation of oil palm and timber. Some foreign timber companies have made this island nation a hell by felling the important forest areas.

A novel use of satellite images has revealed that a major portion of forests have been felled which threatened a large number of bird species living in these forests.

The researhers have compared high resolution images of the island between 1989 and 2000 to determine the extent of detorestation, and then over laid the maps of forest loss with habitat preference maps of the island's birds.

It is estimated that 12% of the forest cover was lost between 1989 and 2000, with 20% in lowland forests.

In many areas, the deforested land were replaced by oil palm plantations. The researches calculations showed that 21 birds species have suffered significant declines following this deforestation. The forest land is rapidly being cleared for oil palm plantation. This further reduced the important rain forests in the island.

The mangroves : Mangroves Bio-diversity is disappearing at an alarming rates. At present, more than 20% mangroves have been disappeared. Crices 3.6 million hactares of mangroves were lost between 1985 and 2005, equivalents to world's 20% of the total mangrove area.

This rate of loss is higher than that suffered by other forest types, yet the loss of mangrove forests can have dire effects on the ecosystems, livelihoods and tourism.

The major drivers behind mangrove forest loss are population pressure, conversion of forests for shrimp and agriculture, pisciculture, infrastructure development and natural causes such as pollution and global warming.

The situation may not improve in the near future. There is deforestation at an alarming rate from 187,000 hactare annually in the 1980s to 120,000 hactare annually between 2000-2005.

Desert Bio-diversity : The desert bio-diversity is quite different from that of tropical forests. The desert areas are with scattered grassbushes, desert plants and very small vegetation at some places. Open berren land isolated huge tracts of land are there with sand mounds.

The Horn of Africa : The Somalia is called the Horn of Africa. It is surrounded by Gulf of Aden and Indian Ocean. Most of the part of Somalia is a desert covered with scanty grass and very low dwarf trees are seeen for several kilometers. Very few part of land is fertile and there is rampant poverty in the country. Although it is surrounded by ocean from two sides even then it has not developed greenery or moisturous environments in the desert. Theft, decoity and sea pirates are common seen on the coastal cities of Somalia.

The crime rate is growing up and the development is not upto the expectation of the people of the country.

The Namib Desert : The Namib desert is in Namibia in Africa. It is in the north of Kalahari Desert which is most wild, dangerous to track and often fatal with violant animals. There are some nomadic communities livings in Kalahari desert.

The Deserts of Patagonia in Andes : The deserts of Patgonia is the fourth largest deserts in the world. It is spread in 480000 km^2. Some of its part is icefield full of glaciers and a larger portion is dry open barren desert land. The vegetation is rough and with thorny bushes which is a characteristic of Patagonia deserts. The storm here which are known as fatal winds move at a speed of 200 kilometers per hour. These winds are quite devastating and move away fast with the things which come in to the way. There are several huge, rocks, bushes and wetlands also in Patagonia deserts. These deserts are known for vicuna, Guineas pigs, rabbits and other small animals. Puma the desert tiger exists here.

The Turkistan Desert : The deserts of Turkistan have some characteristics in their vegetation. The sparse vegetation with small bushes and dwarf trees, the Turkistan Deserts have distinct desert ecosystem in the world and are known for their natural beauty and arid open landscapes.

Some deserts in the world are quite harsh and hard to trek. The landscapes are touching and remains into our memory for a longer time. The Desert of Turkistan and Patagonia are somewhat beautiful but quite harsh to trek. The other deserts of the world are quite hostile. Every desert in the world has its own natural history and distinct ecological systems.

The Australian Desert : The Australian Deserts have different Ecosystems and environment in the world. The vegetations and soil cover and micro vegetation have distinct impact with sparse growth of trees and bushes after a distance.

There are some peculiar instances of ecological variations of deserts in Australia.

The Great Sandy Desert in the North of Western Australia and Great Victoria Desert in the South Australia are quite popular among the trekkers and explorers of the world. The Great Victoria Desert is spread upto a large part of Western Australia. This has an unique ecosystem in the world.

Just South of the Great Victoria Deserts lies the most fertile land : The Nullarbar Plain, and after the Nullarbar plain there is a vast beach resort of the Great Australian Bight which is the main attraction of the worlds explorers and trekkers. This is the largest natural curved beach in the world and the people explore it through vehicles, planes or on foot.

Some of the natural places in Australia are of greater significance for the tourists and explorers. Coral Reef ecosystem and the coral island ecosystem are some of the best locations to study the environment and the bio-diversity of reef islands.

Antarctica : Antarctica is a continent covered with vast sheets of snow with glaciers in it . It is the fifth largest continent, with an area of 14,245,000 square kilometers : twice the size of Europe or Australia. It is surrounded by the South Atlantic and Southern Oceans. The land has high mountains and huge plateause covered by a vast ice sheet. Nine tenths of all the ice and seven tenths of all the freshwater on earth are held in Antarctica.

Antarctica is the coldest place on earth, with temperatures as low as –89°C, and there are frequent blizzards and gales. There is no permanent human population in it but this harsh environment is home to millions of animals including seals, whales, penguins, terns; gulls and more than a hundred species of cold climate fishes.

Antarctica belongs to none, although many countries have claimed parts of it for themselves. These claims have been suspended and the continent is controlled by the Antarctic Treaty.

The international agreement on Antactica was signed in 1959, by 12 nations. Since then more than 20 nations have signed and a further 17 have agreed to abide by it.

The Treaty states that Antarctica should be used for peaceful purposes. It forbids the use of land for military activity, nuclear explorations or radio active wastes. It calls for scientific research and cooperation in Antarctica.

The treaty is at the heart of Antarctica conservation policy and, within the Treaty, two conventions have been organised. One protects and conservers seals and the other preserves living marine animals. Many conservationists say that once mining begins Antarctica's special environment will be destroyed forever.

The Antarctica Treaty came into effect in 1961 but it was agreed that after 30 years any of the 12 original signing nations could request a meeting to review it. This was to request in 1991 but it did not because of the opposition of the world environmental agencies. Antarctica's future as a wilderness is not yet secure. We all the citizens of the world should do our best to protect it.

Green Peace (NGO's) Campaign : It is an international environmental group which want to make Antarctica preserved forever. Their own research base is there. (1) Give complete protection to all wild life and their habitats. (2) Keep Antarctica as a region of scientific research and co-operation (3) Keep Antarctica as a zone of peace : no military or nuclear weapons would be allowed there. (4) Ban any extraction of minerals (5) Ban the disposal of poisonous, radioactive or other harmful waster there. Green Peace is doing its best to protect the Antartica and make it a zone of peace in the near future.

Borneo Sumatra: The orang utans (man of forest) are the great apes who live in the forests of Sumatra. It is estimated that there are 2000 orangutans in the nature reserves. Another 2000 live outside the reserves. Those who live outside the reserve forests, their chances of survival are small as the forests are being reduced at a greater speed.

Philippines : Philippines is a country of islands. There are hundreds of islands in the Philippines Archipelago. These are known for most beautiful birds and mammals. There are 9 species of colourful kingfishers in Philippines.

The bio-diversity of the world can be calculated through various species of mammals from different category. (1) Carnivores. (2) Hoofed Mammals, (3) Primates (4) Sea mammals, (5) Marsupials (6) Rodents (7) Insectivores (8) Bats. In systematic orders the carnivores are: tigers, lions, civets, African Palm civet and Hyenas. Madagascar carnirores are wild dogs, bears, Raccoons and Weasels.

Thailand : Thailand is known for its beautiful rain forests and amazing wildlife. It is popular for Hornbills, elephants, and turtles. Thailand is known for its beautiful beaches and international tourism activities. It is known for its beautiful birds. There are 12 species of Hornbills found in the dense forests of Thailand. There are total 52 species of Hornbills in the world. Thailand have largest species of Hornbills in the world. Some of them are being studied by Hornbill Research Foundation, Mahidol University, Thailand. The primates and reptiles are also very impressive animals here.

Rare Monkies in Vietnam : Tonkin snub-nosed monkey is the rarest animal in the world found only in the Khera ka forests of Vietnam. At present the population of the monkeys is 200. Fauna and Flora International is conducting a project in Vietnam border forests to protect this monkey. Vietnam is also known for most beautiful birds in the world. There are some amazing species of reptiles and primates. The another beautiful monkey Cao Vit Gibbon (Nomascus nasutus) is found between the border forests of China and Vietnam. The monkey is vanishing away because of habitat loss, regular hunting, limited carrying capacity of remaining habitats. The local peoples groups, voluntary organizations are doing their best to protect the Cao Vit Gibbon monkeys (Nomascus nasutus). The forests are being protected with the help of NGOs and mass support.

Uganda-Rwanda and Congo : The forests of Uganda, Rwanda and Democratic Republic of Congo (formerly Zaire) are quite popular for the habitats of mountain gorillas : (Gorilla gorilla beringei beringei). Since the civil unrest in the early 1997, the mountain gorillas have suffered a big setback as the encroachment of forests by the effected population. This has disturbed their population as some 60 gorillas were killed by the poachers in two decades. The Mountain gorillas with a world wide population of about 600 are found only in Uganda, Rwanda and the Democratic Republic of Congo. Many of the births in DRC have occurred in families that have been disturbed in the past three years as a result of the conflict in the region. The park authorities in partnership with the International Gorilla Conservation Programme (IGCP) are rehabillitating park region and re-equipping the park guards. The park staff is to monitor the status of the gorilla groups and to protect them against poaching and working with the communities surrounding the park.

Decline of Boa Snakes : Boa tree snakes are quite popular is the world. They are found on Boa trees in Round Island near Mauritius. For some reasons, their population is on the decline. Boatree snakes (Casarea dussumeri) have always been diffcult to breed in captivity. Collected in 1977 and 78, the snakes bred successfully in 1980s but since 1990 the eggs have either been infertile or failed to hatch modifications made to Boa's diet, accommodation and sound environment, ultra sound scans to check reproduce cycles and finally the supplementation of the diet with calcium and vitamin D_3 have achieved the desired results. In August 1998, 12 clutches of eggs hatched successfully.

Bonobos Threat in Congo Basin : A survey was conducted on bonobos, pigmy chimpanzees found in the congo basin. Once, this basin was a stronghold of bonobos. The survey was conducted in Salonga National Park in the Democratic Republic of Congo and covered an area of 12,000 square kilometer. No live bonobos were encountered and sightings of nests and dungs were made in only a quarter of the area surveyed. It is now thought that bonobos population is 10,000. 80% fewer than was previously thought. The survey found abundant evidence of human encroachment into the park and of poaching. Salonga National Park was created in 1970 especially to protect bonobos. It can be assumed that the species is in crisis across the Democratic Republic of Congo.

Protection to New Zealand Plants : New Zealand is internationally renowned as a plant-bio-diversity hot spot. 80% of the country's vascular plants are endemic. The flora has been on decline and in recent conservation assessment four vascular taxa plants were listed as extinct. Other 199 native vascular plants were classified as acutely threatened, a further 102 taxa plants are in serious decline and so the taxa plants are at risk.

The New Zealand Plant Conservation Network is doing its best to protect these plants with other government departments. The network is getting popular with its conservation efforts to save the taxa plants.

5

Bio-diversity of the Oceans

The oceans are the rich in bio-diversity. It were the oceans where life originated and evolved first. Later on, the life originated on the earth. In this way, oceans are the great source of marine life. For example coral reefs, the whales, sharks, dolfins, sword fish, shiner, seals, walrus and various other marine animals are an excellent examples of living world in the seas.

There are a dozens of seas and have their own marine ecosystems. Most of these are known for their characteristics of marine life.

(1) Crabs, mollucs, crustaceans, (2) Fishes of cold and warmer oceans, (3) Whales and sharks, dolphins, seals, walrus, penguines cord fishes, shiner, manatees and river fishes. (4) Small animals of the oceans are also found in the warmer seas as well as colder seas.

There are ten main species of whales found in the oceans. Among them most known are 1-Humpback, 2-Great Right 3-Sei, 4-Bowhead 5-Minke, 6 Fin, 7-Great killer, 8 Blue Whale (the largest) 9-Great sperm and 10-Grey whale.

The Bering Sea : This sea is in the extreme north of Kamchatka Peninsula of Russian and Aleutian Islands. This is the colder sea and known for several dozens of cold climate fishes, crabs, and whales.

The North Pacific Right whales Eubelaena glacialis is an endangered species of whale now. For two days the locations of Right whales were searched out in the Bering sea. According to the scientists of the National Oceanic and US Marine fisheries the numbers of the Right Whales was found double in this survey. These new sightings increased the number of whales from 13 to 25. The Right Whale is one of the most amazing discovery. There has been a small but a recovering population in the Eastern North Pacific sea but illegal harvesting has had a serious impact and there have been concerns that the species was fighting for its existence. Recently, there have also been sightings of several threatened blue Whales in remote waters in the Gulf of Alaska.

Leatherback Turtles in South Pacific : The leatherback turtles is South Pacific Ocean Islands are being protected with a broad based programme.

The environmentalists and local villagers from all over Melanesia recently met in the Horiara in the Solomon Islands to develop 93 year plan of priority actions to support regional Turtle Conservation Programme in the South Pacific Ocean Islands.

The plan focuses, particularly on the leather back turtle (Dermochelys coriacea) whose numbers in the pacific regions have fallen by 97% in 22 years.

Protection to Krills of Antarctica : Krills are the shellfish in the colder oceans and are the main food of whales. The whale lovers all over the world are trying to protect the krills in the oceans. If there are krills in the sea, there are whales and if the krills (the shellfish) is gone, the life of the wales is always in danger as the krills are their main food chains. Citing to a reliable report there is 40 percent decline in the population of krills in the seas. The main reason of this is considered pollution and global warming.

A research team from the British Antarctic Survey has suggested that the krill population is declining with the retreat of the winter slice, which most scientists believe is being driven by global climate change. Krills are mainly caught as food for domestic animals and fish, and while the fishery relatively small at present, most observers expect that to change rapidly as technology allows krill to be harvested more efficiently. The commission for the conservation of Antarctic Living Marine Resources, which regulates southern ocean fisheies, travels to have a new monitoring framework in place before any boom on the krill fisheries.

Basking Sharks at UK Seas : Basking shark is being protected at the 200 nautical miles at the UK seas. The basking sharks (catorhinos maximus) are among the rarest sea-animals and are found in British waters and expanded colder waters. The basking sharks have been listed on Appendix I and IInd of the Bonn Convention on Migratory Species (CMS), strengthening protection measures in international waters. The UK Marine Conservation Society has compiled a proposal which was submitted to Convention on Migratory Species Conference of Parties, which was held in Nairobi in November. Listing the Basking sharkes under the convention means the country should work with the adjascent sea nearby states.

Basking sharks have been protected in UK waters since 1998 under the Wildlife and Countryside Act but beyond Zoo nautial boundary of UK jurisdiction, the species is vunerable to exploitation. It is widely accepted that fishsing for basking sharks are not sustainable due to the species life history characteristics of low numbers of offspring per adult and slow growth rates.

Gray whales in the North Pacific Ocean : The declining of Gray whales in the waters of North Pacific Ocean has worried the whale lovers and conservation organizations all over the world. The Grey whale's feeding grounds are around

Sakhalin Island. It was thought that there were only 23 breeding female western gray whale-out of a total population of 100.

International Whaling Commission in a meeting had explained in July 2004 that there was a great need to protect the gray whales. The UK had put forward a resolution which was accepted by 57 member nations. Any construction, drilling and development work in and around Sakhalin Island has been banned for sometime forbidden.

New Marine Parks for South Africa

The South Africa sea coasts are amazingly beautiful for their scenic beauty. The marine bio-diversity is known for its richness.

The South African government has created some new Marine Parks in the coastal area. In this way the country's protected Marine-coastline has increased from 11 to 18%. The four areas are : The Aliwal shoal a sub-tidal coral reef off Umkomass that protects threatened sharks, Pondoland, including 90 kilometer coastline near Port St. Johns, which extends 15 kilometers seawards, marking the start of the "Sardine Run' Bird Island in the Algoa Bay that includes many rare and threatened seabird species, and Cape Peninsula, that includes all coastal waters around Table Mountain National Park.

A fith marine protected area is planned off Namaqualand at 9,70,000 hectare will be South Africa's largest marine park.

Fish stock dead in North and South Antarctic Ocean : The United States of America is the largest exporters of seafood to the world. The North and South Atlantics most of the richest fish colonies have been depleted because of over fishings.

It is a well established fact to it that North and South Atlantic Oceans have been popular fish stocks of different species. Because of over fishing most of the stocks of fishes were depleted. The four stocks are (1) White flounder (2) Blacktip sharks (3) South Atlantic and (4) Gulf of Mexico.

Later on, over fishing was halted for spiny dog fish, summer flounder, South Atlantic yellow snapper, North Atlantic swordfish and black tip shark. Out of a total of 894 federally managed fish stocks 76 are classified as over fished and 60 are experiencing overfishing.

Coral Sea and Marine Bio-diversity: Coral sea has a richest bio- diversity in the world. The name coral sea is given because of coral reef from Gulf of Papua New Guinea to the North West of Queensland State of Australia. The coral sea is amazingly known for its marine bio-diversity. The coral sea is spread between 45° to 160° Longitudinal of the Globe along Queensland state of Australia. It is popularly known for its amazing fishes, molluscs, crustaceans, sponge, clams, sharks, whales, crocodiles, turtles, Dugongs dugons, water birds and other marine animals are found in large numbers.

The Great Barrier Reef : The Great Barrier Reef has been divided in 70 bio-regions of which 30 are reef bio-regions and 40 are non-reef bio-regions. In the northern part of the Great Barrier Reef, ribbon reefs and deltaic reefs have been formed. These structures are not found in the rest of the Great Barrier Reef System.

There are no atolls in the reef system and reefs attached to the mainland are rare. Fringing reefs are distributed widely but are most common towards the southern part of the Great Barrier Reef System. These Fringe reefs are mainly attached to the high-lands. Among them are WhitSunday Islands, Lagoonal Reefs are also found in the Southern Great Barrier Reef, but some of these are found further north, off the coast of Princess Charlotte Bay. Crescentic Reefs are the main features of reef in the middle.

The Great Barrier Reef supports a rich bio-diversity. Some of them are quite vulnerable or endangered species, some of which may be endemic to the reef system. The fishes are with many colours, shapes and sizes. These are the most impressive creatures in coral sea. There are more than 1500 species of fish live on the reef, including of the clown fish, and coral trout. Fortynine species are known to the mass spawn, with eighty four other species found on the reef spawning elsewhere in the range. There are thirty species of whales, dolphins and porpoises has been recorded in the Great Barrier Reef, including the minke whale, Indo-Pacific humpback, dolphin and the humpback whale. Large population of Dugongs live there, six species of sea turtles come to the reef to breed : The green sea turtle, leather back sea turtle, harksbill turtle, logger head sea turtle, slatback turtle and the olive ridley turtle. The green sea turtle have two distinct population : one on the northern part of the sea, the other in the southern part. Fifteen species of sea grasses in the beds of islands attracts Dugongs and turtles and provide a habitat for fish. The most common genera of sea grass are Halophile and Holodule. There are salt water crocodiles with low population diversity.

There are 125 species of sharks, stingray, skates or chimera which live on the reef. Around 5000 species of molluscs have been recorded on the reef, including the giant clam and various nudibranches and cone snails. Fortynine species of pipe fish, nine species of sea horse have been recorded. There are seven species of frogs in the islands.

The birds are major attractions in the water as well as the islands. 215 species of birds (25 species sea birds and 92 species shore birds) are attracted to the reef for nesting, roosting on the island including white belied sea eagle and roseate tern. Every year 1.4 million to 1.7 million birds are using the reef as breeding ground.

Four hundred species of corals, both hard and soft corals are found on the reef. Majority of corals sperm gametes; breeding in mass spawning events that are controlled by the rising sea-temperatures of spring and summer, the Lunar cycle and the diurel cycle.

The Great Barrier Reef is the largest coral reef system in the world. It is composed of over 2,900 individual reefs and 900 islands. The Great Barrier Reef is spread upto 2,600 kilometers over an area of 344,400 square kilometers. The reef is located in the coral sea off the coast of Queensland in northeast Australia. The Reef's structure is composed of and built by billions of tiny organisms, known as coral polyps. The Great Coral Reef has been declared the World Heritage Site in 1981. CNN has considered it among the 7 natural wonders of the world. The Queensland National Trust has named it state icon of the Queensland.

The Reef first became known to European when the Hum Bark Endeavour, captained by James Cook, ran aground there on June 11,1770 sustaining cousiderable damage. It was finally saved after lightening the ship as much as possible and refloating it during an incoming tide. One of the most famous wreak saw that of the HMS Pandora, which sank on August 29,1791, killing 35 people. The Queensland museum is conducting archeological digs at the site of Pandora since 1983.

Endangered Turtles of Hawaii: The sea turtles of Hawaii archipelago are always trapped into the fishing nets of the fishermen. Every year several wounded sea turtles are killed by fishing nets during fishing. The fishermen also use fluoresent lights to lure cordfish to the hooks and these also attract turtles. These trappings become quite fatal for the sea turtles. The turtles when trapped in fishing nets for hours they live in the sea water and this makes them difficult to breath as a result they die in the nets.

The Earth Justice Legal Defence Fund is taking legal action against those fishermen who kill the turtles.

Dugongs in Coral Sea : Dugongs Dugon an amphibian mammal will be protected in the Great Barrier Reef. The Australian government has proposed a 6000 kilometers increase in the Great Barrier Reef Marine Park so that the entire system is protected. A number of the new protected areas include sea grass beds that are of vital importance to dugongs (Dugong dugons) once the Queensland government approved the proposals, the new areas will be included in the Park under the Great Barrier Reef Marine Park Act. 1975.

Tuna Stocks depleting in Atlantic Ocean: The continuous fishing and over fishing in the seas have depleted the rich stocks of fishes in the ocean. The stocks of Tuna in the Atlantic ocean are depleting sharply. The International Commission for the Conservation of Atlantic Tunas has failed to take appropriate action to help severely depleted population of bluefin tuna (Thunnus thunnus).

It is acknowledged that Western Atlantic bluefin tuna are severely overfished and the commission has increased the catch question of three nations involved in the fishery i.e. Canada, Japan and USA.

Ban on the Shrimps: The shrimps and the crabs in the Bering sea and Atlantic Ocean are continuously depleting because of the fishing. The Bering Sea shrimps and crabs contractors catch every day of the value of 5 million US dollars. The other contractors may also kill the shrimp and crabs of the same value of less or more than this. The over exploitation of such marine animals is making their stocks exhaust.

Secondly, the World Trade Organization has ordered the VSAT lift the ban on imports of shrimps cought in nets that ensured and kill an estimated 1,50,000 endangered sea turtles every a year. India, Malaysia, Pakistan and Thailand claimed that the embargo on their shrimp exports was discriminatory and unfair waver to free trade. The USA may face retaliatory trade sanctions if the embargo is not lifted.

Monk Seals of Mediterranean Sea: The monk seals in the Mediterranean sea are on the verge of extinction off the coast of Mauritania. It is estimated that only 600 Monk seals (Monachus monachus) survive in the Mediteranean sea. They live mostly in small groups. The death of 200 Monk seals out of 270 is a subject of great concern to marine life lovers.

It is said that a dolphin micro virus similar to that causes distemper in dogs is being blamed for huge deaths toll among the Mediterranean Monk seals.

Orissa Sea Turtle in Danger

The sea beaches of Orissa are considered the safe haven for the nesting of sea turtles, particularly olive ridley turtles. For the the past several years, it has been found that olive ridleys (Lepidochelys olivaceae) nesting areas are being disturbed by the fishermen, dogs and eagles. The marine turtles are found dead several times during the period of nesting.

A record high 13,575 olive ridleys were found dead on the breaches of Orissa in 1997-98. The major cause of death is entanglement in Mechanical fishing gear, specially that is used for shrimp. Even through, mechanized fishing within 5 km. of the Orissa coast is illegal. The Wildlife Institute of India had recorded in 1999 that in four years duration 40,000 dead turtle were washed ashore.

New Species in Indonesian Sea: Every year there are some new species in the ocean of Indonesia. There are six new fish species, 15 new coral species found in the surrounding ocean. A multinational team of marine scientists has surveyed the Tongean and Banggai Islands in the central Sulawesi, Indonesia. A preliminary finding is the relatively high numbers in Tongean Islands. In less than three weeks, the team found four marine fishes that are perhaps exclusive to these islands. The coral reefs are fresh and in much better state than the other parts of Sulewesi and nearby Ceram.

This is the only place in the world where the Banggai cardinal Fish (Pterapogon cauderni) is found. This is highly valued fish in the world. The fish is in much demand in USA, Canada and Europe for their aquariums. The illegal smuggling of some fishes have reduced some species from sea.

The Sturgeon fish population decline : The overfishing of sturgeon (Acipenser oxyrinchus) have reduced its almost all the stocks in the Atlantic ocean. Seeing the continuous decline in the population of sturgeon, the Atlantic States Marine Fisheries Commission has banned the catching of fish along the entire cost for the next 40 years. The catch has dropped 90 percent over the past one century.

British Columbia's Sea Lions: Seeing the endangered sea lions of Southern British Columbia, some conservation groups have purchased South Winchelsea Island, north of Nanaimo in British Columbia, Canada. It is also one of the most important sites in Southern British Columbia for steller's or northern sea-lions. (Eumetopias rubotus) and California sea-lions Zalophus Californianus that come to feed on herring each winter.

Coelocanth in Indian Ocean : A small population of coelocanth is expected in the Indian Ocean. It has been seen in Indonesian waters also. On July 3o, 1998 a coelocanth (Latimeria chalumnae) was caught in a deep set gill-net off the island of Manado Tua, north Sulewesi, Indonesia, almost 10,000 kilometers from the only other known population in the Commores Islands in the Indian ocean. The first living coelocanth was caught in the 1938 in the Commores Island waters. Earlier, it was believed that it has already been disappeared from the seas. In the year of 1995, the presence of coelocanth in the fish market of the island surprised the marine biologists. Since then, many fishermen disclosed the catch of coelocanth in their nearer seas.

The Atlantic Cod Endangered

The population of Atlantic cods is depleting continuously because of overfishing. The Committee on the States of Endangered Wildlife in Canada has listed 307 endangered (or species at risk) species.

The Atlantic cod (Gadus morhua) is among the new sea animals listed as endangered species.

The Alaska Sea and killer Whales : The killer whales are known as orcas (orcinus orca) are preying on Alaskan sea otters (Enhydra lutris) and have nearly wiped out other colonies in parts of the Aleutian Islands. The orca whales also feed on sea urchins. The urchins feed on kelp but kelp is disappearing from the sea now.

Orcas feed usually on the much larger prey : Seals and sea lions-whose population have collapsed in the region in the past two decades. As a result, the orcas switch to new prey. Populations of sea urchins have declined and kelps bed on which urchin feed are disappearing.

Kelp is the base of the coastal food web and provides habitat for fish, its loss may affect adversely sea birds, bald eagles and other near-shore species of animals.

Caviar Stocks Exhausted in Caspian Sea : The Caviar fish population in the Caspian sea has been depleted due to continuous overfishing. The Caspian sea is surrounded by the Azerbaizan, Iran, Kazakhstan, the Russian Federation and Turkmenistan. These countries had agreed to reduce their caviar export quotas for 2004. The combined 2004 export quota for beluga, the rarest and most valuable of all sturgeon was 50% of the 2003 levels, while 2004 quotas for stellate sturgeon was 40% less and for Russian and Persian stage on 10% less than 2003 levels. It is estimated that world's 90% caviar comes from the Caspian sea. The high level pollution and, illegal trade has threatened the species.

The Whales in the Sea: Some countries are continuously killing the whales despite the strong Moratorium of International Whaling Commission.

In 1933, 30,000 whales were killed and the number rose to peak in 1960s. For sometimes this began to decline. In 1962, 67,000 whales were killed and in 1972, the 40,000 whales were killed every year.

The over killing made them scarce in the seas. Some of them have come to very close to extinction. Now there are only 1,000 blue whales, 4000 humback whales in Antarctica waters. Before whaling begans, there were about 2,50,000 blue whales and 3,00,000 humpbacks. The fin whale has fallen from 1,400,000 to 4000 in fifteen years.

Loss of Bio-diversity: It is estimated that once the largest species of the fishes in the seas are extinct now. So is the fate of other marine animals. The crabs and shrimps were much more larger but we witness their very minute form now. The loss of some valuable fishes, sea cucumber, coelocanth, snake fish and pipe fish in the seas is a serious warning bell for the existing animals living in the sea.

The continuous killing of sharks, dolphins and some small fish species like porpoises have become rare into the seas. The shark hunting countries do not realize the fact that their population is limited in the sea and their over exploitation may make them extinct.

Pollution in the Ocean: The pollution in the sea is increasing in millions of tonnes every year brought by floods and rivers. Every year, urea, CO_2, CH_3, CaCl, DDT, CH_4 and other harmful pollutions are rushing to the sea. The oil spill is creating a big trouble for water birds and marine animals. On December 7, 2004, the Malaysian freighter Selendang Ayu broke into two pieces after running aground off Unalaska Island in the Aleutian Island chains. The ship was carrying 4,83,000 gallons of heavy bunker fuel and 21,000 gallons diesel fuel. The amount of fuel spilled is unknown. The fuel spill threatens an area identified in 1977 WWF and the Nature Conservation as one of the highest properties in Bering sea. The spill is likely to have an impact on important commercial fisheries as well as local fishing and sensitive wildlife. The overfishing in the bering sea has made several fish, crabs, prawns and mussels endangered. At present the American ships are on the spree of commercial Fishing in the seas. Every year the river floods are flowing with millions of tonnes of garbage, salt, chemicals and poisonous substance which is fatal for fishes, whales, amphibians and sea snails.

Polythenes and oil slicks: The oil slicks, garbages containers and polythenes have polluted the environment of the Oceans. This has badly polluted the sea beaches and beautiful coastal areas as the sea waves sweep all the dirt to the coastal areas and beaches :

Acid and Detergents: Acid, detergents, insecticides, DDT and other poisonous substances are flown every year to the oceans.

Global warming : Impact on the Oceans

Global warming has effected our oceans at a larger scale. The sea bottom fauna, fishes, whales and delicate animals of the oceans have been effected. The coldwater animals are worst effected by the increasing temperatures of the oceans. The Crabs of Bering sea, prawns and cold water fishes are badly affected.

The growing temperature in the ocean base encourage the formations of coral reefs. (Coral polyps develop and multiply in the warm temperature.) But growing pollution has reduced their growth. Global warming has hampered the growth of cold water fishes. The Arctic Islands and Antarctica continent are melting at a higher speed. This well help in rising the sea level upto one meter and the coastal cities and villages will submerged into the ocean water. This will completely vanish away the small islands from the sea which at present are one meter above the sea level. Several atolls and coral islands will be submerged into the sea water. In some way, this will destroy the sea beaches, hotels, restaurants and human population which live near the coastal areas of the oceans.

6

Bio-diversity of the Rain Forests

The rain forests over this earth are of great importance to human being as well as to wildlife. These forests are found both sides of the equator. These are tropical moisturous forests and are called the lungs of the earth as they absorb more CO_2 and release O for us to create a good balance of oxygen in the environment. These forests can affect the environment of the earth, even the place at which we are sitting and talking.

The Amazon rain forests are the largest wilderness in the world. These are two thirds of the total area of the world's rain forests. In 1987, 2004,00 square kilometers of the rain forests were burned to clear land for agriculture. In 1988, the figure was slightly smaller, about 121,000 square kilometers. It is estimated that the total area of rain forests in Amazon is 4 million square kilometers. In Amazonia, 48000 square kilometers were virgin rain forests. Guatemala, Honduras Nicaragua, CostaRica, Panama, Colombia, Equador, Peru and Brazil have rain forests. In African continent, Ivory Coast, Ghana, Togo, Benin Nigeria, Camaroun, Gabon, Congo, Zaire, Uganda, Kenya and South Eastern Madagaskar are the best examples of rain forests and rich bio-diversity. In South East

Asia, Western Ghats of India, some North Eastern states of Java, Sumatra, Borneo, Sulawesi, Papua New Guinea, Halmahera, Taiwan Hainan, North Eastern Australia are among the best examples of rain forests in the world. The bio-diversity is varied and amazing in the South East Asian Countries. The land animals and the marine animals have a great distinction.

The forests of Amazon which have been destroyed, burned or damaged is equal to an Australia.

The worst suffered is the bio-diversity of the rain forests of Amazonia (The Amazon wilderness are the best cover of rain forests in the world.) Almost one third of the rain forests have been cleared in the last four decades.

The affect of this destruction on the climate is quite evident from the devastating natural calamities. The changing pattern of weathers has effected the wildlife and marine animals also.

Among the most endangered animals are the amazing primates with beautiful form and impressive voice. These depend entirely on forests for their food habitats. The wooly spider monkey is the first primate to die out when the ecosystem of rain forests is disturbed. It is estimated that there are only 100 spider monkeys left alive in the rain forests of Brazil. This is the most fragile animals to die out first.

The Rain forests of Java, Sumatra and Borneo: The rain forests of these countries are moisturous, dense and full of amazing bio-diversity.

The orangutans of Sumatra are the most endangered primate species now. It is estimated that as many as 2000 orangutans exist in the nature reseves of Sumatra. Another 2000 live in the forests outside of the reserves. Their chances of survival are small because of the rate at which the forests are being cut down. The same story is awaiting the fate of other harmless and beautiful animals in the nature.

The Species lost forever: The rainforests contain a greater number of plants and animal species than other habitats on earth. Many species of animals are still unknown to scientists. It is estimated that by the year 2015 a large number of forests will vanish away from the earth. So, is the fate of bio-diversity existing in those forests.

The worst thing is that the rain forests are vanishing away at an alarming speed. Every year thousands of hectare of rain forests are being cleared for agriculture, human settlement, burning and slashing, and permanently damaged by the vehicles and staff of logging crew. Around 15000, square kilometers of rain forest are damaged alone by wild fire and the logging crew.

The Great Apes

The worst sufferers are the Great Apes as their population is on the verge of extinction. It is estimated that some of the Great Apes could be extinct in the wild within a human generation. It means within 50-60 years, the Great Apes may be vanished away from the earth. This theory has been explained through many sources. The future of the remaining Great Apes: the Gorillas, Chimpanzees and Bonobos of Africa and the Orang-utans of South East Asia (Sumatra, Java, Borneo) is in danger. The Great Apes are the monkies without tails.

The Sumatran Orang-utans are critically endangered great Apes which number 7,300 in the rain forests. They mainly are found in Aceh province at the northern tip of Sumatra. The state saw an armed conflict for decades between the Indonesian government and separatist rebels which suffered heavily during December 2004's Tsunami.

The Mountain Gorillas

The mountain Gorillas of Democratic Republic of Congo and the Cross River Gorillas, found on the border between Nigeria and Cameroun are also categorised as critically endangered, with numbers, estimated 700 and 250, respectively. The habitats and food resources of the Gorillas are vanishing away with the felling of trees.

For gorillas and Chimpanzees, ebola fever is also emerging as a significant threat. This fever is quite fatal and takes the lives of several apes every year.

Bio-diversity of Rain forests of Brazil: There are world's one fifth bird species in the Great Amazonian wilderness of Brazil. Some of birds are most amazing and beautiful. Some are large and some are small in shape and size.

The Caiman Crocodiles

The Caiman crocodile is found in Brazil wetlands. It can be seen in Amazon Wetlands and Pantanal wetlands (2,10,000 square kilometers). The largest Rodent of the world is also found in Pantanal.

Protected Areas of Brazil : Brazil Ministry of Environment announced the creation of two protected areas in October, 2005. These are in the states of Santa Catarina. The 12,481 hactare, Araucarias National Park and 6,563 hactare Mata Preta Ecological Station are both of great importance in protecting remnant forests of the Prana or Brazilian pine (Araucaria angustifolia). The Araucaria pine forest of Southern and south eastern Brazil, a distinctive formation of the Brazilian Atlantic forest, once covered more than 20 million hectares but, devastated by the timber industry reduced to remnants covering a mere 2% of that area. The Brazilian pine has been on the Brazilian threatened list since 1992.

Birdlife UK

Birdlife (UK) has received 2 million US$ to protect the Atlantic forests of Brazil. Now, the amount for the conservation of Amazonia has a target of 21 billion US$. The Birdlife is doing its best to protect bird fauna and wild animals all over the world.

Deforestation of Amazonia is increasing every year. This has caused great concern among the environmentalists and rainforest lovers all over the world.

The Continuous Deforestation

Deforestation in the Brazilian Amazon had reached by 27 percent in 1998 with 16,800 square kilometers were cleared. Since 1972, 532068 square kilometers, 13.3 percent of the entire Amazon region, has been lost. These figures could be underestimated because satellite monitoring cameras identifies only deforested areas over 6 hactares.

It also misses 10,000-15000 square kilometers a year that are severely damaged by logging crew and fire damage to standing forests.

The Amazon National Park : The Brazilian President in 2006 had passed a resolution to expand the world famous Amazon National Park further by 1,50,000 hactares and had created seven new protected areas in Para state. The main reason to create these parks within Amazonia was to make them living laboratories of the fauna and flora found there and protect them for a longer time in the history of the bio-diversity conservation campaign of Amazonia.

Further more, one of the decrees establishes, Brazil's first Sustainable Forest District, which aims to futher sustainable development in the country.

In total the decrees will increase the size of western Para's protected areas to 6.4 million hectare, while the Amazon region as a whole will include 45.8 million hectares of protected area. An increase of one third compared to 2003. The seven new protected areas are in the way of planning to protect the amazing bio-diversity of Amazon. Unfortunately, logging is continue in some areas of the Amazon forests which has created more problems for the surival of bio-diversity there.

The global warming is creating trouble to the existing amphibians in the Amazonia and other tropical forests of the world. The life of the marine animals has been effected in the oceans. The chytrids fungus (Batracho chytrium dendrobetidis) has been implicated in amphibian extinctions in the American tropics and at some places the population of amphibians have declined systematically.

America provides evidence that higher night time temperatures are creating optimum conditions for Batrachochytrium dendrobatidis growth with 78-83% of extinction occurring during usually spin off from global warming, will also benefit the fungus as cloud cover promotes moist conditions and shield the fungus in amphibians of the tropical areas.

The Rhinos of Congo Rain Forests

There are some amazing species of Rhinos in the forests of Congo. At present, Africa'a total Rhino population is 14720 of which 3630 are black Rhinos, which have seen an increase of 500 (15%) in 2002 and 2003.

There are currently 11,090 white Rhinos. There are 20 northern white Rhinos, an special species from the northern forests. The race of northern white Rhino is reduced to tiny population in Garamba National park on the border of Democratic Republic of Congo and Sudan. The increase in the number of black Rhino is encouraging after a decline from 65,000 in the 1970,s to only 2400 in the mid of 1990s.

However, there are still reckoned to be 90% fewer black Rhinos than there were 30 years ago.

Kibale National Park, Uganda

The selective logging has caused a great disturbance to the bio-diversity of Kibale National Park in Uganda. This has effected the primates in the Park with gastrointestinal parasites. The bacteria in Redtail monkeys (Carcopithecus ascarius) has effected 92% population of monkeys in the logged forest and 29% in undisturbed forests. This compels monkeys to eat more and more infected invertebrates in the forests. This causes gastro-intestinal disease in monkeys.

The Amazing Primates

In contrary, Red colobus monkeys (Pilio Colobus tephrosceles) and black and white colobus (colobus guereza) from logged and undisturbed forests showed no significant difference in parasite loads, possibly because logging does not affect the diet of these species.

Malaysian Rain Forests : The cloud tigers, pangolin, anteater and other wild animals are found in Malaysian rain forests. The primates are of several species with different nature and habits. The bird fauna is quite amazing and diverse. The strange species of mammals is found in the forests of Malaysia.

The Milky Storks

Habitat loss, human disturbance and poaching have caused a big threat to the wild birds and water birds. The milky stork (Mycteria cinerea) of Malaysia. The Malaysian Nature Society has announced that only 10 birds remain in Malaysia, making extinction within five years a distinct possibility. The estimated global population of the Milky stork is 5550 individuals, with about 5000 in Sumatra.

However the stork's habitat in Indonesia is also under threat, from agricultural expansion and development schemes. For the conservation of Milky storks and their captive breeding, the mangrove development and expansion plan remain continue. Global warming and habitat loss have effected the population of milky storks.

Most Ancient Rainforests of New Guinea : Papua New Guinea is a haven for fauna and flora in the world. This island nation is known for its rich bio-diversity. The large red civets, big mammals, insects, birds and amazing flowering plants are exported from this island to other parts of the world. The export of birds, animals and plants have made them economically strong. Here, we can see the bio-diversity as business.

Amazing Bio-diversity

A team of scientists visited the island nation in the year 2006 and found it amazingly rich in bio-diversity. The rain forests here are now one third of the entire forest area. The Conservation International found here the most isolated jungles in Asia. The Foya Mountains in Western New Guinea has found dozens of new species including a honey eater, 20 frog species and four species of butterfly. The expedition also obtained the first photographs of the spectacular Berlapsch six wired Bird of Paradise, thereby confirming the location of the range of this remarkable species. The interior of the Foya Mountains Range, which consists of more than 300,000 hactare of old tropical forest growth, form a part of Bird Life North Papua Mountain Endemic Bird Area (EBA).

The Endangered Amphibian Animals: The amphibian animals in the rain forests and tropics are vanishing away because of global warming, habitat loss and fungal diseases in the forests and the wetlands.

In a first global survey conducted in 2004, it has given a bleak picture of amphibian animals in rain forests and Tropical areas.

The amphibians are under great threat than birds or mammals according to the results of the first world wide survey. Almost a third of the 5,743 known species of amphibians are threatened and 427 species (7%) are classed as "Critically Endangered."

Environmental Change: Main Threat

The resources for the declines are largely unknown and in almost 30% of species there are not enough data to discover population trends.

Amphibians tend to have smaller ranges and are less tolerant of environmental change than birds or mammals, making the more vulnerable to habitat loss and overhunting.

It is thought that the fungal disease chytidiomycosis may be responsible for severe declines but the fungus was present well over 10 years before decline began.

The fungus itself can be controlled in captive frogs but not apparently in wild populations.

Canada's Great Bear Rain Forests: Canada's 20,000 hectares of rainforests known as the habitats to Great Bears is being protected by country's NGOs, environmental organizations, industry leaders and the indigenous groups. The people are celebrating after their campaign to protect the Great Bear Rainforest has finally brought fruit, 10 years after its conception.

Conservation Efforts

The Canadian Government has agreed to legislation that will protect one third of the forest from logging and ensure that the remaining two thirds are logged using sustainable practices.

The total area of the forest is 20,00,000 hectare which is more than twice the YellowStone National Park.

The Mekong Bio-diversity Revealed

The Mekong Delta is among the first largest wetlands in the world. The Lower Mekong Basin compares parts of Laos, Thailand, Cambodia and Vietnam, and covers 6,20,000 km^2 of mainland in South East Asia. Myanmar's small share of the Lower Mekong Basin is 3% of the entire Mekong Basin. The Lower Mekong Basin is the home of 60 million people. About 80% of the population are predominantly rural and rely heavily on natural resources for their livelihoods.

The Greater Mekong Region

The extraordinary diversity of the Greater Mekong Region of South East Asia, where over 100 new species have been found in the last one decade, equating to two new species every week. Many of the species are spectacular to look at

400, such as bright pink dragon, millipede, and the world's largest huntsman spider, with a lage span of C-30 cm. Most of the species were discovered in the rainforests and wetlands of the Mekong. The spot highlights the importance of ensuring that development of local livelihoods and the conservation of rich bio-diversity.

Bio-divesity of Siau Island : A new species of tarsier, recognised as one of the world's 25 most endangerd primates, has been described from the tiny island of Siau, North Sulawesi part of the Sangihe Island chains a volcanic arc stretching north from Sulawesi towards the Philippine island of Mandanoa. The species is called Tarsius tumpara with tumpara being the name for the tarsier used by the inhabitants of the island. Siau is about one fifth of the size of Singapore and has a human population density of 311 people km square. More than half the island is an active volcano and the remaining habitat for this species is minimal. It is overhunted. Local inhabitants eat the tarsiers as sauce food they call tola tola and the species has been extirpated over much of the island as a result.

New Snub-nosed Monkey Found: A new species of Tonkin's snub-nosed monkey has been found in the Chinese border forests with Vietnam. The new population of Tonkin's snub-nosed monkey is critically endangered in Vietanam. The interviews were conducted in villages and it was found that the Tung Via commune had observed the monkeys after seeing film footage of the species supplied by FFI to a National Mission Network. Following the interviews the FFI led team of researchers located a group of 15-20 individuals of the species including three, juveniles, in a small forest patch in Queen Ba District.

Loss of Habitats: The Snun-nosed monkies are on the verge of extinction

The monkeys seemed wary of people. The main reason for their dectine is hunting for the bushmeat trade. The habitat destruction and pollution are major threats to the survival species of their.

There is a great need to reduce the human pressure on the ecosystems of the Vietnam forests.

Green Frogs in the Cambodia's Cardmom Mountains

FFI has conducted surveys in Cardmom Mountains and unearthed a species of frog previously unknown to science. Description of the new amphibians, samkos bush frog make it an interesting study. It has a green blood and tungusrise bones that are visible through its translucent skin. The reason for this coloration is that the frog does not process the waste product believed in its liver but instead this green pigment is passed back into the frogs blood. Since 2000 the FFI is working in Cambodia which has resulted in the discovery of more them 40 species including 4 frogs, not previously seen in the country. In 2008 FFI published the first field guide to cambodia's amphibians which is available in Khmer and English languages from the office of Fauna and Flora International.

Cambodia's national list of amphibians now stands at 63 species.

Bio-diversity of Galapagos Islands: The islands are a heaven for tourists from all over the world. These islands were favourite destination of the scientist Sir Charles Darwin who proposed the theory of evolution. The Charles Darwin Research Centre is working here since 1836. The Galapagos Islands are famous for their living bio-diversity. The elephantos tortoise (the Giant tortoise : Geochelone elephantopus) is found here. Now this tortoise is on the verge of extinction. This tortoise is quite different from the tortoises of other islands. Earlier, Geochelone elephantopus was endemic to the island of Florence but became extinct following intense human exploitation. Investigations into the genetic data of extant giant tortoises from another island in the archipelago; Isabela, showed that some living tortoises on this island are genetically extinct from the rest of the tortorises on the island.

The DNA Tests

Interestingly, the non-native tortorises from Isabela Island are of recent Florence Island ancestry and were found to have DNA that closely matches that of the extinct Geochelone elephantopus, indicating that the genetic lineage of this extinct species persists in descendants occupying a different island. These islands are also known for water birds, lizards, crabs, snakes and other small birds in the rainforests. The small mammals are also found in the islands. These islands are under the administration of Ecuadorean Government. The bio-diversity of Ecuador is quite amazing and impressive.

Orchids and Ferns of the Rain forests: The tropical forests are a heaven for floral diversity. There are so beautiful flowering bushes, amazing trees and plants rich in variety and beauty. Because of evergreen plant it becomes a scenic spot for the explorers. The ferms and orchids of Colombia, Peru, Ecuador, Venezuela, Guyana, Surinam, French Guyana, Brazil, Bolivia, Chile, Argentina, Paraguay and Uruguay are not only amazing botanical plants but a great creation of nature for human being. These plants are of a great value and recreation.

Colombia, Venezuela, Peru and Brazil are a heaven for most of beautiful orchids and Ferns of the world.

The City of Orchids

Moyobamba is a city of orchids in Peru. The population of this city is 50,000 and the orchids found here are 2500 species. That's why this city is called the City of Orchids.

The Orchid Flora

There are most beautiful species of orchids found int he forests of Thailand, Singapore, Borneo Java, Sumatra, Phlippines, New Zealand and Australia. There are best export items.

Particularly, Thailand and New Guinea are rich in orchids and fern plants. Thailand is the best exporter of orchids today. USA is also a best orchid exporter and buyer country.

Butterflies of Rainforests : There are several amazing species of butterflies the rainforests. Several species of them attracts the tourists from found in far and wide. The butterflies attracts the people with their beautiful colours and varieties. In a single species there are several colours and spots. The wetlands, wetclay, flowering bushes and trees are the best places for butterflies to visit and inhabit them. The butterflies of British Columbia, Mexico, Venezuela, Brazil, West Africa, South Africa, Madagasker and South East Asian forests have most beautiful species of butterflies.

Insects of Rainforests : The orthopoda is the largest world of insect group in the world. There are numerous species of insects, butterflies, moths, caterpiller, mantis and other species found in large numbers in the rainforests. The rainforests have sufficient moisture which is enough for their breeding and growing population in the wild. The rainforests of South America, Africa, South East Asia, have most beautiful and amazing species of insects. Some insect species have good habitats in rain forests of the world.

Macaw of Rainforests : The rain forests of Brazil, Venezuela Columbia, Ghana, Gabon, Congo, Cameroun, Borneo, Sumatra, Papua New Guinea have the species of most beautiful and large parrots in the world. Some countries like Papua NewGuinea are exporting some plants, trees and parrots to Western Countries. The export of wild animals and plants is the main economic backbone of Papua New Guinea.

The Amazing Bio-diversity: The rainforest growth in Pupua NewGuinea is amazing and unique in the world as these two island nations are surrounded by tropical sea.

The bio-diversity of Papua NewGuinea is rich and varied. The amazing wild animals are found here. The country is quite popular for its ornamental flowering plants in the world.

These tropical plants are in great demand for interior decorations in rich nations.

Reptiles of Rainforests: The world of reptiles is amazing, varied and impressive in the rain forests. The lizards, iguana, chameleon, giant lizard, monitor lizard, gecko lizard, boa tree snakes, king cobras, python, Antiguan Racer, green snakes, Anaconda snakes and some water snakes are found in the rain forests. The turtles are common sights in the rainforests. The common fresh water turtles, lake and pond turtles and wetland turtles are quite impressive sights in the forests.

Bird Fauna of Rain Forests: The birds are most beautiful and amazing creatures in the world. A large number of them are in the densely populated forests of tropical countries. One fifth of the bird fauna of the world is found in Amazon forests. Colombia and Venezuela have maximum species of humming birds. Africa and South East Asian have beautiful parrots, kingfishers, hornbills and birds of paradise in the world.

Mammals of Rainforests: The mammals in the rain forests are more violent and amazing. The mammals are in several categories: (1) The Carnivores (2) hooffed mammals (3) Primates (4) Sea mammals (5) Marsupials (6) Rodents (7) Insectivores (8) Bats. There are several species of violent mammals including lions, tigers, jaguars, clouded tigers and bears found in the rain forests.

Reasons of Loss of Forests, Loss of Habitats: It is a fact that the loss of forests is the loss of habitats of the wild animals. The primates, gorillas, chimpanzees, gibbons and pigmy chimpanzees, bonobos, orangutans are an endandgered species of because of reduction of forest areas at a larger scale. Almost one third of the forests of the world are gone in the last four decades.

Timber companies main hurdles: The timber companies are badly damaging the main forests at a larger scale. One third forests of the rain forests have been cleared in the past three decades. Besides agriculture expansion, urbanization and developmental projects have destroyed the rain forests at a greater scale.

Human Pressure, Agriculture and construction: Human pressure, agricultural expansion and construction of dams have destroyed several forests and natural areas. The growing population and massive urbanisation have destroyed natural forests.

Increasing Pollution: Increasing pollution, garbage and chemicals are polluting the environment with a greater speed. Polythenes, juice cans, several boxes and plastic bottles have been dumped in the forests and natural areas. This has created a big problem for the growth of plants, trees and medicinal herbs. For rain forests it is more destructive as it lowers the level of moisture in the forests. The wild animals and plants both are affected by this pollution.

Global Warming: Global warming is the main enemy of new forest growth, moisturous environment and local bio-diversity. The changing weather patterns have destroyed the balance of the ecology of rainforests. The mammals, avifauna, reptiles, orthopoda and several amazing animals found in the rainforests of the world are on the verge of extinction. One third of the rainforests of Brazil have been completely wiped out by the timber companies, agricultural expansion projects, farm houses and ranches recently established there. This has badly damaged the ecological system of the Amazon forests. It is said that for the reforestation of Amazon, there is a need of 21 billion US $. Several NGOs and voluntary organizations of the world have raised their voice in support of the fresh conservation activities for the protection of Amazon forests.

7

Conservation of Bio-diversity

Meaning of Bio-diversity: The animal and plant kingdom in a particular eco-system is known biological diversity. For example, the plants and animals in a forest ecosystem are known as bio-diversity. Various animals, plants, trees and micro plants are a part of a thriving bio-diversity. There are small eco-systems as part of bio-diversity. For example, wetland ecosystem, rainforest eco-system, Atlantic forest ecosystem, Alpine forest ecosystem and Shivalik Hills ecosystem also contain a large numbers of animals and plants. This balance of animals and plants in nature is known as bio-diversity. The floral diversity of the Himalayan mountain ranges is quite well known among the botanists and ecologists of the world.

Bio-diversity within two km square: The bio-diversity in various parts of the world varies from place to place. According to ethnobotanists and floral experts, the bio-diversity within a geographical area varies after two kilometers. The mountain herbs, trees and plants show some variations exhibiting different ecosystems after a distance.

Ecological Changes After a Long Distance

The orchids and fern species exhibit some ecological changes after a long distance. The plants and animals at a higher altitude create a distinct ecosystem. The faunal-diversity also shows some distinction and change in some species after along distance in the area. The plants, bushes, trees and wild animals found in the area have a great quality of adaptation in the nature. Global warming disappearance of water sources and increasing pollution have created an ecological imbalance on the planet. As a result, a large numbers of plants and animals have been disappeared in the last one century. Among them are kakato Hornbill: Philippines, Himalayan Quail, Mountain goat, patiyabagh, leaf-tiger (a panda like animal) Uttarakhand. Several other species of wild cats mother of domestic cats and colourful birds have also been disappeared from the ancient forests.

Fauna And Flora: The fauna and flora depicts the range of bio-diversity in a particular place. How much bio-diverstiy is there. The biodiversity consists of plants, trees, herbs, wild animals and micro animals present in a particular area. There is a different range of bio-diversity within two km^2 range, 10 km^2 range and 100 km^2 range. A typical bio-diversity pattern is found in a certain geographical area, forest land and vst wild lands. All of them have their typical ecosystems. That is obvious in the wetlands, moisturous forests, heathlands and highland pastures. Some birds and animals have distinct features in pine forests (pinus himalayensis) and different features in Deodara cedrus forests. As some animals have traditional affection and closeness to some trees, bushes and plants. The birds make their nests in certain plants of their liking. The presence of distinct flora and fauna in a particular place is known as a spot of rich bio-diversity. Some birds have traditional history of nesting on some ancient trees and bushes of some particular species and origin.

Bio-diversity and Conservation Activities: The bio-diversity of the world is on the brink of destruction because of continuous deforestation, loss of traditional habitats, increasing pollution and global warming. Global warming and pollution have killed many plant species and wild animals in last one century. The conservation and protection of wild animals and plants is necessary for the citizens of the world. The continuous reforestation of native plants and trees is necessary to avoid the migration or extinction of wild animals. The extinction or migration was noticed after a long interval in the forests which were deforested within a decade. The mammals, the reptiles, the avi fauna, orthopoda and other micro organism in the moisturous forests. The main reason of the extinction of the wildlife was (1) deforestation (2) pollution, (3) global warming (4) hunting (5) expansion of agriculture (6) housing and development. (7) Loss of Wetlands (8) Growing Population.

In some regions of South America, African continent and South East Asian Nations, there is continuous hunting of birds, mammals, reptiles and primates for food and charred meat is offered to their guests and visitors.

Reforestation of Native Plants and Trees

The native plants and trees are the soul of local environment. If a forest is cleared within a year, the reforestation activities should be initialed the same year. The natural process of plantation, reforestation of native plants and trees should be maintained to recreate the environment once lost.

In Himachal and Uttaranchal several species of native trees and plants were reforested during monsoon season and this was proved very successful for the growth of new forests. In the original place of the plants cleared in the past one year new plants were raised. The plantation of foreign species proves harmful to the native plants as the invading species destroy the local plants and trees. Impact on the environment and the wild animals is also adverse and they too do not feel comfortable with the growth of foreign species. For example, the Eucalyptus, American bushes and subabool trees have destroyed the local plants and trees in the last two decades in the mountain region of India. In India, new growth of native plants and trees should be allowed to raise up. The invading plants and trees should be destroyed.

Loss of Amazon forests: The loss of Amazon forests is the loss of the environment and an important ecosystem of the world. The traditional habitats of the wild animals in Amazon rain forests have been completely wiped out by the timber companies and logging crew staff. This has resulted the migration of wild animals i.e., tigers, elephants, primates, deers and reptiles to other parts of the wilderness. One third of the Amazon forests have been completely wiped out by the farmers for agricultural expansion, housing, construction of roads and dams. This has resulted in the disappearance of wild animals, orthopoda and woolly monkies. The whole ecosystem of these forests is disturbed because of uncontrolled felling of trees regularly. This process has reduced the rainforest area in Amazonia by one third. By now 20,00000 km^2 forest land in Amazonia has been destroyed by timber companies for ranches and agriculture purpose. Now, there is a great need for reforestation work in the region. The NGOs related to the protection of these rain forests want to raise US$ 21 billion for the reforestation and rejuvenation of Amazonia ecosystem.

Rain Forests of Australia: Australia's Wet Tropics Queensland World Heritage Area covers 897,420 ha. It is located in the North East Coastal Region of Queensland State. This World Heritage Area comprises a proportion of 1,849,725 ha Wet Tropics biogeographic region. Cheludi old Growth forests is located 50 km. North West of Dorrigo and 100 km from Grafton. The area contains over 7,000 ha of unlogged ancient forests. The grasslands of Australia are amazing and quite useful for cattle raising and dairy farming.

Rain Forests of Africa: The rain forests of Africa are known for their rich bio-diversity. The forests and plain grasslands are quite popular among the tourists from western countries. The Wildlife Parks are amazing and full of evergreen cover of trees and plants. Here also, two third of rain forests has been cleared out by timber companies, agricultural, housing and other developments. Ivory Coast, Ghana, Togo, Benin, Nigeria, Cameroun, Gabon, Congo and Zaire are known for their densely populated rain forests and famous grass lands : Savannas.

Rain forest Bio-diversity of South East Asian Countries: Thailand, Laos, Cambodia, Singapore, Java, Sumatra, Borneo, Philippines, Papua NewGuinea and North Eastern Queensland, Australia are known for their amazing rain forests rich in bio-diversity. In these countries, one third forests have been vanished away or destroyed for agriculture by the concerning governments or by timber companies. Some social and environmental organizations have raised their voice against the continuously felling of rain forests for timber and other developmental activities. But this campaign is not very successful to create mass opinion all over the world. The Rainforests Protection Clubs and NGOs are doing their best to protect the rainforests. They have campaigned against continuous felling and logging. The continuously felling of trees and logging by commercial companies have reduced the world forests to one third. All the timber and furniture is imported by the Western countries. The forests of Papua New Guinea have been cleared by the timber companies. The wild life of those forests is vanishing away slowly.

The Conservation Campaign

Several environmental and conservation organizations will have to do their best to create public opinion to protect the forests and wild life of Papua New Guinea. The voluntary agencies, the government and the local communities have created country's first national conservation area. The YUS conservation Area is named after three rivers : Yopno, Urua and Som rivers. This is a 760 km^2 area of tropical forests on the Heon Peninsula. From this conservation area, the endangered Kangaroo, a marsupial that occurs in the newly protected forests will be saved. The local people also benefit from the protection of the resources and services provided by the forests. It is estimated that all forests will contain 13 million tonnes of carbon that will now remain locked up in the forests. The land is under the private ownership and the villagers have campaigned to prohibit all hunting and development work in the area.

Conservation of Nigerian and Cameroon Chimpanzee: The rain forests of Nigeria and Cameroon are in danger as they are being cleared at an alarming rate. This will effect the habitats of chimpanzees. In Nigeria and Western Cameroon a large population of Chimpanzees exists. The secalouris are near the Niger River and Sanago River. This name was given by John F. Gray in 1862 on the basis of a specimen he received from the explorer Richard F. Burton. Gray believed that Burton had collected the animal from Mount Cameroon but released by John Oates, Colin Groves and Paubina Jonkins has indicated that, impact, the type specimen cama Mbata Gabon, to the south. The name Vellerosus is, as such a junior synonym of Pantrogladytes troglodytes. The next available name chosen by John Oats and his colleagues was Pan troglodytes ellioti, a specimen from bas ho Cameroon, described by Paul Mitschie in 1914, who gave it the name, in honour of Daniel G. Elliots support in the study of ape's natural history.

The Bio-diversity of Congo Rain forests: In the last one century the Congo forests have been disappeared by two third. There are only one third forests existing in the northern and southern Congo. The elephants, monkeys, gorillas and chimpanzees are on the verge of extinction because of poaching, hunting and skin and ivory smuggling.

The international organizations like Fauna and Flora International has done its best to protect the forests and the ancient habitats of elephants, gorillas and chimpanzees in various parts of these countries.

The Wildlife Survey

A survey was conducted in Ndoki forest of northern Congo and it was revealed that forest elephants disperse at least 96 plant species from 36 different families. Forest elephants which are smaller than their savannah-dwelling relatives, are therefore responsible for dispersing more seeds than any other species or genus of large vertebrates in African forests. Additionally, elephants carry the seeds farther than any other dispersers, with GPS telemetry showing that they travelled upto 24 km in 24 hours.

These finding underline the importance of large vertebrates for tropical forest structure and functioning.

The loss of elephants and other large-bodied herbivores from these forests could lead to recruitment failure among animal dispersed tree species, and shift the compositions of these forests towards tree species that are spread abiotically.

The future of Gorillas: The continuous felling forests in Africa has spread a warning bell among the conservationists all over the world. The rain forests are a habitats of rich bio-diversity and their continuous felling can lead to the disappearance of many wildlife species.

The Increase in Gorilla Population

A team of rangers from Congolese Institute for Nature Conservation has carried out a survey of the habitats of gorillas of the Administration Republic of Congo's Virunga National Park; finding that gorilla numbers in the park have increased by 12.5%. The habituated gorilla population now numbers 81individuals with babies having been born since the last survey in 2007. Despite, the good news, there is still concern for the long term safety of the gorilla population, with fighting in the region starting again recently following the arrest of the rebel leader who had controlled the sector of the Park where the gorillas are found.

Gorilla Monitoring

An agreement in 2008 had allowed the return of the rangers to the Park's headquarters, from which they had previously been evacuted, and thus the recommencement of gorilla monitoring.

The ecology of Congo rain forests is most suitable for the breeding of gorillas and other primates and hence should be protected by all means.

The Rain Forests of Madagasker

The rain forests and wetlands of Madagasker are slowly reducing. The reasons are urbanization, constructions of roads, increasing population, pollution and global warming. The forests are mainly cleared for agriculture and for the purpose of timber trade. There is a common opinion that the number of amphibians is declining across the globe.

A a large percentage of people in this planet have no proper knowledge about wildlife management and the amphibian biodiversity. Particularly in the tropical countries. At present, one third amphibian species have been disappeared from the planet. These animals are more vulnerable to global warming and pollution.

The researchers have shed light on amphibian bio-diversity hotspot of Madagasker by examining morphological bio diversity and genetic variation of the islands amphibians. The results obtained from DNA sequences of 2850 speciemens from over 170 locations, indicate that the current number of 244 described amphibias in Madagasker may increase two fold, to a minimum of 373 and upto 465.

This means that continuous habitat destruction in Madagasker may be affecting more amphibian species than previously thought and it is also likely that amphibian diversity has been under threat elsewhere in tropical countries.

The frogs from Mexico, Cambodia and Tanzania

The golden frog from Mexico rainforest is quite impressive and is in perfect golden colour which is most beautiful species among the wild frogs in the world.

There are reports of green blood frog found in the Cardamom forests of Cambodia. The Fauna and Flora International team has launched a campaign to find other frog species in the Cambodian Cardmon Mountains and densely populated rainforests.

It is also quite surprising that there are some perfect red species of frogs on this planet which are quite impressive. Some of them are also found in the rain forests of Amazon and Cambodia.

The Red frog species from the forests of Tanzania is also one of the most impressive species in the world. This country is surrounded by lakes and beautiful rivers. The moisturous forests have some good species of frogs.

The Frogs from Andes

The Andes Mountain Range have the most spectacular natural and most impressive views to watch. There are found some beautiful species of frogs from mountain slopes to moisturous environment.

Reintroduced Toads in Puerto Rico: The population of reintroduced toad in Puerto Rico islands is in progress. The captive breeding has been one of the successful experiments.

In 1993 captive bred tadpoles of Puertro Rico, crested toad (awild rough frog with bulging eyes) Pettophryne lemur were released into a specially constructed pond in Puerto Rico as part of a programme to conserve the species, which was only known to breed in a single pond at Tamarindo in Guanica forest.

In November 2003, there was the first evidence that these tadpoles had matured and returned to the natural pond to breed.

Monitoring of releases is difficult as toads take shelter deep in limestone crest rock to avoid danger in the sub tropical dry forest.

The programme to help save this species is supported by a number of zoos in the US and Canada.

The Poison Frog

The Poison snow frogs (Poison-dart frog: Dendrobetes sp.) found in the foothills of Ecuadorean Andes. The poison secreted by poison dart frog has been found useful to human being. It is a powerful pain-killer which has no side effects.

Some countries have taken these frogs to extract medicines without the permission of Ecuador can Government. The environmentalists from Ecuador want to seek the compensation in place of these frogs, because this collection of frogs has reduced the population of poison-dart frogs in the Ecuadorean Andes.

The Bolivian Frog: Bolivia is quite popular for its beautiful frogs. A new species of frog in the genus Telmatobius has been described from 3050 meters at Chuspipata, Provincia Nov-yungas Departanto La Paz Bolvia. Telmatobius is different from all known species of the genus, except for Telematobius yurcare, by the presence of an externally projected humeral spine. The frog inhabits shallow streams in cleard forests on steep slopes.

The Decline of Bull frogs: The bull frogs are amazingly beautiful frogs found in the forests of Ontario, Canada. It's scientific name is Rana catesbeiana which is endemic to Petersborough county in Ortario, Canada. There is a 90% decline in the population of the frog. Ontario's Ministry of Natural Resources had banned the collection of frogs for commercial purposes in 1995 and for personal needs in 1996, but the extent of illegal captures is not known.

The only bullfrog poacher who has been caught and charged had 2000 adult frogs in his possession. Pesticides are believed to be a major factor in the decline they can cause mutations where exposure occurs early in the developmental stages. In ponds in agricultural areas of Minnesota and Wisconsin, USA and Ontario and Hull Quebec, Canada, 65-95 percent frogs are deformed.

Foya Mountains And Frogs: The most ancient forests in Foya Mountains of Western New Guinea are a home of 23 different impressive species of frogs, honey eaters, four butterfly species, six-wired Bird of Paradise is also found in these forests. The other frog species are also expected in the Foya Mountains.

The Frogs of Ghora Dhungee and Daaleegaad: The water frogs and toads of Ghora Dhungee and Daaligaad (Shivalik Mountains India) are quite amazing. There has been continuous decline in the mountain toads and river frogs of Gaad Paar since 1976. The limited rainfall, dryness of land, pollution in the valleys, the reduction of river waters in the mountains has reduced the population of mountain toads and river frogs.

The mositureous valleys which are considered equal to rain forests in the mountains, have dried up in the past three decades as a result there is continuous decline in tadpoles and frog populations in the open mountainland and small rivers. In the high and dry monsoon season, the frogs lay their eggs in the water filled ditches or wet clay and soon the tadpoles convert into frogs. This is also a miracle of nature which we (the writers and environmentalists) have witnessesd in the mountains.

Frog Harvest, A cause of Danger: The reasons of decline in the population of frogs in different countries is different i.e. diseases, prey animals like snakes, mongoose, mouse and other small mammals also prey on forgs.

The amphibian decline is linked to a diverse number of factors ranging from climate change (Global warming) to disease.

Global Trade Pattern: In an investigation of Global Trade Pattern the frog legs are being exported on a large scale. The export of frog legs over 20 years period have increased manifold. Using a UN data base it provides an insight into the levels of amphibians harvesting from the wild.

Global trade in frogs legs has increased over the past 20 years, with the major importing countries comprising France, USA, Belgium and Luxembourg.

The major exporting countries of frog legs are: Indochina, China, Belgium and Luxembourg. The market for frogs in Indonesia is scrutinised in particular, the domestic Indonesian market is thought to account for 2-7 times, the volume exported internationally 15,600 tonnes in 1992). The fat wild frogs legs are in high demand in European market. The poor nations are killing the frogs from wild to earn foreign revenue. This has caused the decline of some frog species from the wild.

Glass Frog: (Cochranelsl buenventura): This beautiful glass frog has been described from a small mountain range in the cordillera occidented in South Western Ecuador. This frog is having lemon green hands, with yellow discuss and a yellowish-silver irid with marown reticulations. An adult male 20.9 to 22.4 milimeter long. There are at present 11 glass frog species in the area.

The disease: The amphibians extinction is exacerbated by higher temperature. The chytrid fungus (Batra chochytrium dendrobatidis) has been implicated in amphibian extinctions in the tropical countries. A study of Harlequie frog extinctions (Antelopus spp) in South America provides evidence that higher night time temperature are creating optimum conditions for Batra chochytrium dendrobatidis growth with 78-83% of extinctions occurring during unusually warm years in the tropics. Additionally, increased cloudiness, a spin off from global warming, will also benefit the fungus as cloud cover promoter moist conditions and shield the funges from excess heat.

Rain Forests Ecosystem for Bonobos

The basin of Congo is a heaven for wildlife. The primates, mammals, reptiles and birds are found here with great varieties. The Bonobos are amazing pigmy chimpanzees found in this world famous wildlife region. Every year the survey is conducted on the population of Bonobos in this area and the population of Bonobos in on the decline. Once these pigmy chimpanzees were dominating this basin, now their population has reduced to 5000 from 10,000.

The World Wildlife Found, UK and Fauna and Flora International have been conducting regular surveys on Bonobos and various other species in the area.

The first detailed survey of a known stronghold was conducted for Bonobos or pigmy chimpanzees, the species which is found here in large numbers. This survey was conducted on the Salonga National Park in the Democratic Republican of Congo and covered an area of 12,000 km^2. No live Bonobos were encountered and sightings of the nests and dung were made in a small area of land. It is now thought that the Bonobos population is C. 10,000, 80% fewer than was previously thought. The survey found abundant evidence of poarching and human encroachment into the park. Salonga National Park was created in 1970 specially to protect the Bonobos. In Africa, monkeys and other primates are killed for food. The population of Bonobos his reduced since then.

Gorillas of Virunga National Park: The world famous Virunga National Park is famous for various species of birds, reptiles, mammals, and primates. The last link of modern wise man (Homeo Sapiens) is found here in the form of Gorilla (Gorilla beringei beringei). This park is spread into 8,00,000 hactares straddling the borders of Rwanda, Uganda and Democratic Republic of Congo.

The Mekino Area

There are reports of massive deforestation and encroachment in this park in Mikeno sector. The farmers and pastoralists and local NGOs, village organisations have jointly constructed an Eco Wall of stones to spread to 20 kilometers to stop the encroachment and to stop the park from deforestation. This is an ideal example by the local communities to protect the park through an Ecowall. In this campaign 2000 people's work force, 12 Congoan groups and some Rwandan community associations took active part.

The Need to Conserve the Wildlands: There is a great need in the world to conserve and protect the wildlands which are also the big hotspots of wildlife. At present, the natural areas and impressive wildlands are disappearing at an alarming rate. Some of the most beautiful natural areas and wetlands have been disappeared in the last one century. The tropical forests, the beautiful grasslands, valleys and wildlands with natural beauty are on the verge of destruction.

Mountain Forests: The two third of the mountain forests which once were thriving with wildlife and plant species, are now left into a fragile state. Most of the ancient forests and habitats have been disappeared from the mountains all over the world. The forests have been cleared for housing, agriculture, road construction, dams and other development work in the area.

The timber mafias, contractors and local authorities have felled them for timber, fuel and housing. The timber also transported to larger cities to sell to rich people for housing and furniture trade.

Rain forests: The rain forests are the lungs of this earth. These forests are rich bio-diversity hot spots and are very useful to human life. These are spread in the countries both sides of equator. The two third rain forests of the world are found in Amazonia, Brazil. The others found are in Ghana, Gabon, Cameroon, Congo and adjoining nations. Some of the rain forests are spread in South Est Asian nations. The wildlife is varied and amazing in these countries. There is a great need to protect the rainforests and bio-diversity found in those countries.

Wetlands: The world's wetlands are a thriving ecosystem for a large number of animals, trees and aquatic plants. The ferns orchids and Taxa plants are found near the popular wetlands. The popular wetlands are: (1) The Queen maude Gulf Migotory Bird Sanctuary, Canada (2) Congo Basin world's second largest wetland (5,908,074 hectare) known for Gorillas and different primates including pigmy chimpanzees. (3) The Pantanal wetland Brazil (2,10,000 km^2) (4) Mekong Delta (6,20000 km^2), (5) Yancheng marshes, (6) Kushiro Marshes, (7) Sunderbans, etc. are among the best known wetlands in the world.

Conservation Efforts : There is rich bio-diversity in the tropical forests and Himalayan Ranges in the world. Great efforts should be made to protect them. In Southern America, Africa and for South Eastern Countries the tribals kill the wild animals for meat, skin and medicine.

There is a great need for mass awareness campaign in those countries, so that a large numbers of wild animals may be protected.

Marking the Boundaries of National Parks : The best way to protect the National Parks and reserve forests is to mark them properly through fencing or through Eco Wall (The stone wall) erected by the volunteers, community leaders, citizens and the NGOS working for the protection of forests, wild life and beautiful natural surroundings.

Encourage Eco-Tourism: The eco-tourism activities may disturb the environment but it creates a great public opinion and awareness regarding the protection of wild lands, wild life and paves the way for sustainable tourism and development.

Marking The Eco walls of the Forests: There is always some encroachment in the forests and wild lands by the local communities. To protect the wildland there should be erected some eco walls and marking spots in the forests which separates the protected forests from the encroachment and developmental work.

There is a great need to fence the ancient forests and pristine wildlands through marking them with stone chaukis or Eco-walls made of rock stones of the same place. Such walls and fencing marks have been successful in protecting the wild lands in developing countries.

Stop Invading Species: The invading species are the worst enemies of native plants as they do not allow them to grow. Such species from plains should be stopped to invade the mountains as this creates more warming and the local plants are wiped out by the growth of foreign species. Such foreign species are being planted in the mountain areas in the name of fuel, fodder and timber which has proved harmful to the growth of native plants in the mountain slopes. The foreign species or invading species should be completely wiped out from the forests. No foreign plant species should be allowed to grow there. The devstating examples of such species are as Madagasker, some pacific islands and coastal countries where the heavy reforestation was done two hundred years ago by the colonial rulers to produce coal from the wooden logs.

Need of the Hour: Continuous Reforestation: The continuous reforestation should be maintained in the mountains. The deforestation of forest growth has resulted into the loss of habitats and bio-diversity. The native plants should be planted in place of felled trees. This task should be accomplished within two years, continuous felling of trees should be stopped for some years and local plants should be allowed to grow. For example Oak, Myrica esculenta Rhododendron are found in a single ecosystem in the mountains and they should be allowed to grow in the mountains and hills. The Deodara cedrus grow at 7000-8000 ft. and pine forest 4000-5000 ft. height and should be allowed to grow freely within their ecosystem.

Reforestations of Native Plants and Trees: In some experiments, in the past it was found that the growth of native plants was seen marvellous after some months of reforestation. The native plants were planted to make up the lost forests. After some years, the bio-diversity of that forestland was maintained perfectly well. The fauna and flora again came to life with massive plantations.

Complete Protection to Water Sources: The wetlands and water sources should be restored to its original forms. The moisturous forests areas should be protected by planting native species. To maintain plantation, soil moisture and forest eco system the reforestation should be done during rainy season.

Participation of Local Citizens and Communities: The local citizens and forest communities should be invited in the reforestation and wetland management programmes. The volunteers, NGOS, and tribal associations should take active part in the conservation activities.

Reduce Pollution: We should create a pollutionless environment over this planet. The whole world is effected by pollution of nuclear wastes, polythenes and different types of garbage. This has badly ruined our environment.

The local people legally consume the non-timber forest products required for the human needs. The forest wealth should be protected and harnessed in the interest of human needs and the efforts should be continued for its conservation.

Growing Population: The continuous growth of population in different continents and absence of infrastructure has resulted into unemployment, poverty, corruption and terrorism. This has badly damaged the economic backbone of several nations.

Construction Activities: The construction of dams, road, rail network, housing and clearing the forests for agriculture has damaged natural areas and wild lands.

Global Warming: The whole world is effected by global warming. This has badly damaged the environment of colder regions like Arctic and Antarctic continent, Himalayan Ranges, the Alps and the Andes mountains. The worst sufferer are rainforests and moisturous vegetation areas of the world.

8

Bio-diversity and Wildlife Tourism

Importance of Bio-diversity: The study of bio-diversity of the world is necessary for the higher research work on wild life and tourism. The floral diversity encourages us for botanical studies and herbal treks. Anation plays an important role in maintaining its environment and important water sources creating a vital link for the survival to all living creatures in the surrounding. It largely depends on the significant works of the local governments to protect the local ecosystem. The growth of a bio-diversity regions depends on a healthy eco-system of animal foodchains, symbiosis, natural process of growth and supporting the natural system of co-operation and natural balance of give and take process over this planet. Now it is well understood that the nature's laws are to balance mutual exhange of food among animals and plants into an automatic process that encourages natural growth and survival of species over this planet. In this way, biodiversity is a world of animals and plants which harbours the process of natural balance among various plants and animal species within a particular ecosystem. To introduce the human being with the amazing world of plants and animals into a recreative way is a form of wildlife tourism or eco-tourism.

The study of bio-diversity hot spots introdues us with a vast world of wildlife and plants. We should protect them to encourage wildlife tourism.

Bio-diversity Hot Spots in the world: The bio-diversity is an amazing world of plants and animals which creates a natural balance of eco-system over this planet. There are rich bio-diversity hotspots in the world. Among them, 30 new hot spots have been underlined for their thriving ecological system over this planet. Some of them are amazingly beautiful and are being utilized as the best spots for wildlife tourism.

Importance of Wildlife Tourism: Bio-diversity is a boon to this entire planet. The citizens of the world are alive today because of this bio-diversity. Wildlife tourism has become a subject of learning and earning world wide. The study of wildlife has become quite popular among the biologists: environmentalists and nature lovers all over the world. The trekkers, explorers and travellers enjoy the sight seeing in the wildlife protected zones. The importance of wildlife tourism has increased manifolds as it has given a new life to the "Safari Parks" and "Game Parks" all over the world. The protection of wild animals for the purpose of tourism and human recreation has transformed the world of wildlife Parks and Wildlife Reserve Areas in some countries. In South Africa, there famous Safari Parks and Game Parks for the recreation of businessmen and big budget tourists. In many countries, wildlife tourism has become an immediate source of foreign exchange.

Rain Forests Bio-diversity: The floral diversity is quite amazing for the botanical studies and herbal treks. The bio-diversity of rain forests is rich and varied. Both fauna and flora are found abundantly and with many species which is a source of immense recreation for tourists and explorers. The traditional habitats of lion, tiger, bear, jaguar and other carnivores are found in rain forests. For example, the mammals in rain forests are different and distinct to encourage wildlife tourism. (1) the Carnivores (2) Hoofed mammals (3) Primates

(4) Sea mammals (5) Marsupials (6) Rodents (7) Insectivores (8) Bats. Among the Carnivores are : Cats, civets, Genets and Oyans, African Plain Civet, Hyenas, Mangoose, Madagaskar Carnivores, Wilddogs, Bears, Red Panda, Raccoons, weasels and their relatives. The rainforests are a living world of bio-diversity and their conservation is necessary for their survival for a longer period.

A large numbers of international tourists visit the rainforest countries to enjoy wildlife tourism. South America, Africa and South East Asian countries are the best source of wildlife tourism.

Himalayan Bio-diversity: The bio-diversity in the Himalyan region is quite distinct and different than the other parts of the world. The high altitude plants and animals for their different ecological zones. (1) The Alpine zones (2) Semi Alpine and (3) Temperate zones. These ecological zones are the main characteristics of mountain wild life and floral diversity. The Himalayas are the highest mountains in the world and these bring climatic changes with heavy rainfall and snow storms in the snowclad mountains. The cold waves during winter are full of chill. There are different ecological belts at different heights of the Himalayan Ranges.

Desert Bio-diversity: The bio-diversity of desertland is quite different from that of mountains and rainforests. The deserts are hotter during summer and colder during winter. The thorny bushes and scattered sand grasses grow within a small distance. Cactus is the main plant of the desert. The Govi desert, Sahara desert, Atacama and Patagonia deserts, Thar desert in Rajasthan and American deserts have a distinct eco-system in the world. Some amazing species of plants and animals are found there. The Patagonia desert in South America has become a tourists paradise.

Ocean Bio-diversity: The bio-diversity of oceans is quite amazing and rich. Among them are the Atlantic ocean, Pacific ocean Indian ocean, Mediterranean ocean, Coral sea, Tasmania sea, Caspean sea. Azov sea, Wadden sea, Bering Sea, Arabian Sea, Red sea, Antarctic ocean are among the oceans which are rich in bio-diversity. The mammals are with unique varieties. The fishes, sword fishes, whales, sharks, dolphins, otters, dugongs, turtles seals, sea lions, walrus, water birds, shore birds and sea-bottom fauna are found with amazing beauty and diversity. Both coastal areas tourism and ocean tourism have got a solid impetus in the areas of ocean exploration activities to observe marine life.

Wetlands Bio-diversity: The wetlands play a major role in keeping the plants and trees evergreen and environment colder and moisturous. This creates a pleasant environment to the nearby communities and wildlife. The aquatic plants and the bird fauna in the lake ecosystem. The wetlands are known for the growth of wildlife, aquatic animals and plants. The caiman crocodile found in the Pantanal, Brazil is an amazing example of amphibians. The frogs, turtles, snakes are also found in the wetland. The tiger, jaguar, bear, fox, marsh deers (60,000) are found in the marsh wetland of Pantanal. This wetland is an amazing place tov isit among the tourists of the world. Several water birds and animals are found in the Pantanal wetland. The other famous wetlands are Azov sea, Wadden sea, Mekong Delta, Sunderbans, Congo basin are well known for their rich bio-diversity and uniqueness in the world. These wetlands are visited by millions of tourists every year.

Grassland Bio-diversity: There are amazing grasslands all over the world. Some are as small as 3000 hactare, some are spread to hundreds thousand square kilometers. The Kansas Tall grass prairie in the Flint Hills of North Eastern Kansas are well known for their eco-systems. The mammals, birds and reptiles found here are quite distinct. Mongolia's Green swords grasslands are quite different in the world. The North West European grasslands are dominated by perennial herbs. The grasslands are found in several countries in different climates. It varies in height and geographical formation from place to place. For example, Tallgrass fields in South America, Savannas in Africa, Steppes in Siberia, Downs and Velds in Australia are some of the best examples of grassland ecology. The milts, insects larvae, nematodes and earth worm are found into deep soil. The grassland mammals roam here and there in search of food. The famous grasslands are explored every year by thousands of tourists.

Island Bio-diversity

The Islands surrounded by oceans have different, moisturous and lively climate. The islands in colder seas and the islands in the warmer seas have their own ecosystem and patterns of climatic diversions. The vegetation in the colder islands is different from that of warmer islands. So is wildlife. The Hawaii Archipelago, Low Archipelago, Galapagos Archipelago, Madders, Archipelago, Phoenix Archipelago, Aleutian Archiolago, Tuvalu Archipelago etc. have their different bio-diversity and climate. The otters are shorebirds are common in some islands. The colder climate Islands like Aleutian Islands have different vegetation and wildlife in it. The island bio-diversity varies from place to place. The ecologists have observed a distinct ecosystems in every island.

Antarctica Bio-diversity: The Antarctica Bio-diversity is cold climate bio-diversity. Although, it has no prominent vegetation as it is covered by snow the year round. But it has cold climatic animals which are amazing and strange in nature.

The penguins, blue whales, orcas, colossal squids and fur seals are found in the Antarctica sea. The Antarctica krills are important food for whales and seals. The seals, squid, ice fish, penguins, albatrosses and many water and shore birds are found here. The emperor Penguin breeds during winter while another species of Penguin breeds in the summer. Rock hopper Penguin had distinctive features around the eyes giving appearance of eyelashes. King Penguins, Chimstrap Penguins and Centra Penguins also bred in the Arctic. The

Arctic fur seal was very heavily hunted in the 18th and 19th centuries by USA and UK.

Bio-diversity and Tourism: Bio-diversity is themain source of tourism in many countries. Bio-diversity of a forest or wildland encourages us for travelling that part of land to see the amazing wildlife and floral diversity there. For this purpose, wildlife tours are organized by several travel and tour companies to attract more tourists to observe wildlife in the Safari Parks of Brazil, Colombia, West Africa, South Africa, India, Thailand, Cambodia, Borneo, Sumatra, Java and Australian continent. The Ningaloo Barrier Reef in Timor sea and The Great Barrier Reef and Atolls in coral sea are some of the best examples to enjoy marine bio-diversity there. The Gorillas and Pygmy Chimpanzees in Congo Basin, clouded jaguars in Java, Tigers and orangutans in Java and Sumatra forests are a great examples of rich bio-diversity. The above countries are the best destinations of wild life tourism.

Wildlife Tourism: In recent years wildlife toursim has become a hot subject to enjoy wildlife in developing countries. The National Parks, bio-diversity hotspots, amasing wilderness and natural areas are a great source of recreation for the tourists from foreign countries who come to enjoy life with great learning sense and expenience.

Some countries have achieved tremendous success in wild life tourism. These are British Columbia (Canada) Yellow stone National Park (USA) Amazonia Wilderness (Brazil), Colombia, Venezuela, Peru, Ecuador and Andes Mountain Ranges which are famous for their Bio-diversity and natural beauty. It is a great combination of wild life and amazing natural areas.

National Parks: The National Parks in some countries have done great business in wildlife tourism in the world. Among them are Columbia Wilderness, St Elias National Park USA, Mana Pools National Park, Zimbabwe, Kruger National Park (South Africa), Pampas Galeros National Park, (Peru), Manu National Park, Andes (Peru), National Park of Colombia, the

Amazon National Park (Brazil), Rajaji National Park (Dehardun), Corbett National Park (Ramnagar), The Great Himalyan National Park (Kullu), Kaziranga National Park (Assam) The Manas National Park (Assam), Sagar Matha National Park (Nepal) Ran Thambhor National Park (MP), Dorjee National Park (Bhutan).

Reserve Forests: The Reserve Forests are the main bastion of bio-divesity hot sports. About 70 percent wildlife inhabits in the reserve forests in India. The National Parks and Reseve Forests in India are in good state comparatively to other countries of the world.

Special Protected Areas: There are some special protected areas in the world just to protect the fauna and flora of that region in a small forest area. These protected areas are nature's living laboratory. In the Himalayan States of India there are some ancient forests of oaks, pine, Deodar, Myrica Sepida and Rhododendron. These are found at the height of 4000 to 7000 in the Indian Himalayas. The Oaks and Pines are found in lower heights while the Deodara cedrus is found above 7000 ft. In India, Uttaranchal and Himachal also have such protected areas. And the wildlife is protected with rules of the law. In some other countries such special protected areas are Atlantic Forests in Brazil, South Africa, Congo basin, Foya Mountains in Papua New Guinea. The ancient forests are found in the South East Asian Countries. These forests are very ancient and still unexplored for wild life. The concerned nations and governments are protecting them for nature tourism. Unfortunately, the tribals and poachers in these countries continue the hunting of wild animals.

Amazing Animals and Safari Tourism: There are vastly, expanded areas of forests in the form of wildlife parks. The most amazing animals are found in the wilderness and wildlife parks of Canada, South America, Ghana, Gabon, Congo, Kenya, Uganda, Zaire and South Africa. The tourists go to see them in particular. The Gorillas and Pigmy Chimpanzees of Congo basin, the Orangutans of Java, Sumatra and Borneo are a living labotory of Great Apes. The countries are known for their amazing rain forests. These forests have become a great source of Safari tourism in the world.

Elephant Conservation Project : India is a leader in Elephant conservation projects. (Asian Elephant): The Aisan elephants are knownf or their habitats and mode of life. Indian elephants have become immediate source of research for the research scholars all over the world. For examples, the Asian elephants of Raja ji National Park in Dehradun are a great source of this research. The tourists and explorers from all over the world come here to see the Asian elephants and the Asian Safari Parks.

Lion: The lion is the king of forests. This is the strongest animal in the wild which can kill every animal including the elephant. The lions of Gir forests, the white lions of India are unique species in the world. The Indian panthers, tigers, leopards and mountain tigers are unique wild animals. The Asian tigers and Asian lions are also quite valuable species in the world. The lions create an impressive sight when they are on the hunting spree. There are great efforts to protect this wild animal all over the world. The roaming area for them has been increased in different wildlife Parks in India. The Asian lions have a unique characteristics of hunting, habitation and roaming in avast expanded wild land. They should be given protection.

In the case of tigers, the Government of India had launched a project named "Tiger Project" in 1972. Since then, a lot of practical efforts have been made to protect this wild animal. There are several species of tigers inhabiting-different forests in Indian sub-continent. (1) The mountain tigers (2) The tropical tigers (3) The rainforest tigers, (4) Bamboo forest tigers (5) Mountain bush tigers, (6) Snow tigers are known among the big cat lovers in the world. The Asian tigers in various forest areas are a subject of study. Their habitats, mode of living, natural surroundings and style of hiding under the bushes is quite amazing.

The tourists like to visit wildlife parks with the animals described below.

Leopard: The leopards are from a cat family. They are found in Africa and South Asia. The leopards can climb the branches of trees and after observing their prey jump over them. The leopards of Africa and the leopards from South Asia are quite different genetic species.

Jaguar: Jaguars are the yellow skin tigers of Central America. Known for round spots, cloudy skin and large black strips. The jaguars are the night hunters of the rain forests; particularly of central Amazonia.

Panthers: Panthers are the large black cats also known as Puma. It is also known as the black leopard.

Bears: There are several species of bears which are quite popular among the tourists. (1) Grizzly bears of Alaska (2) Kodiak bears of Alaska are largest carnivorous in the world (2.5 meters) (3) Bespectacled bear of Colombia and Andes (4) The brown bear of Himalaya (5) Black and red bear of Shivalik Hills (6) The bears of Sunderbans and South East Asian nations. The bears are herbivores and carnivores both. In Indian Himalayas, the bears are herbivores.

Bespectacled Bear: This bear is found in Colombia, Amazon, (Brazil), Peru and Andes Mountains. The bears in Colombia and Andes are of rare and of different genetic species.

Polar Bears. They are white like cottons and are solely depend on sea food i.e. fishes, dolphins, sea lion, seal, walrus and sharks. The polar bears are great hunters. They live in the caves of snow and roam over a large part of the polar regions.

Grizzly Bear: The grizzly bears are found in Alaska and British Columbia's coastal forests and waters. They are black and are aggressive hunters of local fishes. They catch the fishes in the running waters. The population of the grizzly bears is on the verge of extinction and most of them are killed by the local hunters in Canada and Alaska. Global warming is also a great reason to their extinction.

Antelopes: These are the species of small deers found in the Tibetan plateaus and other parts of the world.

The North American horned deers move with a herd in the night and spend their most of the time on the steep rocks for their safety.

The stag deer in Rajaji National Park (India) move with a herd. The horned deers in the world are on the verge of extinction as they are being hunted by skin sumggless for horn and meat also. The (impala deers of South Africa are the fastest runners in the world. So is the name of a Impala car.

Marsh Deers: The marsh deers are found near the dense forests and wetlands. For examples Kaziranga National Park, Assam, India, Rajaji National Park, Uttaranchal, Pantanal Wetland, Brazil have a good number of marsh deers. At present the Pantanal (2,10,000 km^2) has 64,000 marsh deers near the flood plains of Uberaba lake in Brazil.

Rhinos: The one horned Rhinos are the great attraction of Kaziranga National Park, Assam. The Rhinoceros unicornis is the main species in India. It is considered that the number of Rhinoceros unicornis in Kaziranga is more than 1500. More than 12,00 Rhinos have been killed by the poachers for its skin, bones and single horn. The price of its single horn in the international market is US $ 60,000.

Giraffe. Giraffe are the tall and most impressive animals of South African Parks and are in large population i.e. 10,000 and more. These species are hunted by lions and leopards in South African forests. These animals are always victim of the violent animals in the park. These have dark spots on their coat. Giraffe is sincere and gentle animal with a long weak and small head. These are found only in African continent.

Zebra: Zebra are a relative of horses. They are dark strips animals found in the South African National Parks like Kruger National Park, Cape Peninsula including Table Mountain Park. The Garden Beach, Kwa Zulu National Parks and mountains. The other parks are known for their natural beauty to observe from a distant land. The Kruger National Park is a haven for wild animals.

Wild Ass. Wild Ass are main wild animals of Tibetan Plateaus. The Chang Tang wild life Reserve includes these species. The wild Ass are the main characterstics of bio-diversity in Mongolian deserts, Sichuan China and other parts of the mountain deserts. They are visible in large numbers in Ladakh valley also.

Yak: Yak is a Tibetan version of cow. The Tibetans carry baggage and food grain over the back of the Yak. The Yak are milching animals (female Yak) and Tibetan people have domesticated it for milk. Yak are the multipurpose animals for the Tibetan population. The wool, skin, head-trophy, tail for spiritual values. The yak is killed for meat by Chinese hunters in Tibet. Unfortunately, their number has been reduced to a few hundred.

Wild Birds: The wild birds are a feature of Manu National Park. There are some 800 bird species recorded in Manu National Park in Colombia. World's 25 percent birds are found in South America and one fifth in Amazonia wilderness in Brazil. Some 200 species of humming birds are found in Colombia.

The Great Bustard: The Great Bustard is the bird of Western Himalayan foothills and only comes out in the night. It grazes particularly in the moonlit nights and hides itself into the bushes. It lays it eggs in side the bushes without making a nest. In the name of nest it makes it half ft. deep pit with two three grass leaves in it and after some days four to eight eggs lay in it. The baby birds come out after hatching for some days. The chicks follow their mother and after smelling some danger they hide themselves in the grass covered with bushes.

The Monal Pheasant: The Lophorus impejanus is a bird from the high mountains of Western Himalayas. It was an endangered bird in 1980. In 1984 the bird was seen in Chanshal valley in Himachal Pradesh. Earlier, it was thought that the bird is extinct.

The Cheer Pheasant: The Cheer Pheasant is a small species of Monal found in the low hights of Himachal Pradesh. Its scientific name is Catereus wallichie and is found at 6000–9000 feet in the mountain valleys.

Eastern Himalyan Monal (Sclater's monal) is found at the height of 4000′–9000′ in the Arunachal hills. Its length is upto 35″ and hight 15″–18″.

The Himalayan Quail: The bird is an inhabitant of Western Himalyan foothills. It has not been seen or recorded since 1868. But the ornithologists say that the bird still exists in a very small population in the Western Himalayas.

There is continuous decline in the population of wild animals in the forestlands in our country. In the coming decades in India alone 81 mammals, 38 birds and 18 raptiles may be vanished away. The loss of habitats reduction of forest land, developmental work, pollution and global warming are some responsible factors to make them more vulnerable.

Among the 45,000 plant species 15000 are flowering plants. It is estimated that among them 10 persent plant species either have been vanished away or are on the verge of extinction. These species have disappeared in the last one century.

Bird Watching: The bird watching is an easy and comfortable pastime hobby and more and more people are taking interest in it. It has become a part of recreational activity in the world. To watch beautiful birds, observe their habitats and write something about their important areas makes us happy.

Nature Watching: Nature watching is the best pastime hobby and the intelligent people all over the world are enjoying it through the spells of nature tourism. The best natural areas in the world are : The Himalyas, North East India, the Alps, Canada, Southern America and Andes. British Columbia, Colombia, Venezuela, Peru and Brazil are some of the best places to enjoy nature watching.

Trekking and Exploration: The trekking and exploration activities in the wild are among the best hobbies to keep one fit and healthy. Three states of India Himachal, Uttaranchal and Sikkim have become Trekkers paradise from the tourists from all walks of life.

Trekking in the mountains is the most enjoyable exercise for fitness and good health. Trekking and exploration activities are becoming more popular among the trekkers and mountaineers of the world. Both the activities are co-related and beneficial to human health. The Younger generation in India is more aware about trekking expeditions.

Mountaineering: Mount Everest, Nepal is the best example of mountaineering expedition in the world. The mountaineering in the world is the best adventure sports. The mountaineers all over the world come to climb the Indian Himalayan peaks, the Alps in Europe and Nepal Himalayas including Mount Everest. The Nepal government is earning an excellent amount of revenue from the foreign climbers of the Mount Everest. This has encouraged mountain tourism in Nepal at a large scale.

In India, more than 100 mounain peaks are suitable for mountaineering and trekking expeditions. The government of India is trying its best to encourage the mountaineers to visit India every year to scale the highest peaks in the Indian Himalayas. The peaks of middle heights are quite popular among the mountaineers of foreign countries. This has given a new insight to the people of the world to visit India to ride the best mountain peaks in the world. The dome shaped, triangular and steep mountain peaks have become a great attraction among the foreign mountaineers. The Indian peaks are getting 30-40 teams or more to ride the average mountain peaks regularly.

Sometimes, the number of tourists or climbers is much more in trekking season.

Hiking: The wildlands always have been attracting the hikers from the very ancient time: The educated class which want to experience the beauty of natural areas, trekking is the best way to reach place to place. Hiking is a good sport to explore wildlands, wilderness and natural areas.

Camping in the Wildlife: The camplife is the most enjoyable in the rural set up where there are forests, wild lands and most beautiful natural areas. Such activities always encourage rural tourism. This helps both in nature conservation, wildlife management and provide new dimensions in nature tourism.

Mountain top: The mountain top camping is an unique experience in life as it provides us an insight into the camping, natural beauty and adventure spirit in the wild. Experiencing the enjoyment of a new life among the classmates or teammates makes us happy. The mountain top camplife provides us a heavenly experience. It is always an inspiring and adventuresome sport for the newcomers.

River Valley Banks: The river valley always inspires us in many ways as it provides us beautiful landscapes, sand dunes and wide panoramic banks with white shining sand cover. To camp in the wide sand covered banks provides new thrilling experience of life near the gushing crystal water of the river. To observe wild birds, fruit trees, insects, butterflies in the wild enriches us with new experiences of life.

Amidst the forests: To camp amidst the forests, always provides us an amazing insight into the nature's peaceful paradise. The large deodar and oak trees, flowering bushes, ferns, orchids, moss and velvet grasses always inspires and welcomes us with a new spirit of life.

Particularly in the month of February and March, camping in the forests is more enjoyable activity which recreates and entertains us into a big way.

In the open Pastures: The camping in the open pastures is an ever remembering activity. It always provides us immense pleasure and enjoyment when we camp amidst a lush green pasture in the higher altitudes. The whole pasture is covered with wild flowers, evergreen velvet grass, and sweet smelling herbs. The pastureland is sometime surrounded by a vast Deordar and Oak forests, which attracts us in many ways.

Between the Rocks and Caves: When there is bitter cold during heavy rain in August or cold waves during December and January months we always prefer to camp between rocks and safe caves just to protect us from cold waves and wild animals. Such rocks and caves in Himachal, Meghalaya Uttaranchal are a nature's gift to protect us from natural calamities, and the violent animals in the wild. We camp between the safe rocks or in the caves in a protective way.

Open Barrenlands: The open barrenlands in the mountains are covered with a small dwarf grasses and bushes with some scanty growth of trees and dwarf plants. Such lands are quite attractive and pleasant to the people who want to establish their camps amidst the open barren lands. The natural areas are sometime surrounded by delicate plants and thorny bushes and some domestic plants and trees. Such barrenlands and mountain pastures are in Kathapuria Cheena, Bageswar district in Uttaranchal. In Pauri hills, Simtoli, Baheli, Jaspur Kandai, Bubakhal, Maandaakhaal, Ghandiyaal Khaal and

Seeku Dhaar are among the most beautiful barren lands in Uttaranchal.

In the Mountain Forests: Among the most beautiful berren lands and forests and pastures are in: Daaligaad, Nagar jaa Dhaar, Seeku Dhaar wildlands and forests, Ghoraa Dhungee, Thandaa Paanee, Katraa Siyaaraa, Shilvaanee; near Simtoli village. The other areas are Taal forests, Gwaad forests, Damdeval forests and openlands and trees. The small plants are orchids, ferns and mosses which grow on old saal trees. The fern forests, sweet smelling plants and herbs are quite beneficial to human being. The camplife here is quite enjoyable but the main fear prevails: the attack from violent animals. So, the teammates should be cautious and always keep explosives with them to drive them away. The saal forests are good for bird watching and exploration activities. There are epiphyte orchids on saal trees.

Near the Marshland and Open pastures: In the Teraai region, the marshlands are a heaven for water animals and aquatic plants. At one corner, the beautiful marshland and at the other corner the plain pasture land surrounded by Saal, Tendu, Semal and other important species of trees create a moisturous climate. To enjoy camplife amidst the forestland of Saung river and Toya river is a heavenly experience. The crystal clear river water creates most impressive sights during the sunrise, sunset and at the right noon time. It is an immense fact that the mashlands and pastures in the mountains have quite impressive landscapes and natural beauty. The pastures and marshlands in the Terai region have their own beauty and charm. The marshland of Chidderwala in Toya river bed and pasture land exhibit a most impressive view of the forest land, pastures and gurgling river waters. The Gaad Paar river and Thandaa Paanee a pure water source in Pauri hills (Shivalik Range) have their own beauty and charm and create a most beautiful panoramic view during spring and rainy days.

There is a great need to encourage, bio-diversity conservation and wildlife tourismin India. The beautiful pastures, densely populated forests, deep river valleys are a great source of wildlife tourism and natural areas-based tourism.

The countries who are the leaders in wilderness and wildlife tourism are Canada (British Columbia), Brazil (Amazon), South Africa (Kruger National Park), and Australia (Kakadoo). The rainforest countries of Africa and South East Asia are a great source of wildlife tourism.

9

Bio-diversity Hotspots in the World

What are the bio-diversity hotspots? The bio-diversity hot spots in the world are those places where there is a heavy composition of wild animals, plants and insects. For example in the terresntrial bio-diversity, the rainf orests ahve richest composition of wild animals and plants. In ocean bio-diversity, the coral reefs have a rich marine like. (plants and animals). The large forests and wild lands where various species of wild animals, birds and plants are foundinlarger numbers are known as bio-diversity hot spots. The rainforest of Amazon, Thailand, Borneo, Sumatra, Congo, Kenya, Uganda are bio-diversity hotspots in the world.

Bio-diversity as a Recreation: There are 30 new biodiversity hotspots in the world. The rain forests are evergreen forests and rich in bio-diversity. The carnivores, mammals are a unique sight there. Among them are lions, tigers, panthers, jaguars, leopards, Civets, Genets, African Palm civets hyenas, mangooses, Madasker Carnivores, wild dogs, Red Panda, Racoons, weasels and their relatives. The mammls in the world are of several types i.e (1) Carnivores (2) Hoofed mammals (3) Primates (4) Sea mammals (5) Marsupials (6) Rodents (7) Insectivores (8) Bats. These animals are of great attraction to human being. The wild birds with different colours and species are a great pastime recreation while watching them amidst the dense forests. The reptiles like turtles, lizards, snakes, and crocodiles create a beautiful sight while observing their movements. Several plants, trees, flowering bushes, ferns, orchids and mosses are a great attraction to the botanists and plant lovers all over the world. In this way bio-diversity is a great recreation to human mind.

Bio-diversity Hotspots in the world : There are several bio-diverstiy hotspots in the rain forests, mountain forests, wetlands and oceans. The rain forest bio-diversity and Coral Reef Biodiversity are the richest in the world. For example, The Amazonia in Brasil, Western African forests, South East Asian Rain Forests and North Eastern Rain forests of Australia are considered the richest bio-diversity hotspots in the world. These forests are scattered both sides of Equator toward 20° North and South. The mammals, reptiles, avies, orthopoda and other animals are found in large numbers. There are various species. The marine life is also rich in bio-diversity in Coral Reef Barrier, Ningaloo Barrier Reef and the Great Barrier Coral Reef in Australia are pure rich in marine-bio-diversity. The fishes, Emperor fish, pipe fiesh and snake fish are quite impressive sea animals. Besides this, the whales, sharks, dolphins, turtles crocodiles, sea snakes are common sights in Coral Reefs and Coral sea in Australia.

The other bio-diversity areas are Parrots Island, Lizard Island, Snake Island, Antigua, Mauritania Coastal Marine Park, South Africa South Coastal Marine Park, are some of the rich bio-diversity hotspots in the world. Besides this, the Foya Mountains in New Guinea are newly searched out bio-diversity hotsports in the world.

British Columbia: British Columbia in Canada is most beautiful place which has a rich varieties of wildlife and natural areas for the purpose of tourism in the world. Known for its fresh water lakes, rivers, fishes and grizzly bears, British Columbia is world leader in wilderness tourism. In 2004, the direct revenue was $ 9.5 billion with 1,17,500 full time jobs to the people. The natural landsscape of British Coulmbia is amazing in natural beauty. The beautiful meadows spread upto thousands of square kilometers, the river valleys, the Columbia mountain ranges are some of the most beautiful natural areas which boast of British Columia's leadership in wilderness tourism. British Columbia attracts millions tourists every year to see the vast tracks of natural wonders of this state. The bio-diversity is quite rich the cold climate mammals, polar bears, grizzly bears, wild foxes, beautiful birds, water birds and shore birds are found in large numbers. Mountain tiger, mountain Goat and Bighorns are also found in snowclad mountains.

Amazonian wilderness in Brazil: The rain forests of Amazon are most popular among the tourists of the world. The Amazonia wilderness are the largest wilderness in the world spread upto 5 millon square kilometers. World's two third rain forests are found in Amazon and one fifth of world's bird species exist here. The most violent carnivore mammals are found in Amazonia. A large number of poisonous snakes are found here. The water snaks Anaconda is found in the Wetlands and rivers of Amazon.

The Amazon National Park is the best example of the amazing wild life in the world. The Government of Brazil is doing its best to protect the wildlife of Amazon through this National Park. The birds, reptiles, amphibians, primates and armadillos are being protected in this park.

The rain forests of Amazon are being felled at a large scale every year. Most of the forests are cleared for agricultural development, housing complexes, ranches and roads. The timber merchants of some timber companies have more than 15 lakh kilometer square forests of Amazon.

This is a big loss for cleared the habitats of wild animals. The loss of rain forests is the loss to all the citizens of the earth. These rain forests are the lungs of earth as they absorb

CO_2 from atmosphere and in exchange release oxygen for us. These forests affect human life all over the world. We all the citizens of the world should protect these precious forests.

Atlantic Pine Forests: The Atlantic pine Forests are some of unique and rare forests in the state of Santa Catarina in Brazil. The Araucarias National Park is spread up to 12,481 hactares and Mata Preta Ecological Station is spread in 6,563 hactares. Both are of great importance in protecting remnant forests of the Parana or Brazilian Pine Araucaria angustifolia. The Araucaria pine forests of Southern and South Eastern Brazil, a distinctive formation of the Brazilian Atlantic forests, once were covered in more than 20 million hactares but were devastated by the timber industry and continuous felling today has reduced the remmants covering a mere 2% of that area. The Brazilian oak is one of the Brazilian threatened species list since 1992.

Salonga National Park: Salonga National Park is famous for Bonobos (Pigmy Chimpanzees) in the Democratic Republic of Congo. The Park is spread upto 12,000 km square forestland and is a bio-diversity hotspot in the world. The first detailed survery on the presence of Bonobos in Congo Basin was conducted in 2005. It was found that there was little evidence of Bonobos presence species occurring in the Salonga National Park. No live bonobos were seen and sightings of nests and dungs was found only in a quarter area of the forest. It is now thought that the Bonobos population is 10,000, 80% fewer than previously was thought. The survey found abundant evidence of human encroachment into the park and the incidence of poaching. Salonga National Park was created in 1970 specifically to protect Bonobos. If the situation is this in Salonga National Park it can be assumed that the species, is in danger across the Democratic Republic of Congo.

Virunga National Park (Rwanda, Uganda, Congo): The Virunga National Park is a bio-diversity hotspots between Uganda, Rwanda and Democratic Republic of Congo. The park is spread in 8,00,000 hactare. This is the home of the threatened Mountain Gorilla (Gorilla beringei beringei) there is a massive deforestation in the Mickeno sector of the forest. The encroachment by pastoralists, agriculturists, and local communities have threatened the existence of forestland as well as mountain gorillas here. The other wild animals, reptiles and birds are also on the verge of extinction as there is continuous felling of the forestland.

An Eco-wall of stones has been erected in the park up to 20 km. This will help to stop encroachment by local people. This wall was erected by 2000 workforce, six Rwandan community associations and 12 Congolese associations with some NGOs have contributed in this wall. Now the encroachment has been stopped permanently.

Kruger National Park (South Africa): The Kruger National Park is called the King of Parks in South Africa. This National Park is spread in 21,000 square km. This Park has become economic backbone of South Africa's Tourism Department. There is a metalled road upto 200 km. 700 km. road is in good state. In this Park, there are 10,000 elephants 3500 Rhinos (White), 500 Rhinos (black), 25,000 wild buffalows, 2000 lions, 900 tigers, 250 cheetahs, 5000 Giraffe, 13,000 wildebeast, 1,40,000 Impala dears, 900 stagdeers, 30,000 zebras roam more freely in the Kruger National Park. Besides this, 507 beautiful bird species 114 species of reptiles, 34 species amphibians, 49 fishes, 336 tree species are found in the Park. The water birds, shore birds are found in the wetlands and coastal areas.

Yosemite National Park (USA): This park is spread upto 3082 square km and with most beautiful scenic spots like Sierra Nevada. The Park is in the Yosemite Valley which is 11 km. long and 1.5 km wide. There are Glacial Point, Cathederal Rocks, Elcapltan and Sentinel Rocks. Among the highest water falls are: Ribbon Fall 491 meter high, the other large falls are Bridaliveil, Sentinel, Vernal and Navada. Yosemite Park is in the nine of Trans human drives its name from a tribe Transhuman AmerIndians who seasonally occupied the valley.

The valley was discovered in 1830s but it was quite difficult to reach there for many years.Here, the black beer, ptarmigan, mountain bluebird, three toed woodpecker and other song birds are also found here. Besides this, mountain Rocky goats, bighorn sheep, grizzly bears and water birds are also found in large numbers.

Hornbill National Park (Thailand): The Hornbill Research Foundation in Mahidol University, Thailand is conducting a research on the important species of Hornbills found in the rainforests of Thailand. There 12 species of Hornbills which are found in Thailand.

There are 9 specias and sub species of Hornbills found in the Islands of Philippines. The rain forests of Philippines have most beautiful species of hornbills in the dense forests. A large species of hornbill from an island of philippines has been vanished away in the last few decades. This was a big loss to bird lovers.

Mauritania National Park: The Park is a most beautiful and amazing wetland with rich sea and coastal biodiversity. It cover 12,000 square kilometers, equally distributed between land and sea and is Africa's largest Coastal National Park. It is a wetland of international importance registered under the Ramsar Convention and UNESCO World Heritage Site. The Park was founded in 1976 mainly for its birdlife. To allow the sustainable management of the fish population in the Park is allowed since then.

Halma Hera National Park: The Island of Halmahera has been declared a historical park. The Aketa Jawa-Lolobeta on the Island of Halmahera, Indonesia has been declared a National Park following more than 8 years of discussion. The Park will protect 167,300 hactares of hill and lowland rainforests. The Park is vital for at least 23 bird species endemic to North Maluku, including Wallace's standardwing (Semioptera wallacei) and three of Halmahera's four endemic bird species sombre Kingfisher (Halcyon funebris), Halmahera cuckooshrike (Coracina parvula) and dusky oriole (Oriolus phaeocromus).

The Park is also home to the seminomadic tribals Tobelo Dalam whose traditional life style has been under increasing pressure as forests are logged and cleared for settlements and plantations.

Great Barrier Coral Reef, Queensland (Australia): The Australian Government has proposed a 6000 km. increase in the Great Barrier Reef Marine Park so that the entire system is ptorected. A number of the new projected areas include seagrass beds that are of vital importance to dugongs (Dugong dugon). Once the Queensland Government approved the proposeals, the new areas will be included in the Park under the Great Barrier Reef Marine Park Act, 1975.

The Great Barrier Reef is the largest coral reef in the world. It is composed of over 2,900 reefs and 900 coral islands spread upto 2,600 kilometers an area covering 344,400 square kilometers. The reef is located in the Coral Sea off the coast of Queensland State in the Northeast of Australia. This Great Reef is the world's single largest structure made by the living organisms. It supports a rich bio-diversity and was selected as a World Heritage Site in 1981. The CNN has considered it one of the seven natural wonders of the world. The Queensland Government has named it a State Icon of Queensland. The researches shows that the complete reef structure was completed 6,000 years ago. The bio-diversity in the Reef system is rich and varied. There are whales, dolphins, porpoises and fishes in the Greet Barrier Reef including dwarf mink whales, Indo-Pacific humback dolphin and the Humpback whales. A large population of dugongs live there in the grass beds.

Six species of sea turtles come to the reef to breed. The green see turtle, leather back sea turtle, hawksbill turtle, loggs head sea turtle, leatherback sea turtle, loggers head sea turtle, flat back turtle and olive ridley turtle come here to breed.

The Green Sea turtle show two genetically distinct population: at Northern part and the other on Southern part. Fifteen species of sea grass beds attract the dugongs and turtles to breed. There are 5000 species of mollusks, 125 species of sharks, 49 species of sea horses in the reef system. There are seven species of frogs on coral islands. Some 215 species of birds including 22 sea birds, 32 species of shore birds come to the reef to breed and nesting. Every year 1.7 million birds come to the islands.

The northern islands have some 300-350 plant species.

Seventeen sea snakes live on the Great Barrier Reef. No sea snake was found in Great Barrier Reef World Heritage Area. There are more than 1500 species of fish including clownfish, red bass, red throat, snapper, coral trout on the reef.

The common soft coral on Great Barrier Reef belong to 36 genera.

500 species of marine algae or sea-weed is found on the coral reef. There are thirteen species of genus Helimeda, which deposit calcareous mounds up to 100 meters wide creating marine ecosystem on the surface are compared to a rain forest cover.

The rising temperature in 2002 and 2006 has bleached the coral reefs to a large extent. The growing pollution and global warming have affected the marine life of the coral sea.

PuMat Nature Reserve: Vietnam is a heaven for wild animals. The strange mammal saola (Rseudoryse nghetinhensis) is found here. The species of Bovid was first discovered in Vietnam on May 1992. Later, the same species was found in Laos. The Pu Mat Nature Reserve Contains one of the largest blocks of forest remaining in the Truong son Mountain range on the border below Laos and Vietnam. Since mid 1997 it has been the focus of project supported by European Commission designed to halt its destructions and degradation.

These forests are considered among the most ancient forests where a large numbers of mammals, reptiles, amphibians, avies and primates are found in good state.

Taxa Plants, New Zealand: New Zealand is internationally known for its plant bio-diversity. This country is considered rich in bio-diversity. It is a hotspot in various species of Taxa Plants. 80% of country's vascular plants are endemic and some of them are on the verge of extinction.

Among the country's taxa plants 119 species are native vascular plants which are acutely threatened. A further 102 taxa are seriously on the verge of decline and 502 Taxa are at risk.

The role of New Zealand Plant Conservation Network has been admired by the environmentalists worldwide. The network had started a campaign to protect these plants with the help of botanists, botanical gardens, zoos, local authorities, local councils, universities and the Government Department of Conservation. The project has been successful in creating mass awareness among the people in New Zealand.

Milky Storks of Malaysia: The milky storks, the rare storks in the world are on the verge of extinction. The habitat loss, growing pollution and global warming has reduced their survival. Human disturbances and poachig have threatened their existence. The milky stork (Mycteria cinerea) is an endangered species in Malaysia. The Malaysian Nature Society has announced that only 10 birds remain in Malaysia, making extinction in the next five years. The work of the Malaysian Nature Society has been quite admirable in the conservation of Milky Storks.

Mount Hkaborazi National Park: The Park was created by Myanmar Government on October 10nth 1998. This Park exists between Tibetan Border and Myanmar. The Park covers 3812 square kilometers of snow capped Himalayan Peaks, sub-alpine habitats and tropical evergreen rainforests. It gives shelters to mammals such as takin, red panda, goral, musk deer and black barking deers. Unfortunately, it does not cover the range of the recently discovered leafdeer a species of muntjac. This area should also be covered, under the Eastern Himalayan Park. The above unique species should be protected by all means.

Butterfly Sancturies, Mexico: The three forests in Mexico have been declared the Butterfly Parks as several species of butterflies breed and move freely in the moisterous forests, of Mexico. The butterflies arrive here from Canada, USA and breed here at a particular occasion and again move to other countries.

The butterflies in some countries are on the verge of extinction. In Europe, there are 567 species of butterflies and 69 species are threatened: 17 at global level and 52 at a European level.

A survey on butterflies was conducted in 50 forests of Uganda and it was found that the sites of butterflies were under threat. It took five years and a fund of $1600,000 was spent on the survey and research work. In a Valley in Colombia has resulted in the discovery of a new species of butterflies. It has been put in Natural History Museum, London.

Kakadoo National Park, Australia: Kakadoo is a vast wilderness and National Park in Australia. This park is a living laboratory of wild animals and amazing beautiful plants and trees. The life in Kakadoo is more enjoyable when some people track the wildland for recreational activities like bird watching. There are some amazing bird species here like kakatoo, kingfisher, hornbill, woodpecker, water fowls and wild fowls. Some water birds come here to breed and enjoy life during winter as well as summer. The large trees, bushes, dwarf plants and grasslands full of long green grasses provide shelter to mammals, reptiles, avies, primates, small mammals, rabbits, porcupine and relatives of Weasels.

The birds are amazing and beautiful and chirp with beautiful songs.

Danube Delta: This is a most beautiful Delta of Danube river and also the home of several wild animals, plants and birds. This is the ecologically most sensitive wetland. Ukraine has come under international pressure to halt the construction of a shipping canal through the ecologically sensitive environment of Danube delta. The work is continue on the spot despite the worldwide protest. The Ukraine authorities explain that the project carries no serious environmental risk but conservationists fear that the work will destroy bird and fish habitats there. In the past four months, the US and EU have officially asked Ukraine to stop all construction work pending on independent scientific assessment. This construction may hamper the bio-diverstiy and also erode the Delta on a larger scale.

Yavorovski: National Park, Ukraine: The Yavorovski National Park of Ukraine is spread in 7078.6 hactares. The park was established in Yavorovski District, Lvov oblast, Western Ukraine. The park provides protection to more than 1340 species of vascular plants, 27 of which are listed in the Ukraine's Red Data Book.

The park also consists more than 250 bird species, 12 species of amphibians and 8 reptile species. It has a distinct mosaic of soil types that give rise to some 20 types of forest community.

Ukraine Wetland and Water Birds: The Wetlands of Ukraine are some of the best wetlands in world which protect various species of birds and water animals. The Sivash wetland is near the border of Azov Sea in Southern Ukraine. From time to time several scientific surveys were conducted to support the conservation project of the wetland and locate the exact numbers of different species of birds there. In a recent survey, it was revealed that there were more than 1.4 million waterbirds including 23,000 grebs, 30,000 cormorants, 208,000 swans, gees and ducks, 340,000 coots, 515000 waders, 167,000 gulls and 96,000 terns. The Survey confirmed that

Sivash ranks alongside the Wadden Sea and Banc d' Arguin as one of the most important wetlands for birds in the Western Pelaearctic flyway. This is the traditional flyway and nesting place of most of the migratory birds. This wetland is a heaven for most of the water birds and shore bids for roosting.

Chilean Endemic Forests: A beautiful, rare and endemic forest in chile is on the verge of extinction. Continuous encroachment for housing, timber and agriculture has vanished away some of the most important forests of the world. In Chile some forests are quite rare and important for human life. The Ruil Nothofagus alessandrii forest, a rare and endemic temperate forest in central Chile, could disappear in 10 years. By 1999 only 352.2 hactare of this forest type remained in 183 fragments surrounded by a matrix of Pinus radiata plantations. Only 42 hactares of forests are protected in a public reserve. The forest is also being invaded by introduced species. Conservation efforts involving land owners and public agencies are required, both inside and outside the protected areas.

Welsh Islands, UK: Uk's Welsh coast is a heaven for waterbirds and shorebirds. The islands of Skomer, Skokholm and Middleholm, are off the Welsh coast of UK. The islands are most important breeding sites for the shearwater puffinus puffinus. A survey has revealed that C. 150,000 pairs of this bird breed here which is 50 percent of world population. The species is only bird breeding in the UK to migrate to South America where it spends winters in the South Atlantic, Off Argentina, Brazil and Uruguay. The Welsh Islands are a heaven for the breeding of Puffinus, a bird of local origin.

Rajaji National Park. Rajaji National Park is a favourite destination for the safari tourists from all over the world. It is a world famous bio-diversity National Park which is known for its Asian elephants and tigers. The Park covers 1225 kilometer square area and is a heaven for kingfisher, laughing birds, yellow paradise, white paradise, hornbills, karaoon, saraoon (magpies), kaljeenth (black magpie) Hilansh, Kaffoo, koel and several other species of magnifiscant birds. Some 65 wild birds including several species of cranes are found here in the Saung river banks in the Park.

The bears, sambhar, stagdeer, boars, wildcats, several species of primates, mongoose, rabbits (black and red), marsh deers and several other wild animals like porcupine are found in the park. The toads and water frogs are common in the park.

Besides this, several evergreen trees, plants, flowering bushes, fruit trees and berries are found in the park. The The Park is a heaven for honey birds (humming birds and longstalked flowering bushes.) It is known for its fresh water mangroves. Two orchid species are found in Rajaji National Park. These are : Obenoria and Vanda Cristata. Orchids are quite popular and are found on the moisturous Saal and Semal trees in the Park.

Kaziranga National Park: Kaziranga National Park is a natural biological Park in the world spread upto 759 square kilometers. This park is a heaven for several amazing wild animals including elephants, rhinos, deers, hogdeer, wild buffalos, swamp deers, sambbar, wild boars, hog badgers, bears, fishing cat, cobras, python, civets and rabbits are found in this beautiful park. The park is a heaven for wild birds including small song birds. The monkeys and langoors are common sight here. The one horned Rhino (Rhinoceros unicornis) and wild buffalo are found here. It has been declared a World Heritage Site by UNESCO.

Kaziranga National Park is being disturbed by local hunters and Poachers. The continuous hunting has reduced the unique Rhino (Rhinoceros unicornis) population in the Park. Besides this, the flood effects the wildlife in the park every year. This has badly damaged the population of every wild animal here.

Kaziranga National Park in Assam is a World Heritage site and main stronghold of Great Indian Rhinoceros (Rhinoceros unicornis). The population of Rhinos was badly affected by floods in 1998. There were three periods of flooding: fist in June 1998 but third from 3 to 8th September, caused the deaths of large numbers of animals, either by drowning, or being killed by peoples vehicles. Thiry two Rhino drowned and four were poached. Five elephants, 20 wild buffalos, 400 hogdeers, 8 swampdeers, 10 Sambers, 14 wild bears, 5 hogbadgers, 1 bear, 9 porcupines were killed. At Southern edge of park, 1 elephant, 28 hog deers 3 wild boars, 2 hog badgers, 1 fishing cat, 2 cobra, 1 python and 2 civets were found dead because of devastating flood.

During the flood 47 animals were rescued including 1 rhino calf, 42 hogdeers, 2 swamp deers 2 wild boars and 1 elephant. The hogdeer and deer population was reduced to 50 percent in the flood. This was a devastating loss to the Kaziranga.

Every year several animals including elephants, rhinos, bears and deers are killed by devastating floods as well as the poachers. The teeth of elephants brings US $ 1,00,000 and the horn of rhino US $ 50,000 in the international market. The network of the smugglers, poachers and whiskers is so strong that the park authorities are almost unknown about the ghastly killing of those wild animals in the park.

At present, there are 2500 rhinos in the world of which over 1500 live in Kaziranga National Park. It is believed that in the last one decade. 1200 rhinos have been killed by the poachers.

Kaziranga is a living natural laboratory for its rich bio-diversity. This the natural habitat for Rhinocesos unicornis and wild buffalos. We should protect the rich bio-diversity of Kaziranga.

Wildlife of Arunachal Pradesh

Arunachal is a living laboratory of the bio-diversity in the world. The forests, meadows, pastures and valleys are a beautiful manifestations of nature. This state is rich in beauty as well as wild life. The medicinal herbs, moisture loving plants, orchids and ferns and several specis of wildflowers attract the tourists from the world over. The state is a heaven for the mountaineers, trekkers, explorers and camplovers. The mountain deers, tigers, bears, primates, porcupines, rabbits and weasels are found in the state. The wild animals of cold climate are a distinct feature here. The wild pheasants and song birds are common sight here. One small species of the Himalayan Monals is found in the forests of Arunachal. The landscape and bio-diversity of this state is most enchanting and amazing in the world. Some species of monkeys from Arunachal are quite unique and different from the rest of the world. The mammals, reptiles, avies, primates and orthopoda animals are quite unique and amazing. The border areas and wildlife of Arunachal Pradesh should be protected by all means. Arunachal Pradesh is the heaven of India and we should save it from foreign encroachments. Indian Army personnels have done their best to protect its borders and environment with great dedication.

Bio-diversity of Central Asia: The Archa (junipers) forests once covered the areas of Tienshan and Pamir-Alai, in Kyrgyzstan and Kazakhstan, have been reduced to some rammants. Once spread to 20,000 km^2 now remain 4000 km^2 in the mountains of Soviet Central Asia. In these areas, the practice of livestock rearing, grazing in the forests has destroyed all possibility of natural vegetation. The most beautiful forests of Archa (Juniper) have been destroyed by the timber traders, farmers, local communities and livestock grazers.

The other Russian Natural Forests are unique and most beautiful scenic landscapes in the world but lack of maintenance and publicity the areas remain unnoticed. The Zapovedniks Reserve forests, Katunsky Biosphere Reserve are among the most enchanting and sacred forests in the world. The Snowmountains, juniper forests and the open plain grasslands create an amazing ecosystem and moulds them into a beautiful scenic land.

Ecosystem of Sumatra: The Ecosystem of Sumatran forests is rich and amazing in the world. It is the combination of rain forests, evergreen plants, moisture and heavy growth of shade loving herbs. The orchids and ferns have given a true colour to floral diversity. Among the mammals: tigers, cloud tigers, boars, bears and primates of different species are found here. Some wild animals and birds here are quite amazing and rare in the world. Most of the species of primates are endemic here.

The orang-utans (The man of forest) are found in the ancient forests and National Parks of Sumatra. The rain forests are being felled at an alarming rate. It is estimated that one-third of the rain forests in the country have already been wiped out. The future of orangutans is in danger as there are only surviving between 3000-5000 orangutans in the forests of Sumatra.

The ecosystem of Sumatra is affected by global warming, encroachment, loss of habitats and pollution in certain areas of Sumatra.

Importance of Bio-diversity Hot-spots: There are only certain natural areas, wilderness and forests in the world which are known for their rich bio-diversity. Some regions of the world are rich in amazing floral diversity. These certain areas are known as "Bio-diversity Hotspots in the world. To protect them, we should stop deforestation at all levels. At present, there are 30 global biodiversity hot spots all over the world. Maputaland in South Africa, Swaziland, and Kwazulu Natal are the global hotspot of bio-diversity. The area contains a large numbers of plants and animals which are endemic to this area. There is a continuous threat from unplanned agriculture and town planning. The new map shows the areas that are most important for conserving the regions vegetation types and has just been used by Zulu Natal wildlife, the provincial conservation body, to guide the development of proposed eucalyptus plantations in the area. Among other bio-diversity hotspots are Amazon forests, rain forests of Venezuela, Colombia, South Africa, Ghana, Gabon, Cameroun and Congo Basin are among the best known their amazing bio-diversity.

Conservation Tasks: There should be an excellent policy and strategy to conserve and protect National Parks from timber traders, hunters and tribals. The ancient forests should be protected from local communities, encroachment from farmers, construction of housing, roads and increasing pollution. The timber companies and other illegal activities in the forests have damaged several beautiful spots of natural importance. Several forests areas in the Himalyas, Central Asia, South East Asia, Africa, Australia and Amazonia have been vanished away. The rain forests all over the world have been felled at an alarming rate. The protection of such forests is necessary for balancing the proportion of CO_2 and oxygen in the environment.

Reforestation: There should be proper planning and strategy for the fencing of protected and forests all over the world. The Continuous reforestation on the felling spots is the reality of time to maintain the forest cover through replanting and protecting them for the future. For example, reforestation activities in the Himalyan states of India have encouraged people to plant more trees in the forests which were felled earlier by the timber merchants. The oak, cedar and pine forests have grown into complete trees. In the rain forests too same native tree species should be planted at a larger scale.

Spreading of forest Cover: There is a great need to spread a larger forest cover to make up the lost forests in the mountains, tropical countries and wetland forests in the wetland areas. The Atlantic forests of Brazil are some rare examples of Prana pine. Now, there are only 2 percent remnant forests existing in Brazil. There should be heavy reforestation activities in some countries where a large number of ancient forests have been vanished away.

Protection to Wild Species and Habitats

There are numerous organizations and environmental agencies which are providing protection to wild animal species and their habitats. This is the best way to protect the wild life and their places of shelter. In developing countries, efforts are being made to fence the wildlife Parks and bio-diversity hot sopts to protect the animals and plants within it. Some of the countries have been in political chaos for some decades and a large number of manpower had to settle near forests. A large chunk of a forest was used for fuel and timber and the wildlife was used for food. This has reduced the population of primates in several African countries.

1. There is a huge profit in the conservation of wildlife Parks and bio-diversity hot sports all over the world. Some countries have developed wildlife tourism through National Parks and wildlife sanctuaries. For example, British Columbia, (Canada) is the best example of that sort. Amazonian wilderness, the rain forests of Ghana and Congo Basins are some of the ideal examples. National Kruger Park, South Africa is an excellent example of Wildlife Tourism in the world.
2. There is always a possibility of employment through wildlife tourism. British Columbia earns 9.5 billion dollars every year and provides employment to 1,17,500 people through wilderness tourism. Some 20 Amazon Travel and Tours companies are earning

revenue through their worldwide sponsored tours and creating employment for the younger generation.

3. The Economic benefits are many. We earn a good bunch of foreign exchange. There are hotels, motels, restaurants where the tourists eat food and drink beverages. They use cars, buses taxis and several other things and pay direct money in exchange.
4. To create wildlife tourism, we, the citizens of the world should protect bio-diversity hotspots all over the world.

10

National Parks and Wild Life Management

1. Wildlife Protection and Management: Wildlife management and protection has got a unique awareness all over the world. Several species of wild animals and plants are being protected in developing countries. A large number of wild animals and plants have been vanished away from this planet in the last one century. Global warming, pollution and rapid growth in population are some of the responsible factors. Some of the species had a great importance to man and its biosphere. Now it is a great responsibility of every citizen to protect the environment and wildlife of this living planet.

The protection of wildlife and natural areas is an asset for the development of tourism.

The protection of natural areas is also important for the protection of wildlife. Some of the countries have beautiful wildlife parks and rich bio-diversity just to encourage tourists and earn an excellent amount of foreign exchange. The excellent services to tourists provides best prospects to earn money and make the life style more competitive.

Wildlife tourism or eco-tourism envisages the ways for the protection and conservation of parks through mass awareness campaign. Among the tourists, there are several scholars, environmentalists, writers, journalists and intellectuals and they always write about the loss of bio-diversity in the park and the impact of tourism due to mass arrival of tourists from the foreign countries. The roads passes through the National Parks should be used in one single way: in and out just to protect green plants, trees and to keep the wild animals undisturbed.

Importance of National Parks: The importantance of vast stretches of National Parks, its existing wildlife, floral diversity helps in creating a balance in the environment. For it is necessary for the balance of ecosystems at different levels. For example, the wetlands, plants and animals in it, the gushing river water amidst the forestland, the marshland, the pastures and varied grasslands make it a beautiful recreation point for the lovers of nature and eco-tourism. The biological diversity remains protected inside a National Park as it is a safe habitat for all living animals, plants and micro-organism within a boundary line of the park.

The wildlife tourism can be encouraged through wildlife parks management and maintenance. The studies on wildlife mangement has become quite popular among the younger generation of South American, African and Asian nations. The park authorities should pay more attention on wildlife management and captive breeding research on wild animals.

Expansion of Parks: The continuous deforestation, agricultural expansion and human encroachment for housing and road construction has reduced the areas of forests and National Parks the world over. Particularly, South American and African nations are facing the problems of encroachment. In this way the protection of all wild animals and floral diversity and the expansion of parkland is quite necessary.

Expand the Corridors for Elephants: It is necessary to expand the coming in and going out corridors of elephants. The area should be expanded just to support the roaming area for tigers, bears and elephants so that they may go out in search of their prey. Rajaji Natonal Park, Dehradun has expanded the elephant corridors in the park. This is among the largest corridors in the country.

Expand Roaming Territories for Lions and Tigers. In some countries, the roaming territories for lions and tigers are being expanded in the National Parks. Such territories have been created and expanded in several countries. The corridors for Siberian leopard, African tigers and leopards, South American tigers and jaguars have been expanded. In India, the National Parks are being expanded with its requirements for expansion of a possible roaming area for the wild animals.

Expand the Grazing area for Deers, Zebras, Wild Buffalos, Ziraffe and wildebeests: The grazing area for the grazing animals should be expanded inside the park in the form of pastures or grassland. The vast National Parks like the Amazon National Park, (Brazil), Virunga National Park (Congo) and the Kruger National Park, (South Africa) are some of the best examples of expanded grazing area for the herbivores. In India, Rajaji National Park has an expanded grazing area for elephants and deers. The total area of Rajaji National Park is 1600 km^2.

Improve the Food Chain And Food Resources Within the Parks: It is necessary for the park authorities to expand food chain inside park to balance the population of herbivores and carnivores. The rich food chains provides the survival of carnivores and balance the population of herbivores like bears stags, wild buffalos, wild pigs, deers and marshdeers.

Plant Fruit trees and Beries for Primates: The plantation of wild fruit trees, berries and flowering bushes are important for the population and survival of monkeys, bears pandas, rabbits, and other fruit eater animals. The wild birds are fruit eaters and spread the seeds to all parts of the forests. The fruit bats also eat fruits in large numbers and help in the dispersal of fruit seeds in the forests and distant park areas.

Wild Life Management in National Parks: To develop eco-tourism wildlife management should be adapted with great conservation activity. If wildlife is managed properly the bio-diversity thrives and thepark becomes a safe heaven for wild animals and plants. The park authorities should create new habitats for wild animals, wetlands and manage it within a ecological setup. The population of wild animals thrives in the park with a proper food chain system.

Reforestation Activities: In developing countries two third of the existing forests have been wiped out completely in the past one century. Particularly, the Alpine and Rain forests have been lost in the last 50 years. Once there were more than 20,000 km^2 Archa forests in Central Asia, now, there are only 4000 km^2 existing forests. In South America, there are now 2 percent Atlantic forests surviving which once were covered in 20 million hectares in the state of Santa Catarina (Brazil). The Brazilian Pine (Araucaria angustifolia) is limited in some remnant forests of South Eastern Brazil.

Protection of Habitats: The protection of wild animals in protected forests and National Parks is a positive step towards the conservation of the wild animal species. The great need is to create natural habitats for them and protect the traditional habitats already existing in the park. There is a great need to create some natural covers for bears, tigers, lions and primates near their roaming territories.

Create more natural habitats for monkeys, reptiles and carnivores as these things are necessary in a multipurpose Safari Park. The natural caves for lions and tigers should be maintained in different territories. The habitats for bears and primates should be created at different locations near their traditional resting places.The habitats for reptiles and birds also be created properly.

Conservation Activities: The main task is to continue conservation activities in the National Park. The real meaning of conservation activities is not only to protect the wildlife in a particular area but to multiply and spread the species for the future generation. The protection of wild animals, breeding and spreading their population and help them to live the longer life in a forest park ecologically suitable for their survival.

Breeding of Wild Animals in Captivity: There are some Ecological Research Centre, Wildlife Breeding Centre and Environment Research Centre established in some parks of South Africa, Canada, USA, France and India to breed the wild animals in captivity. Because some species are so rare that their breeding in Captivity is more safe and fruitful. Later on, they are left to their natural places where they adopt themselves according to the nature.

Providing More Natural Environment: In a Wildlife Sanctuary or National Park, the wild animals should be provided more natural environment. The traditional plants, should be planted to provide shelter and nesting to the wild birds.

Stop the Encroachment and other Disturbances: The encroachment in the national park and other human disturbances should be stopped with immediate effect. The poachers, hunters and Wildlife organ smugglers should be punished severely. There should be permanent fencing or Eco wall to protect the boundaries of the National Wildlife Parks. Also, take the co-operation of local dwellers and communities in the protection of the Park and wildlife within.

Important National Parks and Wildlife Management: India is a heaven for national parks and wildlife sanctuaries which are established in different parts of the country. In the past two decades there is an increase in the number of hunting and poaching in the National Parks of India. In Rajaji National Park, Dehradun, Kaziranga National Park, Assam, Manas National Park and various other National Parks in the country are under the secret eyes of poachers and smugglers and the authorities could not stop the illegal activities in the park. Once, there were 67,000 Rhinos in Zimbabwe's national parks but now there are only 3000 surviving Rhinos today in Chebore National Park, Mana Pools National Park and Sainji National Park in the same country. The Smugglers have killed 63,000 Rhinos by now. This too for skins and horns. The elephants too have been killed in African forests in large numbers for its ivory teeth. It is estimated that at the end of this century, some of the wild animals including large mammals will be completely vanished away like the Dinosaurs.

Best Safari Parks in India: There are several best Safari Parks in India which should be maintained for a longer period to encourage wildlife tourism. Among them are Rajaji National Park, Deharadun, Kaziranga National Park, Assam; Ranthambhour National Park, Kanha National Park, Bharatpur Wildbird's Sanctuary, Western Himalyan Wild Bird Sanctuary Sarahan, Shimla, Himachal and amazing wildlife parks are in some Southern States of India.

The large mammals: Among the large mammals of India are: lion, tigers, leopards, elephants, bears, primates, wild boars, Sambhar, deers, marsh deers, stag deers and Neelgai. Among the small Mammals are, fox, rabbits, weasels, mongoose, wild cats, porcupine, hog deers and civets. The other wild animals are found in large numbers in several wildlife parks of India.

Reptiles: Among the reptiles, there are Giant mountain lizards, small lizards (green, red and blue), snakes (green, yellow, brown and black), cobra, python, diamond back snake, crocodiles, ghariyals, turtles, water snakes and several other reptiles. The lizards found on the mountain rocks and tropical rocks are quite different in colour and nature.

Avies: The avifauna is the most important characteristics of Indian National Parks. There are several pheasants, wild fowls, song birds, water birds and other forest birds with strange musical sounds.

Primates: Langoors, monkeys, golden langoor, lion tailed macaque and snub nosed moneys are also found in the mountain forests of northeastern countries.

Small Mammals: Among the small mammals are wild cats, rabbits, porcupines, weasels, mongoose and various other small animals.

Orthopoda: The wildlife parks in India remain full of different species of insects including moths, dragonfly, mantis, honeybees and butterflies.

The Amazing Botanical Plants and Trees: India is a land of amazing herbs, unique, species of ferns and orchids. The ornamental plants, sweet smelling spices, aromatic herbs and aquatic plants are found at different ecological regions.

2. Kaziranga National Park: Kaziranga National Park is among the most beautiful Wildlife Parks in the world. The park is known for its rich bio-diversity. The wild animals like tigers, bears, hogdeer, hog badger elephant, wild boar, Rhinoceros unicornis, wild buffalo, swamp deers, sambar fishing cat, cobra, python, civets, porcupine and rabbits are found here in large numbers. Kaziranga is internationally known for the single horned Rhino species (Rhinoceros unicornis) in the world. Spread into more than 759 km^2, it is a heaven for mammals, primates and wild birds.

Among the reptiles King Cobra, Pythons, and common snakes, turtles and lizards are found here. Kaziranga and Manas National Parks are famous for Golden langoor and Rhinoceros Unicornis. One horned Rhino is found only in Kaziranga in the world.

The Great Bears's Rain forests, Canada: The Canadian Government has agreed to legislation that will protect one third of the forest from logging, and ensure that the remaining two thirds are logged using sustainable practices. The total area of rain forests to be protected from logging is 2 billion hectare which is more than twice the size of Yellow Stone National Park.

Global Warming

The cold climate Ecological zone should be maintained at its original temperature for the Polar bears and Grizzly bears. Already, a large population of bears in the park is facing the "heat" of global warning. This has badly disturbed the Polar Bear Ecosystem and their habitats. Also, a large areas of their food chains, rivers or oceans are in danger as most of the part of it has badly affected in the past four decades.

The agreement to protect the Great Bear Rainforest will also set a new precedent for decision making by local indigenous groups as the forests First Nation Group will be given the rights to define what happens on their land.

Some NGOs and alliance of environmental organization, industry leaders and indigenous groups are quite happy that after their 10 years Campaign to protect Great Bear Rain Forests has been successful.

Serengeti National Parks. This park is established between countries Kenya and Tanzania. The park is spread in 25,000 km^2 area. Several species and their migration movement is being noticed in the park for the past one decade. Several Research organizations from UK and USA are cooperating in this affair. The conservation of large migratory species can be problematic because of their requirements for large protected areas. The movement of wildebeest (connochaetes taurius) in 25,000 km^2 territory of Serengeti Mara. Ecosystem of Tanzania and Kenya has recently been studied using eight individuals collared with Global Positioning Systems. It was noticed that 90% of their time was spent inside the Park and 10 percent of the time was being spent in Ikoma Open Area and Mara Group Ranches, areas that receive limited protection and that are threatened by poaching an agriculture. The Animals are now spending time in Western Buffer Zones, and the development of community run Wildlife Management Areas in such buffer zones is an important step in the process of conservation of the park.

Panna Tiger National Park: The Indian tigers are on the decline beause of loss of ancient habitats and their continuous poaching. The Panna Tiger Reserve is an unique example of tiger protection in the world. The climate is quite suitable for the growth of tiger population in India.

Tropical deciduos forests from the bulk of potential tiger habitat in India, but accurate population estimates are scarce. To solve this 45 day survey, using photographic capture-recapture sampling was carried out in 2002 in the 542 km^2 Panna Tiger Reserve in Central India. Sixty sites were sampled using camera traps. Thirty six photos allowed individual tigers density was 6.9 tigers for 100 km^2. Results of the study suggest that the 15000 km^2 of the remaining Indian tropical dry forests can potentially support population of C. 9,000 wild tigers, if managed and protected as Panna. (2) Indias Palamu and Valmiki Tiger Reserves are collapsing as a result of the failure of national and state governments to release sufficient funds and sometime the staff do not get pay at proper time.

The Marine Parks of South Africa: The National Parks and Vast Marine Parks in South Africa are managed properly keeping in view wild life tourism, revenue generation and creation of employment for the local people in a greater way.

The South African Government has declared four new marine parks in a protected areas that is near the coastal land and the sea. The country protected coastline has been increased 11% to 18%. The four areas known for their natural beauty and bio-diversity are:

(1) The Aliwal Shoal, a subtidal coral reef off Umkomaas that protects threatened Sharks, (2) Pondoland, including 90 km. of coastline near Port St Johns, which extends 15 Km. seawards, marking the start of Sardine Run. (3) The Bird Island in Algoa Bay that includes many rare and threatened sea bird species; and (4) Cape Peninsula that includes all coastal water around Table Mountain National Park. A fifth marine protected area is planned off Namaqualand and, at 790,000 hactare will be South Africa's largest National Marine Park.

Nanda Devi National Park: The park lies in Garhwal Himalyas and covers 630 km^2. The Nanda Devi Park is considered among the best Himalyan Natural Parks in the World. The bird fauna is expected to 168 but only 57 species have been recorded. There are some species of mammals: Muskdeer, thar, bharal and snow leopard. The Park is known for its primates, tigers, bears, wild boars, weasels, rabbits and porcupines. The Musk Deer Research Centre is widely known among the tourists. The park is a heaven for cold climate mountain birds. The song birds are found here in large numbers. This park has become a heaven for tourists from far and near.

Sagarmatha National Park, Nepal: Sagarmatha National Park is the most popular National Park in the Himalyas of Nepal. Located in North Eastern Nepal and covering 1,148 square km, the Park covers the upper catchment of the Dudhkosi river system, a distinct geographical entity enclosed by high mountain range. The Parks northern boundary lies along the main divide of the Great Himalayas, coinciding with the Tibetan border.

With its lower boundary at 2845 meters and containing seven peaks over 7000 meters, the park reaches to summit of Mount Everset 8863 meters (29078 feet), the world's highest mountain peak. The parks four main glaciers Chhukhung, Khumbu, Gokyo and Nangpa La-feed deeply incised valleys which drains into Dudh Kosi and its tributaries to form the part of the Ganges River System. In the upper hight of Gokyo valley, the Ngozumpa Glacier (20 km) is the longest glacier in the park with some 17 small glacial lakes. These lakes are used by water fowls and migratory birds.

The Sagarmatha National Park is an important high altitude breeding ground for birds. Among the 162 recorded mountain birds 36 breed in the park. Some of them are: Blood Pheasant, Robin Accentor, white throated Red start and grandala. Other important birds are Tibetan Snow Cock, Snow partridge and Himalayan monal.

The red panda, Asiatic black bear and snow leopard are found here. The short tailed mole, Tibeten water shrew, Himalayan watershrew and woolly hare are among the smaller mammals in the region. Here, Makalu Barun Valley is the trekker's paradise. The Barun Valley is an important bird's paradise. This will expand park upto 1400 square km more for wild animals. The Park was listed as World Heritage Site in 1979. Nepal is earning enough revenue through Mountain Tourism.

The Chang Thang Reserve (Tibet): Chang Thang is the most impressive and vastly expanded National Park of Tibet. It covers 240,000 square kilometers of the Northern Plain, forming the north western part of the vast elevated Tibetan tableland. It has been converted inot a vast Biosphere Reserve now. It is the largest wildlife Sanctuery outside the arctic or Antarctica. The Reserve protects a number of species that are unique and endemic to Tibetan Plateau. It covers a large part of the remaining range of the wild Yak. Once, this species was widespread in this plateau but was reduced to a few hundred by continuous hunting. There are several other mammals i.e. Tibetan antelope or chiru. Tibetan gazelle, Tibetan wild ass or Kiang, Tibetan brown bear, snow leopard, Tibetan argali (or wild sheep) and bharal or blue sheep. Among the birds, are 67 breeding species, most of palaearctic origins have been recorded. The six of them are known as endemic as: black necked crane, giant babax, Kozlovs, babax, kozlov's bunting, Roborovsky"s rose finch, and Taczanowski's snow finch.

This reserve is a place of large herds of wild ass and Tibetan antelope. Establishment of the reserve will help to control illegal hunting, in particular the commercialized slaughter of wild Yak for its meat and the Tibetan antelope for its wool.

In the west end of the reserve is Memar Lake region where the population of Yak is 1000 and also the traditional breeding ground of Tibetan antelope.

In addition, the Arjin Shan Reserve (45000 km^2) bordering the Chang Tang Reserve in the north east is being extended to the west. This will increase the area of the vast reserve to 390,000 km^2 of land into a single protected reserve park.

The Swiss National Park: The Alps are the most beautiful principal mountain systems in Europe. These mountain ranges passes through various European contries i.e. Switzerland, France, Germany, Austria and Northern Italy. These cover 165,000 km^2. Among them the Swiss Alps are in the most beautiful form of mountains.

The Swiss National Park is located in the canton of crison in eastern Switzerland, where it adjoins Italy's Stelvio National Park (1,482 km^2).

The Swiss National Park lies at a height of 1,500G-3,174 meters. The park is a combination of beautiful snowclad peaks: among them are Piz Quattervals (3,165 meters) separated by deep, narrow valleys. The Engadine Valley, on the park's northern boundary passes its water into Danube river.

The Parks total area, is168 km^2. One third of it is forest, one third grassland and one third is covered with bare rocks and scree.

Dwarf mountain pine is the main tree species here. At the lower heights is a growth of Scots pine, arolla pine, larch and Norway spruce. An excellent growth of broad leaved trees in scattered throughout the park. Among them are white birch, green alder, aspen and rowan.

Above the treeline at about 2350 meters are many herbal plants including edelweiss and anemone. Some 640 species of plants and herbs have been recorded in the park.

Among the mammals are wolf, brown bear, lynx (are extinct now) red deer, chamois and ibex. There is a small enclave of Hotel Furon and Hotel Guron in the park and it is mostly uninhabited.

The main road passes through the park which is responsible for numerous road accidents.

There are 100 species of beautiful birds, with 60 nests in the park. Among them caper caillie, ptarmigan, black woodpecker, nut cracker and golden eagle are common. The smaller song birds are wall creeper, ring ouzeal, alpine accentor, snow finch and Alpine chough. The information about the park and reading facilities can be enjoyed outside the park Zernez. Swiss Alps are among the most beautifully located and ideal for shooting of films. The international filmmakers come here to enjoy natural beauty and shoot their films here.

Manu National Park (Peru) : Manu National Park is located on the eastern side of the Peruvian Andese. This Park is one of the richest in biological diversity. It is situated at an elevation 3640-4000 meters. The park covers an area of 15,328 km^2. According to biologists of the world, it is one of the last great unspoilt wilderness areas remaining on the eastern side of the Peruvian Andes. This is the park of the Peruvian Amazon regions which still is unexploited. Manu's pristine wildlands, diverse habitats and types of wilderness make it biologically richer in the Latin America. This park lies in Selva, the great tropical region of the Amazon basin. The park have an excellent growth of virgin forests with tall trees reaching to the highest of 50 meters (160 feet or more). Most of Peru's Selva animals have been hunted for meat and skin in the past. Some 200 mammal species have been recorded in Manu. Among them, more than half are from Peru. There are some in termingled species from North American origin such as deers and bears with ancient South American forms; marsupials such as oppossums (the only marsupial to be found outside of Australia and edentates (armadillos, sloths and anteaters), The five species of opossums include the rare black-shouldered opossum, known from only six specimens. The endentates are represented by three species of anteaters: the giant anteater, the tamandua or lesser anteater, two species of sloths: the three toed and the two toed sloths and two species of armadillo, the rare giant armadillo and the common nine banded armadillos.

The richness of ecosystem explains its beauty and charm. There are 13 species of primates, among them are woolly monkey and Emperor tamarin. The endangered species are: the giant otter, Jaguar, ocelot, bushdog and North Andean hemul.

Manu National Park is a heaven for beautiful wild birds. Among 1500 species of birds in Peru 800 have been recorded in the park. These are Andean condor, harpy eagle and hoatzin. There are 18 species of macaws and parrots. Two species of endangered reptiles are also found in Manu: black caiman and spectacled caiman are endemic here and both of which are being killed for meat and skins in other parts of South America.

The timber companies, gold companies, domestic cattles and wild fires have destroyed the one fourth of the Manu National Park. The Peru government should take care of it into proper way by fencing and strengthening protection of the Park. Peru is well known for beautiful wild birds, mammals, reptiles, primates and orthopoda found in this National Park. The best thing is that the park is an ideal habitat for Vicuna. The population of Vicunas in the park is increasing in several hundreds. Vicuna's are a relative species of camel. Vicunas are known for its beautiful wool, skin, meat and bone ornaments. In the Andean Countries like Bolivia; Argentina and Chile, the population of Vicuna has increased to 1,20,000. Some thirty years ago, it was 6000 left in the wild of these countries. The Vicuna's are now domestic animals also. The woollen clothes of Vicuna are very costly one and are woven with great care. The park is a heaven for local trees, dwarf bushes and very small grasses.

Amazon National Park: (Brazil) The Amazon National Park is among the top Bio-diversity National Parks in the world. All the Amazon mammals and birds are foud in this park. The Amazing wildlife of this park includes (1) Large mammals (2) Primates, (3) Reptiles (4) Avifauna (5) orthopoda (6) Small mammals, (7) Amphibians.

If the rain forests of Brazil are wiped out, the woolly spider monkeys are first to die. There are just 100 spider monkeys left alive in the rain forests of Brazil.

The Amazon National Park is deep and densely populated wilderness. The marsh deers, bears, armadillos, sloths and ant eaters are found in the park. The Jaguar, giant anteater, the tamandua, or lesser anteater, dwarf and silky anteater, 13 species of primates, woolly monkey and Emperor tamarind are found here. The giant otter, ocelot, bushdog, North Andean Hemul, caiman, crocodile and wild boars are also found here.

Some 1500 bird species, 200 honey birds and 800 birds were recorded in the Park. There are 18 species of macaws; two species of endangerd reptiles. Among the reptiles are, pythons, cobra, boatree snakes, Anaconda and some 30 species of snakes, lizards and turtles. Unfortunately some areas of ancient forests in Amazonia have been felled by the timber companies of Brazil and USA.

A vast area of land has been cleared for grazing for cattles, ranches, and agriculture. A 60,000 sq. kilometers of forests, has been destroyed to convert into a pasture land. This has badly ruined the fertility of the land.

The Largest Marine Park: A water and island territory more than 500,000 k^2 designed as a National Momunent by US Government. This include the marine trend Marine National Monument in Western North Pacific Ocean. This is deepest point on the planet and extends to cover nearby under sea volcanoes and thermal vents.

The Pacific Remote Islands Marine National Monument Covers several areas to the South and West of Hawaii, and includes Wake Island, an important breeding site for seabirds.

The Third Marine National Monument, the Rose Atoll, is located to the east of American Samoa and are known for Ruse.

Some Beautiful National Parks of Alaska : (1) **Katmai Natonal Park :** This park is in Mt Katmai Afognok Island and is known for Kodiak bears.

2. Kenai fords National Park: This is a beautiful park near shipyard Homer. This is in the Aleutian Range area.

3. Wrangell St Elias National Park: This beautiful park is in the north of the water of Gulf of Alaska.

4. Kluane National Park: This park is near the Kluane Lake in Yukon state.

5. Lake Clark National Park (Alaska Range): This park is known in the name of Lake Clark.

6. Denali National Park (Alaska): It is in the background of Mt Mckinley the highest mountain in North America.

7. Glacier Bay National Park: This park is in the North East of Bay of Alaska.

8. Gates of the Arctic National Park: This park is amazingly beautiful park to observe the snow clad beauty. It is surrounded by beautiful snow lands.

9. Mt Mckinley Park (20320 ft.): This park is the most respected mountain Park in North America. This is the highest point in North America and is tourists and trekkers paradise.

These all the parks are located in Aleutian Range of Alaska State and are home to numerous, sea birds, shorebirds and mammals. The natural beauty of this area is amazing and beautiful. The Island tourism can be encouraged in larger scale through star cruise journey.

The islands like Tanago, Kanaga, Adak, Amlia, Atka, Seguam, Kornovin, Ummak, Mkushin, Fox Island, Unalaska Island, Akuton, Unimak Island, Sanak Island, Shumagin Island, Chrikof, Trinity, Sulwik Islands are among the most beautiful cold climate islands to visit. There are some four meters islands which are also with the flavour of snow and natural beauty.

Jigme Dorjee National Park, Bhutan: Jigme Dorjee National Park in Bhutan is known for its Alpine vegetation. It has some beautiful orchids, lily, ferns and herbal medicinal plants. The most beautiful wild flowers and alpine herbs are found in this park. The park has some species of aromatic herbs.

It is said that the mountains are quite popular and rich in cold climatic bio-diversity. Wild animals and plants alike are a combination for mountain environment.

Mauritania National Park: Mauritania National Park Mauritania's Park National du Bank de Arguin and World de Fund for Nature has raised Swiss francs 400,000 for park surveillance and for three new patrol boats. Besides, this capacity building workslops will be organized to educate park's 51500 human inhabitants, the boats will help curtail the threat posed by private fishing boats and help park dwellers to improve their living conditions without being driven to over fishing by competition from poachers. The park was founded in 1976, mainly for the protection its bird life. If covers 12,000 km^2, equally distribute between land and sea and is Africa's largest coastal National Park and a wetland of international importance under Ramsar Convention and UNESCO World Heritage Site.

Katunsky Mountain Forests : These forests are among the most scenic mountain forests in the world. These can be called the wonders of nature. The small peaks remain snowclad, and 200 meters down a beautiful slope with small growth of Archa forests and then Alpine wide pastures with juniper trees and grasslands. This heavenly view in the wide pastures with juniper trees and grasslands is amazing. This view in the morning and evening sun fills our heart with magic when we observe it both the times. It is more enchanting amidst the nature. The other Russian National wonders are Altai mountains and Zapovedniks which have been put in the UNESCO World Heritage Sites. A new National Park in Kazakhstan has come into existence quite recently. The Altais are the most beautiful mountains which extend from Russia into China and Mongolia, encompassing part of eastern Kazakhstan. It contains a full spectrum of landscape and climate zones, bio-diversity and natural resources. The park would be bounded on the north and east by Russian-Chinese borders, to the west by the upper reaches of the Buchtarma River and to the south by lake Markakol, a proposed territory of 13,000 sq. km. It borders Katunsky Zapovednik in Russia and Beluka National Park creating a total of 14,500 square km. protected areas.

The Valley of Flowers, Chamoli, India: The Valley of Flowers is a World Heritage Site since 1986. This is an alpine valley formed by the small glaciers turned into V shape to the valley which is covered by numerous mountain flowers, alpine grasses and herbs. The Flora of this valley has adopted the harsh climate of this region. The Valley is covered with snow from November to May. The whole pasture gives flowers during July-August and the valley is full of sweet fragrance during that time. Some of the mountain flowers are: Anemone, Geranium, Marsh Marigold, Primula, Potentillas, Geum, Aster, Lilium, Himalayan Blue Poppy. Aconite, Delphinium, Ranunculs corydalis, Inula, Saussurea, Companule, Pediculeris, Morins, Importiens, Bistorta, Ligularia, Anaphalis Saxifraga, Lobelis, Thermopsis, Trolliuns, Bistork, Ligulavia, Anaphaleis, Lobelie etc-are found in large numbers. It is estimated that there are 360 flowering plant species in this valley.

Natural Areas Management: A large number of plants and animal species have been wiped out from the natural areas because of encroachment, forests clearing for timber and agriculture. Other development activities in the area are also a reason of wildlife loss. This has ruined the habitats of wild animals and plant ecosystems in the world. Pollution and global warming have added to their destruction. Now it is time to protect the nature and expand natural areas for the future generation. The loss of habitats in natural sites, wetlands and small remnants of forests have been destroyed in the past one century. This has badly damaged the natural sites forever.

Small Forest Land and Wildlife: A small forest area is a unit of a well protected forest. The small remnants of forest in a wildland exhibits its bio-diversity into several ways. The ecosystem of the small forests in the wild display its functions into several ways. It protects the wild birds and provide them shelter in trees for nesting. The reptiles, mammals, primates and insects also take shelter under shade of small forests. These remnant forests provide a lot of support to orthopodas as they are the food for birds, reptiles and local pheasants. The small herbs and plants also grow under the shade and moisture of small forests.

Protecting the Ecosystem: To protect the wildlife, the best way is to protect the whole eco-system of that forest range. The bio-diversity survives there only because of the protection of whole ecosystem. Any change with climatic or physical the whole eco-system is affected immediately. The felling of trees, results into the reduction in wild life or destruction of natural areas affects the whole of environment. It affects even that place where the human beings are living in villages or towns. Growing human population, increasing pollution and global warming have affected whole chain of ecosystems of this planet at a greater speed.

11

Importance of Wildlife Tourism

The wildlife tourism has a great significance to developing countries. It is growing up every year at a faster pace. The tourists and travellers from foreign countries arrive in this country in large numbers. At present 6.5 million tourists arrive in Indian cities from the Western and South East Asian countries. Most of the tourists arrive at Delhi, Bombay, Calcutta and Banglore airports. Besides this, the local airports are receiving the foreign tourists at the larger numbers. The tourists which arrive in India, a large numbers of them come to see wildlife and natural areas. This number can be increased up to 10 million tourists every year. A great emphasis should be given on the development of infrastructure and proper management of wildlife. There should be some good stay points near the wildlife sanctuaries as these things are important to international tourists. Such stay points are in South Africa. The National Kruger Park in South Africa is the best example of wildlife park in the world. Nearly 4 million tourists arrive to see this park every year. All the big animals with large population are found there. The foreign nationals find that park full of recreation. There are some stay points near the park and the tourists enjoy food, refreshments and various types of drinks. In India, Rajaji National Park, Jim Carbett National Park, Kaziranga National Park, Manas National Park, the Great Himalayan National Park, Kullu, Nanda Devi National Park, Western Himalyan Nature Park, Kufri Shimla, Western Himalyan Wild Bird Sanctuary, Sarahan (HP), Bharatpur Bird Sanctuary, Kanha National Park, Ranthambhour National Park, The Wildlife Parks in Kerala, Karnataka and Tamil Nadu are of great bio-diversical importance. These can be turned into tourists paradise. All these parks should be equipped with tourists interested in modern amenities.

Wildlife Tourism in South East Asia: The South East Asian countries are of great bio-diversical importance as they have a large numbers of beautiful birds like white paradise, Kingfisher, hornbills, paradise of forest birds, fish eating owl and eagles are found in large numbers. The mammals, lions, tigers, rhinos, pangolin, anteater, chimpanzees and other beautiful primates are found there. At present, Thailand, Singapore, Borneo, Java, Sumatra, New Guinea, Philippines and Cambodia are known for some of best international parks in the world. Tasmania Island has been developed into an international exploration activity park for the tourists. Besides this, the Great Barrier Reef has become a paradise for marine life lovers all over the world.

The Kakadoo National Park, Ningaloo Coral Reef Park, The Great Barrier Reef Park have become the hot spots of bio-diversity in the world. The international tourists have a great interest for these parks in the world.

Wild life Tourism in America: In USA, the wildlife tourism is more popular in Alaska rather than other National Parks. The YellowStone National Park and other protected areas are popular among tourists but not popular like South Africa and India. The USA government is less or more depend on captive breeding inside the park and then the animals are released in the wild. But such captive breeding is against nature's law and cubs of tigers are not good hunter when they are released in the wild. But several species have been saved from extinction through captive breeding. The theme parks are more popular in USA rather than wildlife Parks. Some of the wildlife Parks in USA and Canada are used as hunting resorts or Game Parks.

Wildlife Tourism in South America: The wildlife tourism in South America particularly in Amazonia, (Brazil) is most popular as 20 travel and tour companies from Canada, USA and Brazil sponsor wildlife tours and earn an excellent amount of foreign exchange. The other countries which are doing well in wildlife tourism are Colombia, Peru, Venezuela and Equador. These countries are a heaven for wildlife and nature tourism in the world. The Andes mountains are considered the most beautiful natural places in the world.

The countries known for amazing bio-diversity are Argentina, Bolivia and Chile. The climate and bio-diversity is considered amazing and distinctive in South America. The plateaus of Bolivia, the deserts of Atacama and Patagonia, the sea coast of Chile and the beautiful islands are not only full of scenic beauty but rich in bio-diversity also. The amazing natural beauty and vast wilderness for exploration activities are not less than the heaven. Argentina's 50 coastal areas are beautiful and popular marine life wetlands.

Wildlife Tourism in Canada: Canada is a paradise of meadows, grasslands and beautiful natural areas. British Columbia is a heaven for nature tourism. It is a country of cold climate, snow clad lakes and Islands. Islands are known for their Arctic ecology. Wildlife tourism in some Islands is on the rise. Nature tourism in British Columbia State is on its peak. This State is known for Polar bears, grizzly bears, mountain tigers, and other wild animals of human attraction.

At present, British Columbia in Canada is a world leader in Wilderness tourism, exploration and trekking activities.

Wildlife Tourism in UK: UK is a small country but has a good sense for nature tourism, national parks, zoos and unique forest lands. The British people have a good sense for the conservation of natural areas and wildlands and like to explore them from time to time. Several British NGOS are working for wildlife conservation, tourism and nature exploration activities. Fauna and Flora International is working for wild life conservation and Ecotourism in developing countries. The trekking, mountaineering and camping in the wild are important activities among the UK citizens.

The younger generation in UK is more sensitive towards reforestation, conservation and eco-tourism activities. The students go on adventure tours on holidays.

Wild Life Tourism in Africa

The African nations have atleast one third of rainforests. Two third of Africa's rain forests have already been wiped out by timber smugglers, citizens encroachment for housing and road construction and agricultural activities. There are several beautiful National Parks, wetlands and grass lands in African countries i.e. Ghana, Gabon, Congo, Nigeria Cameroun and Zaire. Some of them have most beautiful rain forests, wetlands and grasslands. The bio-diverstity in some forests and national parks is rich and varied. The wildlife parks which remain undisturbed are founding in good state. The protected areas are quitre amazing and rich in wildlife species. Wild life Tourism is more enjoyable in the Safari Parks of Ghana, Gabon, Congo, Cameroun and Zaire. Uganda, Kenya, Tanzania and Zambia are also doing well in wildlife tourism. Some of the National Parks here are not well managed as the hunters, poachers and criminals have made these parks their hunting resorts for some time to enjoy hunting. They drive over the forestland and kill the animals for horns, bones, skin and flesh also. Some National Parks in Africa are continuously being encroached by local population and displaced citizens.

Wildlife Protection Through Toursim

The wildlife protection can help in encouraging tourism in large scale. When there is mass awareness in wildlife conservation activities the National Parks receive a large numbers of tourists. The awareness helps in maintaining wildlife parks in developing countries. The writers, journalists, poets, botanists and environmentalists visit these places and create a mass awareness campaign through mass media and workshops on wildlife protection and nature conservation activities.

Wildlife Tourism: Economy: Revenue and Employment: Wildlife Tourism in many countries have developed their economic backbone into a quick foreign exchange earner. Tourism has improved their economy, created large scale unorganized employment in different sectors by reducing the workload and sharing their responsibilities in the areas of intrastructure development. This has created new projects for wild life tourism, its formation and development to make it more popular and comfortable for tourists coming from foreign countries.

The Natural areas and original forests in the developing countries should be protected just to encourage wildlife tourism. The protection of wildlife and natural areas plays an important role in encouraging wildlife tourism in developing countries.

12

Wildlife Toursim in India

Wildlife Conservation : India is a land of most beautiful wild lands and natural parks, rich in bio-diversity and heavily populated forests. At present, there are 450 National Parks, Wildlife Sanctuaries and protected areas in the country. Some 3000 most beautiful natural areas and wildlands are known for their scenic beauty. These can be used just to encourage wildlife tourism and natural tourism in the country. At present 6.5 million tourists are visiting India annually and most of them are wild life tourists or tourists interested to visit natural areas. Wildlife protection and conservation activities should be encouraged to boost up wildlife tourism. We can take it from countries like: South Africa (The Kruger National Park). The Amazon National Park (Brazil), Gunung Leuser National Park (Indonesia), Thai National Park (Thailand) are among the most adimired wild life parks in the world. In India, Rajaji National Park, The Great Himalyan National Park, Kullu, The Valley of Flowers, Jim Corbett National Park, Kaziranga National Park (Assam) and Kanha National Park are popular among the tourists for their rich biodiversity. Besides, this Kerala, Karnataka and Tamil Nadu have some most beautiful wildlife sancturies known for their amazing beauty and rich fauna and flora.

There is a great need to encourage conservation work through creating natural habitats, expanding the park area, stopping deforestation and encroachment by farmers, pastoral people and timber smugglers.

After creating a peaceful and pleasant environment, the tourism should be encouraged at a larger scale. There is some impact of tourism but it can be overcome by some skilful ways of park authories and staff.

Importance of Wildlife Tourism in India: There is great need to encourage wildlife tourism in India as it has a rich and varied wildlife in the forests. By encouraging wildlife tourism it will pave the way for wildlife conservation thus creating a mass awareness among the people of the country.

Wildlife Tourism: In modern times nature tourism and wildlife tourism is attracting the foreign tourists at largerscale. The scenic spectrum of natural areas is always attracting the lovers of nature. The amazing wild animals are a great source of human recreation.

In several countries wildlife tourism has become the backbone of their economy. In South Africa, there are only Seven National Parks and all of them are doing well in wildlife tourism. The Kruger National Park is a largest wilderness in South Africa and is the king of all natonal parks. The park is getting four to six million tourists every year and is a haven for all the wild animals in South Africa. The park has been fully commercialised by the South African Government. It functions as largest Game and Safari Park for the big businessmen and a large fee is taken from them to maintain the affairs of the Park.

Tourism in National Parks and Reserve Forests : We have already mentioned that there are 450 National Parks and Wildlife Sanctuaries in India. Some 3000 most beautiful natural areas are in the country to provide best recreation to foreign tourists. There are some great findings regarding the protection of rich bio-diversity of the parks and wildlife sanctuaries.

1. All the National Parks and wildlife sanctuaries should be kept in good state. They should be protected into the most modern ways and should be prepared to welcome the visitors into an impressive way. The Safari Parks, wildlife sanctuaries, bird sanctuaries and National Tiger and Rhino Breeding centres should be made more recreative. For example Rajaji National Park, Jim Corbett Tiger Sanctuary, Kaziranga National Park, Ranthambhour Tiger Park have unique bio-diversity. The Great Himalayan National Park, Kullu are some of the most beautiful parks which have great attraction to welcome the visitors.

Nature's Paradise : The wonders of nature are spread into the forms of mountains, forests, valleys, waterfalls, rivers and flowering pastures. The natural spectrum of wildlands always encourage people from far and near to travel the scenic lands. Modern adventure sports should be organised there just to impress the travellers from far and near. Small restaurants and stay points should be established near the natural areas and national parks. For this reason, the tourists explore the way to enjoy life from a different angle.

It has been seen that where there were some restaurants and rest houses near the natural areas or wildlife park, the tourists came there in larger numbers. They enjoyed them during trekking the wildlands. They enjoyed food in the restaurants and took rest in the rest houses. This provides them a good spirit to enjoy life in wilderness. Whenever they felt for food and rest they came back to the stay points and restaurants to relax. After eating food or refreshment they took complete rest and again re-energised themselves to explore the natural beauty of the wildlands. All these events create a positive impression among the tourists coming from far and near and they enjoy the beauty of nature.

River Valleys : The river valleys and waterfalls have become popular among the foreigners in the Andes Mountain Ranges where the river valleys, slopes and water falls create a beautiful spectrum of natural beauty amidst the forests and grass lands.

The waterfalls of Andes and Amazon in Brazil are quite popular among the tourists as they flock there in large numbers. In South Africa there are great scenic spots to enjoy them from very near. We can observe the beauty and beast, in the midst of wildlands. Andes Ranges have most beautiful lakes, waterfalls and natural water springs to entertain human mind.

The most important thing is the amazing wild life in certain natural areas which remain untouched from the outer world. There are some most beautiful and inspiring moments when a group of friends observe the activities of a woolly monkey, opossum, bear or a humming bird. It is worth to mention here that the Andese mountain forests are a paradise for different species of humming birds. The Andes mountains are a haven to the wild life watchers from all over the world. In this way wild life tourism can be most successful in the Andes mountains. These are the most scenic mountains in the world. The natural beauty always encourages the younger generation to visit the wild life parks the world over. Wildlife tourism in India has a very special meaning to the wildlife lovers. There are some different species of wild animals in Indian parks. For example, Rajaji National Park. Dehradun and Kaziranga National Park in Assam have different wildlife species. And most of them are endemic to this particular ecological zone.

Pastures, and Forests : The pastures and forests with beautiful natural spectrum are a great source of inspirations to the travellers and nature lovers world ever. There are most beautiful places of natural importance in developing countries but poverty, pollution and disease have tarnished the charms to visit there. Secondly, political upheavels, civil unrest, communal riots and water borne or airborne diseases are common there. And the governments in these countries are not concerved to remove poverty or to take steps to control the diseases. The tourists do not visit those countries inflicted in wars and diseases. Basically the tourists are a peace loving people and like to enjoy their time in peace and harmony. They require pure, germless water to drink and neat and clean food with great hygienic quality. The beds and stay points with purity and cleanliness are necessary for the relaxation of tourists and explorers. The famous grasslands, highland pastures, prairies, pampas, the plains of reeds (Mekong delta), low velds and downs are such a beautiful grasslands to visit and enjoy the different ecosystem of the world. In this way it is necessary to enjoy life in the open grasslands amidst the trees and bushes.

Safari Parks : The Safari Parks provide great recreations. The vast grasslands and forests are a heaven for wildlife tourism. There are safari Parks to enjoy the amazing beauty of wildlife. For example Amazon National Park (Brazil), the Kruger National Park (South Africa) and Serengeti National Park (Congo) provides best recreation to wildlife watchers. All the wild animals (herbivores and carnivores) in the above parks are there in large numbers. In Kruger National Park there are more than two lakhs of Impala deers, 10,000 elephants, 3500 white rhinos, 400 black rhinos 20,000 bisons, 2,000 lions, 900 leopards, 250 cheetal, 5000 giraffe, 14,000 wildebeests, 1000 stag deers 40,000 Zebras are enjoying natural environment in this world famous Safari Park. Besides this 507 species of wildbirds, 114 species of reptiles, 34 species of amphibians, 49 species of fishes, and 336 different species of trees are found in the Kruger National Park and that's why this park is liked by all the wildlife lovers of the world. The park is spread in 25,000 square kilometers and more than 300,0000 lakh tourists visit the park every year.

Rajaji National Park : Rajaji National Park is spread in 1600 square kilometers and is an ideal Safari Park of India. It has a large population of Asian elephants, tigers, leopards, primates, reptiles, avies and orthopoda to enjoy the beauty of wildlife adventure. Besides this, it has its natural wetlands, plants, trees and herbs in large numbers. The park is being disturbed by timber smugglers, poachers and smugglers of elephant tusks and tiger skin and bones. This has disturbed the peace of this park. The network of smugglers is very wide and they are spread all over the country. Several wild animals were killed by the poachers during 2003-2010 in Raja National Park.

Jim Carbett National Park : Jim Carbett National Park quite famous in the name of British hunter Jim Carbet. The park is an ideal sancturey for leopards and tigers. The international tourists who are visiting this park are from western countries as well as South East Asian nations.

The area of Jim Carbett Park has been expanded from time to time. The area of Rajaji National Park and Jim Carbett National Park function as a single entity for the corridors of elephants and a large roaming area for tigers. Both parks are densely populated and match to each others ecosystem. In this way both the park are an ideal roaming area for the tigers as well as for the elephants.

Bamboo Forests : The bamboo forests in the country are a great source of bio-diversity. In the forests where there is a great density of bamboos small mammals, wild birds and reptiles are found in larger numbers. The bamboo forests of Kotdwara hills, Rajaji National Park, Kaziranga National Park, and forests of North Eastern States, Central India and other parts where there are vast densities of bamboos forests and where marsh deers, weasel, mangoose, rabbits, porcupine, foxes and other animals are found in large numbers. The bamboo forests are a great source of food for the herbivores living in the Shivalik hills.

The bamboo forests are great source of innovative technologies for the farmers and tribal communities. For housing, bridge making, river side housing and open hampsteads bamboos are always a wonder timber for the poor people. The bamboo forests provide shelter to eagles, hawks, vultures, owls, bats and several other birds. For bird watching and camplife bamboo forests are a boon to man.

Wildlife of Saal Forests : The saal forests are a heaven for carnivores as well as herbivores. The large mammals, tigers, bears, elephants, stagdeers, wild boars, primates, foxes, weasels and mongoose are the original animals of these forests.

The reptiles, avies, orthopodas and several other living creatures are found in the saal forests. The wild fowl is the mother of domestic fowls and several cross breeds have been produced from the wild fowls. If the saal forests are gone various species of song birds, parrots, huppoe, woodpecker, wild fowl, water fowl and other birds will be vanished away permanently. The saal forests provide shade and shelter to other shade loving plants under their canopy. The ferns, flowering plants, small growth of trees and several other shadeloving plants which grow under the saal trees are of great importance to human being.

For example, Rajaji National Park, Dehradun, the ancient saal forests of Bhabhar Kotdwara Garhwal are a great source of wild vegetables and natural mushrooms during the rainy season. The rich bio-diversity of saal forests always inspire the man to explore the wildlands and forest patches.

The Mountain Forests : The mountain forests are a great source of courage and inspiration to human being as they are firm, determined and nature's ultimate strongholds. The mountain forests which are fresh, clean and pollutionless always encourage us to trek them or camp amidst the lush green forests. In the Indian mountains April and May months are more pleasant as they are the summer months and there is still some chilling cold in the mountains to make us more active for our trekking schedule.

1. The mountain forests provide us great inspiration while trekking through them.

2. The mountain slopes and valleys are good for camplife.
3. Nature watching is the best pastime hobby.
4. Bird watching in the foothills and valleys.
5. Herbal tracks through the mountain slopes.
6. Ideal camplife in the mountain pastures and grasslands.

Wild life of Shivalik Mountains : There is abundant wildlife in the foothills and valleys of Shivalik mountains. The semi-temperate and moisturous mountains are a great habitats of wild animals, birds, reptiles and orthopoda. There are small fruit plants, berries, for herbivores birds and small deers and rabbits. The bears, primates wild boars are also found in large numbers there. The Shivalik tigers, foxes, primates and porcupines are found in large numbers.

In the foothills, because of moisture and small water sources, there are numerous species of insects, moths, butterflies and other flying insects which are an ideal food for birds, pheasants, lizards, frogs and other small animals.

1. The Shivalik Hills are of medium heights and hence are more enjoyable during summer as well as winter. During summer, they have very warm climate and valleys always protect us from harsh winds during winter.
2. Even, the small forests are a paradise for bird watching.
3. There are numerous natural areas for exploration activities.
4. Trekking routes, passes through the forests and wild lands are most enjoyable.
5. There are some beautiful huts amidst natural areas and some days can be enjoyed in peace and serenity.
6. The small hills of Shivalik Himalayas are pleasant for winter as well as summer days camplife. The Shivalik Valleys are average warm during winter days.

7. The Shivalik wildlands are a great source of celebrating of tea parties and picnic holidays.
8. Natural places for exploration activities.

Wildlife Tourism in Terai : The wildlife parks in Terai are an ideal habitats for the wildlife protection. The terai forests are the particular one where the forests of the mountains as well as from plains meet. This is an ideal place where the wild animals from mountains meet their counterparts from the plains. These parks have an assimilating temperature from mountain hills as well as terai plains and making them an ideal habitation for the wild animals of both ecosystems. In these parks, one can find more birds from mountains as well as plains during winter and spring season. Such wildlife parks have become an ideal habitation and an expanded roaming area for elephants, tigers, bears, deers, wild boars as well as other small animals. The terai regions are an ideal sports for bird watching, nature watching and camping in the wild. The access of a big passage of road to the park makes it more enjoyable and profitable for the purpose of Safari Parking as the tourists face tigers and elephants from a near distance. It becomes more exciting for the visitiors to enjoy wildlife from very near.

Wildlife Tourism in Bharsaar, Pauri Hills

There is rich bio-diversity even in bare small mountains of Pauri hills. Bharsaar is a beautiful mountain Resort in Pabau block. This is a great combination of high mountain Ranges, the apple orchards, pastures and valleys. The mountain tops are covered by oak, cedar, myrica esculenta, rhododendron and other alpine grasses and bushes. The bushes of Hisaaloo, Kingora, Lisimachia punctata: a yellow flowering bush and a medicinal plant is found abundantly in this area. The climate remain colder in the summer months of May-June. The heights of Bharsaar mountain peaks may range to 8000-9000 ft. as during winter the peaks are covered with first snow of the year.

Bharsaar is a Horticulture College and is situated in a wide valley. This place has become immense attraction for the scholars of horticulture science, nature lovers and explorers of the wild lands. Above the Bharsaar Horticulture College, there is a temple of Budhaa Bharsaar in the midst of deep forests which has become immense attraction among the trekkers and explorers of forests and wildlands.

Wildlife Tourism in Khirsoo Hills : Khirsoo is a beautiful mountain forest which has been declared a wildlife sanctuary quite recently. The place is known for its heavily dotted forests and beautiful wildlands. Wildlife is rich and abundant in the forests of Khirsoo. The mountain tigers, several species of monkeys, langoors, foxes, bears, wildcats, wildboars, porcupines, weasels, rabbits are found in large numbers. The small mountain deers Ghweed and Kakhad are found in these forests. The red foxes, porcupines and rabbits are found in warm valleys.

Khirsoo Wildlife Sanctuary is quite popular for its rich bird fauna. The wild fowls, water fowls, turtle dove, Kaljeenth (black magpie). Karaoon (blue magpie), saraoon (redmagpie), white paradise, hilaansh. Kaffoo, Koel, Green and blue coloured birds, Tailor birds, mouse birds, bulbul, surady, hornbill, kingfisher, forest crow, skylark, small species of Monal Pheasants are found in the forests. This is the most beautiful place for the enjoyment of natural beauty and wildlife.

Wildlife Tourism in Maandaakhaal : Maandaakhaal is a mountaineous natural wild land near Boobaakhaal. This is the most beautiful scenic land in the world and is known as the Alps of Shivalik Hills. Maandaakhaal is known as the Heaven of Pauri Hills and Crown of Maandaakhaal Valley.

1. The Natural Beauty : The nature watching from Maandaakhaal is much more exciting like the mountains of Andes in South America. Here we are watching a full view of

Pauri city and a large numbers of the Himalayan Peaks including Chaukhamba and adjoining mountain peaks.

2. Wildlife : The wildlife of Maandaakhaal remnant forests is like a heaven on earth : Mountain tigers, bears, wild boars, foxes, red fox, porcupines, rabbits, monkeys, langoors, weasels and several other small mammals are found here.

3. Among the birds, all mountain birds of middle heights are found here. The valleys of Maandaakhaal are pleasant and warm during winter in comparison to other mountains of the Himalays. During July and August the whole valley is full of greenery and mountain flowers blossom here and there in the pastures and along the roadside. There are oak and pine forests in the valley which are quite popular for bird watching and nature watching. The valleys of Maandaalkhaal are pleasant and nice experience for nature study.

4. There are many beautiful pastures and Ideal Camp Sites for Camplife : The wildlands of Maandaakhaal are an ideal destinations for campsites for trekkers, tourists and explorers from far and near.

5. The whole Maandaakhaal is the most beautiful wildland covered with mountain grass, beautiful bushes, dwarf plants and some scattered cedar, oak and pine trees.

Maandaakhaal is a heaven on earth which is the most suitable example of Alpine climate with a marvellous growth of trees, bushes and grasses in the natural surroundings.

Wildlife Tourism in Ameli Forests : Ameli forests are also known as mountains of rising sun. These mountains are covered with most beautiful, lovely and full of oak, cedar, pine and broad leaf canopy trees. The wildlife is rich and abundant as mountain tigers, bears, deers, wildboars, primates porcupines, ghoral (now extinct), rabbits, wild foxes, weasels, wild cats and several other mountain animals are found in the deep forests and valleys. Ameli mountains are moisturous mountains and wild birds are found here abundantly. These forests are spread upto famous Adhvani forests of the high mountain ranges from Kanskhet, Deewa Danda, Danda Naagarjaa and various other mountains of wildlife importance. Ameli, Adhwani, Deewa and Dandaa Naagarjaa are the holy mountains of Pauri hills.

Among the wild birds, all the birds of semi-temperate mountain ranges are found here in the deep forests and valleys. The forests have an excellent amount of moisture and the orthopoda are found in large numbers. The birds feed upon them.

During summer as well as winter months some migrant birds also come here to breed in the deep forests and valleys which is an ideal place for breeding of migrant birds. After a few months they fly away to their original destinations.

Several species of parrots, hilaansh, kaffoo, koel and laughing birds, are found in the forests of Ameli.

Some 40 years back this forest was an ideal sanctuary for Ghweed and Kakhad (very small deers) but now only 5 or 10 small deers are visible in the forests. The continuous felling of forests in large numbers have destroyed their original habitats and resting points.

Once these forests were so densely populated that the sun rays hardly penetrated through their canopies. In 1960s, a large portion of ancient forests was felled by the wood smugglers, government contractors and local timber mafias. This has badly ruined the mountain forests which once were the living heaven for the rich wildlife there.

1. Adhwani And Ameli are best destinations for exploration activities.
2. Ideal for wildlife camping.
3. Ideal for Trekking.
4. Ideal destinations for bird watching.
5. Wildlife tourism can be encouraged in Ameli and Adhwani forests.
6. The forests are interesting sites for botanical studies.

Wildlife Tourism and Kanskhet Forests

The cedar forests of Kanskhet are the most beautiful and scenic mountains of Pauri hills. The road from Kandolia to Kanskhet is plain serpentine with oak, cedar and pine trees make a beautiful impression when we drive in the sunlit morning with pleasant environment. The sweet songs of birds in the far away forests amidst the nature provide us a good recreation.

The densely populated forests are a living paradise of nature. Several species of birds, most of them song birds exist in the valleys and forests. Small birds fly from one bush to another in search of food and nesting. We can spot several beautiful nests of different shapes and sizes on the branches of bushes, trees and long grasses. Some of the small trees are a heaven for bulbul, mouse birds, tailorbirds and turtledove. There is a great need of some stay points, picnic spots and rest houses near the periphery of Kanskhet forestland. The spring time is quite pleasant and full of delight as we pass through the oak, cedar and pine forests. The summer days are always cool, peaceful and most enjoyable in the valleys.

The grasslands are a beautiful shelter for pheasants, wildfowls and local birds like teetar, chakor and baters etc. These birds are found in the valleys of Shivalik hills.

Adhwani Forests and Daandaa Naagarjaa: The forest area in Kanskhet is not only scenic and beautiful but it is full of natural habitats of wildlife. There are some beautiful vibrations and positive indications in this golden land.

In the same way, the Adhvani forests and Daanadaa Naagarjaa are a great source of inspiration to religious people as well as nature lovers from far and near. Daandaa Naagarjaa is the most ancient temple amidst oak and deodar forests.

Wildlife in these forests is the same as in other mountain forests. The birds are amazingly most beautiful, multicolour and sing the sweetest songs of life.

The moonlit nights : In summer days the moonlit nights are amazingly beautiful, pleasant and enjoyable while walking through the road. The moonlit nights provide us immense pleasure and happiness in the silence of night. At that expensive time all the forests remain silent and provide a real happiness amidst bright moonlit nights.

A large number of tourists have expressed their will ingness to visit these places and see the environment in the moonlit nights, but main problem is that there is not a proper stay point between Kanskhet and Pauri. There is a great need of a permanent Rest House with food at Tekka the beautiful place and a paradise of nature. Tekka is the most pleasant place and a temporary staypoint of village Kewarsh Kewarsh is an ancient village of Pauri Garhwal and Tekka, a beautiful tea point.

Nature Watching in Boobaakhaal, Seekudhaar and Jaspur-Kandai Mountains

The Shivalik mountains are a beautiful sight for nature watching, hang gliding, paragliding, trekking and exploration activities. BubaaKhaal, Ghori Khaal, Pashunda Khaal, Ghandiyaal Khaal, Seekoo Dhaar and Jaspur Kaandai mountain ranges are full of natural beauty. These mountains are best located in Shivalik hills and are known for rich bio-diversity. The forests, pastures and valleys are rich in bio-diversity and plant species.

Jaspur Kandai, Seeku Dhaar, Ghandiyaal Khaal are known for several medicinal herbs and ornamental plants. Among them are chiraita, ferns, orchids, drossera, pitcher plant, lily, Kadwee, Lisimachia punctata, Varbascum longifoliam, Dudhiya-Sunflower, Kandella, Hisalloo, Kingora, Ficus auriculata, timla, bedoo, tunga, jaltanga, black Hisaaloos (Rasp bery : logan bery: black Aanchoo) wild catflower, sweet smelling Buryaali ghaash, aromatic herbs and green tea herbs are some of the best known flowering herbs which are beneficial to human being.

The Land of Wild Flowers : This is the main region in Shivalik mountains where there are abundant wild flower species. There are some 250 most beautiful wild flowers, creepers and small herbs which flower during spring and in the month of August after the rain is over. The whole mountain area and pasture lands are full of mountain flowers. The Berginia Ciliata (Kamaliya) Jangli Piyaaj (Virginea indica), Genthee (Dioscorea bulbifera) family : Dioscorea mushtaka Booti. (Cypeus rotundus) Cyperaceae and several other valuable medicinal herbs and plants are found in the middle heights of the Shivalik hills.

Orchids and Ferns : There are several species of orchids and ferns found in the slopes and valleys of Shivalik mountains. Some of these are of food vegetables and some others are of great medicinal values. The ornamental plants are also found in large numbers.

Oaks, Myrica sepida, Rhododendron, Cedar, Fir, Juniper, Pine : These trees are the main characteristic of the Himalayan flora. Infact, these trees and plants are found together in the Himalayas. Some mountain slopes and valleys are covered by oak, rhododendron, myrica esculenta, cedar, fir, juniper and pine and make a most beautiful and cumulative impact on the environment into a positive way. Ecologically, these plants are the original plants of Himalayan environment and are natural to grow there.

Tubers : Among the tuberous roots are mashal chana, khabarshula, genthee, taidoo, wild yam etc. are some of the important wild tubers with great nutritious value for human being. There are some tubers which provide life saving medicines to human being. They are great cure to skin cancer, blood cancer and bone cancer. The genthee, taidoo, salab mishree are some of the medicinal herbs to cure the fatal diseases.

Lingad, Shishua and Ghanyaa : Some wild food vegetables function like antibacterial medicines and also provide nutrition to our bodies. There are curative properties in lingad, shishua and ghanyaa, the wild vegetables found in the river valleys, river basin and mountain tops. Ghanya is found at 6000 ft. height, lingad and shishua are found near the river bank and river waters.

Lupiya, Loichatta, Pathar Chatta : These are the rock worts and are known for their curative properties. Lupiya is edible wort found at 4000–6000 ft. and is eaten raw. Loichatta and pather chatta are green herbs and suitable to cure the burns, cut and wounds. The paste of Loichatta and Pather chatta is rubbed on the injurious parts and the wound and is cured in two three days. If the blood is flowing continuously, these two herbs stop the blood flow and cure the cut part in a few days.

Mountain Flowers and Vegetables : The mountain flowers and vegetables are of great importance to human being. The wild flowers have some medicinal properties and aromatic in nature produce scents, oils and several other shampoos. These vegetables are a great source of minerals and are used as food vegetables.

Samoyaa, Vanasha, Catflowers : These three flowers are found at the height of 3000–6000 ft in the temperate Shivalik hills. Samoya is a scented, aromatic herb, Vanasha, an edible herb used in tea and milk, catflowers are used in tea, milk and cure the fever and fatigue.

Herbal Tracks : The herbal tracks are encouraged in the Shivalik hills to encourage tourism, knowledge and awareness for herbal medicines in the country. The herbal tracks are conducted several times a year to encourage herbal tourism in our country. The Himalayan low heights and Shivalik hills are a fertile ground for such herbs.

India is a haven for strange mammals, primates, bears, deers, marsh deers, wildboars, avifauna and orthopoda. The variety of climate and ecological adaptation has made India a nursery of rich bio-diversity. From Himalayan states in the north, the deserts of Rajasthan and Gujarat in the west, the Western Ghats and Eastern Ghats in the south, Assam, Meghalaya, Arunachal, Nagaland, Mizoram, Tripura and Manipur and Arunachal in the north east are a thriving laboratory of unique wildlife species in the world.

Because of its rich bio-diversity, the Government of India should encourage wildlife tourism in every national park of the country. Domestic tourism can be made most popular in our country. This campaign can be initiated from schools and colleges. It can be popularized at a widerscale so that the people of one state can learn a lot of things about the people, culture and wildlife of other states. Such things are necessary for communal harmony and national-integration.

13

Wildlife Tourism in the World

There is a great need to protect wild plants and animals for the survival of human life. In the ancient time when there were no crops, the ancient human being were largely depend on wild animals and plants for food. It is also a point to note that there are some game parks in some countries for great game, recretion and adventure tourism. In Canada, USA, South America, Africa and South East Eastern Nations have their game sanctuaries besides a popular campaign of wildlife protection in those countries. Such game parks have become economic backbone of tourism activities in those nations.

Importance of wild life: In this universe our earth is the only one planet where the environment and ecological adaptation is in good state. This is the most lively planet which is the most suitable to humans as well as wild animals and plants. This is the lonely living planet in the universe. In other planets, there is no sign of life, water and grass. Other planets are so harsh in climate that it would be difficult to produce life there.

The wildlife has a greater importance to human being as it is a process of co-existence and mutual give and take theory in nature. The plants, birds, mammals, reptiles, primates and orthopoda create an environment suitable for the living of human being. All the living beings and plant kingdom live in a way of co-existence in the nature. Also, are depend on each other for their survival and regular food chains.

Some regions over this planet are rich in bio-diversity and create a living environment for human beings and other living creatures. For example, the whale is depend on fish species and other marine animals. The man kills the whale for his food. The plants and trees are used for timber, housing, fuel and fodder. The man in the ancient time was solely depend on wild animals and plants for his food. And atlast these all natural things create a living environment for the inhabitation of human being and other living things over this planet.

The Rich Bio-diversity: There are some regions on this planet which are still rich in bio-diversity and natural resources. The amazing wildlife of British Columbia (Canada), Amazonia Wilderness, Colombia, Peru, Atlantic forests, Andes (South America), Altai mountains (Kajakhstan), Ghana, Cameroun, Congo (Africa), South Africa's Kruger National Park, Indian Himalyas, Thailand, Cambodia, Vietnam, Java, Sumatra and Borneo, Philippines, Papua New Guinea, North East Australia, the Great Barrier Reef (Australia) Tasmania Island, Kakadoo National Park are among the rich biodiversity hotspots in the world.

Wildlife Tourism and its Importance

The bio-diversity hotspots all over the world have become immense attraction for international tourists. In some countries there are some most popular tourists destinations in the world. The management and conservation of wildlife areas has helped in encouraging wild life tourism in some countries.

There are numerous natural areas in our country where there is all possibility to tap their natural wealth for nature tourism. The wildlife parks help in the promotion of wildlife tourism. The beautiful large wildlands encourage wilderness tourism in the countries where there are vast areas of wilderness. For example British Columbia is the world leader in wilderness tourism and is earning the largest amount of foreign exchange in tourism.

The Amazonia wilderness: The Amazonia wilderness is the largest natural wonder in the world. These are world's rich rain forests. These forests are being felled at an alarming speed. It is estimated that 2 million square km rain forests have been cleared in the past four decades. If the remaining forests are wiped out, the global warming will speed up and reduce the balance of carbon and oxygen in this planet. The wildlife of Amazon wilderness is amazingly rich and beautiful. World's one fifth of bird fauna is found in these forests. The mammals, primates, reptiles, avies, amphibians, orthopodas are rich and varied in this wilderness. The Wilderness tourism in Amazon forests is at its peak as twenty five travel and tours companies from Canada, USA, U.K. and Brazil are sponsoring wildlife tours in the wild of Amazonia.

Wildlife Tourism in Andes Ranges: The Andes Mountain Ranges in South America are not only rich in the bio-diversity but are a great spectrum of natural beauty. These mountains cover an area of more than 2 million km^2 and are a source of scenic beauty from North to South. Some peaks of Andes are over 6000 meters culminate in Aconcagua in Argentina at 6,960 meters (22834 ft.). Andes covers a distance of 7,250 km. This vast mountain range has an almost unbroken connection with Rocky mountains of North America. This mountain range creates a distinct mountain system extending the full length of the Americas. These extend from sub-antarctic latitudes to the south of the Arctic.

The Andes function as the watershed between the Atlantic and Pacific oceans. On the west they plunge steeply into the pacific and on the east they slope more gently to the Atlantic Ocean. The two sides are equally dissimilar in climate. The Southern Andes is a region of violent winds. Practically all the rain fall from the Pacific is deposited on the Pacific side of the cordillera having the eastern part of Southern Patagonis in a rain shadow that makes it as impoverished as any desert.

The wildlife tourism is flourishing in the Andes i.e. Colombia, Peru, Chile, Bolivia and Argentina have done their best in wildlife tourism in some areas of their country. Argentina, Colombia and Peru are an excellent example of wildlife torism. The tourists come to see the wildlife, forests and beautiful landscapes of these countries.

Wildlife Tourism in Canada : The world tourists visit Canada for happiness as it is a heaven for cold climate Bio-diversity. Its various National Parks are enchanting and amazing with its bio-diversity. The black bears, grizzly bears, mountain goats, wild sheeps, deers, foxes, porcupines, rabbits and other animals of ecological importance are found in Canadian forests.

Canada is a wonder land in natural beauty and wildlife. The bird species are varied and vivid. The national parks and forests of Canada are rich in plants, trees and wildflowers. Most of the forestland is still pollutionless and clean environment. The Canadian National Parks are known for its beautiful forests, scenic beauty and amazing bio-diversity. (1) Banff National Park is a wildland where large amazing goats and other wild animals are found. The park is 6641 km^2 in area. (2) Jasper National Park is 10,878 km^2 in area and is a heaven in natural beauty and wildlife. (3) Kootenay National Park is 1377 km^2 in area and is known for its forests and scenic beauty (4) Yoho is 1,313 km^2 in area and have been designated as Canadian Rockies World Heritage Site. This part of earth is known for its distinct and amazing wildlife, trees and flowering plants.

Wildlife Tourism in Central America: The Tourists, explorers and trekkers visit Mexico in large numbers because of country's pleasant climate, rich bio-diversity and beautiful landscapes. The other countries of central America are

Guatemala, Beliz, Honduras. El salvador, Nicaragua, Costa Rica and Panama are among the beautiful countries to visit. The Maya Biosphere Reserve (16,000 km^2) is the Guatemala's largest protected tropical forest. These nations are depend on agriculture, tourism and transportation. They have maintained their economy in different areas of life. Soberania National Park, Panama is protecting Harpy Eagle (Horpia Harpyja). In Guatemala Laguna de Tigre National Park is quite populaor among the tourists. Some of the species of wild animals are endangered because of lack of management, threat of hunting, habitat loss and use of fishing nets. The highland wildlife tourism in the forests of Mointeverde, Costa Rica is well known among the explorers.

Wildlife Tourism in Africa : The wildlife tourism in the rain forests of African countries is quite pleasant and exciting as all the large mammals are found here is the parks. These nations with rainforests are in good state of bio-diversity. Despite the loss of forests, encroachment and development activities, the national parks are in good state.

Ivory Coast : Ivory Coast forests are being felled at an alarming rate. The tourism is in good state in the country and a large numbers of tourists come here to camping in nature and explore the rich and varied wildlife. The Tai National Park, Cote, Ivoire is famous for the population of chimpanzees.

Ghana: Ghana's National Parks are well known for its amazing wild animals i.e. large mammals, primates, reptiles, avies and orthopoda. The National Parks of Ghana in true sense are some Great Safari Parks which attract the foreigners to its rainforests, grasslands and wetlands. The deforestation is continue in its forests and some species of wild animals may vanish away very soon.

Cameroun : Cameroun is known for its rainforests and wildlife. These highlands extend into North Eastern Nigeria and the offshore island of Bioko. The highland has 53 bird species of which 22 are endemic. There are 55 species of amphibians and reptiles. The most interesting places are mountains of Oku.

Cameroon and Kupe in Cameroon, Mount Malabo on Bioko, and Obudu Plateau in Nigeria are impressive sights. There is a great need of wildlife protection in the highlands. In recent time, 50 new taxa have been found in western Cameroun highland forests.

Gabon : Gabon is also known for its rain forests and rich and varied wildlife.

Congo: The Congo Basin Forests are quite popular for Gorillas, Chimpanzees and Rhinos. The tourists visit these parks to enjoy wildlife from a very near distance. This multipurpose park is a heaven for wild animlas. Garamba National Park is famous for white Rhinos and is on the border of Congo and Sudan.

Zaire, Kenya and Tanzania : The Victoria lake is surrounded by these three countries and have a unique ecosystem to support the tropical mammls, primates, reptiles, avies, orthopoda etc. for a longer period.

The above African nations are having very beautiful national parks but civil unrest, riots and community wars have destroyed the forests at a greater speed. Local forests are destroyed by timber smugglers and encroaclunent by the pastoral people.

South Africa: In African continent South African National Parks are well-maintained and protected. At present, in African continent, South Africa is the only country which is drawing maximum tourists from foreign nations. This country is enjoying full growth in wildlife tourism. The five parks are doing their best in wildlife and safari tourism : (1) The Kruger National Park one of world's largest game reserves (2) The Cape Peninsula (3) The Sun City (4) The Garden Route and (5) The Kwazulu Natal Parks and Mountains.

Madagascar: The Madagascar is a nation island in the Indian ocean just opposite direction of Mozambique. There are beautiful rain forests in the south east of Madagascar. There are ancient fern forests in full density where gentle lemur, a nocturnal monkey is found. Madagaskar is favourite place for sea birds and shore birds. Its wetlands are known for several plants, trees and herbs.

The Meller's duck and other three different species of ducks are found in Madagascar. This Island is tourists paradise from far and near.

Wildlife Tourism in Australia: Several parts of Australia are amazingly beautiful. The beautiful wildlands and expanded wilderness are a great source of recreation.

Kakadoo National Park : Kakadoo wilderness is one of the best Australian National Parks. This is one of the largest wilderness in the world. Here, the long trees, dwarf trees, grasslands and wetlands are an ideal habitats of wild animals, primates and birds. The strange wild animals are jewels of this park.

Ningaloo Coral Reef : These reefs are the most ancient in the North Western Australian coasts. The three hundred km. long fringing Coral Reef is the main characteristics of Ningaloo Coral Reefs. The marine life is rich and impressive.

The Great Barrier Reef: This world famous coral reef was declared World Heritage Site in 1981. This is labelled as one of the 7 natural wonders of the world. The Queensland National Trust has named it a State Icon of Queensland. The Reef is largest reef system in the world. It is composed of over 2,900 individual reefs and 900 coral islands. It is spread upto 2,600 kilometers an area of 344,400 square kilometers. The reef is located in coral sea and has become a popular destination among the world class tourists.

Tasmania : Tasmania island is a part of Australia. It is known for its pandas, marsupials and bearlike animals known as Devils of Tasmania. The forests greenery and wild life of Tasmania island is rich, varied and full of human recreation. The beautiful natural landsapes always attract the tourists from all over the world. The island is surrounded by Tasman sea.

Wildlife Tourism in Indian Parks : The Indian Parks are quite popular among the international tourists. Its rich and varied wildlife and ecosystem is amazingly beautiful. It paves the way for a systematic approach to study the ecosystem and its various National Parks and existing wildlife. There are five types of National Parks in India which are rich and varied from the point of view of bio-diversity and ecosystem. (1) The Himalyan National Parks (2) The Rain Forest National Parks (3) The plain land Tropical National Parks (4) The Coastal National Parks, (5) The southern plateau National Park. The parks are a marvellous examples of wildlife with different species and ecosystems.

India is a heaven for wildlife tourism. In the past one decade India has received 6.5 million tourists every year. The tourists come to see its rich cultural heritage and amazing wildlife. Some examples of the parks are: The Great Himalyan National Park, Kullu, Western Himalayan Bird Sanctury, Sarahan (Himachal), Western Himalyan Nature Park, Kufri Shimla (Himachal) Kaziranga National Park and Manas National Park (Assam), Kanha National Park, Ranthambhor Tiger Sanctuary, Valmiki Tiger Reserve, and Bharatpur Bird Sanctuary, India are among the best Wildlife Parks and wild life sanctuaries. The Silent Valley National Park, Kerala, Kudramuph National Park (Karnataka) are among the best national parks in South.

Rajaji National Park : Rajaji National Park is among the largest Soal and Baan Forest Parks in the country (1600 km^2). It is known for the Asiatic tigers, leopards, stags and Asian elephants. The park is known for various species of mammals, reptiles, primates, avies, and orthopoda. A small species of fresh water turtle is found in the fresh water mangroves of Rajaji Park but it is becoming extinct because of pollution, loss of habitats, global warming and felling of ancient forests at an alarming rate. Rajaji National Park has become a heaven for explorers, trekkers and wildlife lovers. It represents some amazing species of fauna and flora.

Corbett National Park, Ramnagar: Corbett National Park is a heaven for tigers, elephants, bears, wild boars, reptiles, avies, and various insects and butterflies found in this park.

The park is a heaven for the floral diversity also. There are so many species of wild flowers, herbal medicines, aromatic plants, fruit trees, bushes and large trees.

Jim Carbett Park is basically a tiger sanctuary but elephants from Rajaji National Park also visit this park from time to time and thus expanding their roaming area.

Wildlife Tourism in Nepal: Wildlife tourism and mountaineering have become the economic backbone of Nepal. The Chitwan National Park, the Sagar Matha (Everest) National Park, Makalu-Barun Valley are some of the most beautiful National Parks in Nepal. Some of the valleys have become most popular among the Western and Eastern tourists and explorers. Nepal is a heaven for wildlife tourism and high mountain bio-diversity. There is a great achievement in trekking and mountaineering. Everest is the highest peak of Nepal Himalayas and is still a paradise for mountaineers.

The Valleys, rivers, pastures and forests are in fresh state and can be used for exploration and trekking activities. In some valleys, there is a rampant pollution and this should be cleaned with the help of volunteers.

Wildlife Tourism in Bhutan : Bhutan is a very small nation almost landlocked with India. The natural areas of Bhutan are fresh and beautiful and provide a colourful spectrum of natural panorama. The country is rich in wildlife and natural beauty. It has amazing species of mammals, primates, reptiles, avies and a thriving world of orthopoda. About two third of the country is a beautiful spectrum of natural area including mountains, grasslands and forest cover. Bhutan is nature's peaceful paradise.

Wildlife Tourism in Thailand : Thailand is a country of most beautiful hornbills. World's twelve hornbill species are found in Thailand. At present there are 54 rare hornbills species in the world of whom twelve are found in the rain forests of Thailand. Besides this other wildbirds, macaw, large parrots, waterfowls are found there. The tiger, elephants, wild bears, marsh deers, horned deers and primates are found in the dense forests of Thailand. Among the reptiles, the sea turtles, ridley turtles, cobra, python, lizards and others animals are found near the wetlands and smooth seas.

Thailand is known for its beautiful birds (Avies fauna), and insects (orthopoda) including moths and butterflies.

For wildlife tourism, Thailand has become a heaven for toursists from worldwide. Wildlife tourism and seaside exploration activities have become its economic backbone in tourism in East Asia. Besides this, health tourism has become its most luxurious money earning source.

Wildlife Tourism in Cambodia and Vietnam : These two countries have most beautiful rain forests in the world. Some of them are most ancient and remain unspoilt beauty of nature. Some wild animals and birds found here are not found in other parts of the world. These are called endemic species of wild animals. These forests are a haven for such mammals, primates, birds, and reptiles.

The Birds of Paradise are found in both the countries and in the isolated dense forests. The birds like wild fowls, water fowls, six winged birds and long tailed birds (like peacock of India) with different colours are found in the dense forests of Cambodia and Vietnam. The birds with various colours are amazingly beautiful. There are some ancient forests in both the countries where wildlife is thriving secretly and silently amidst the dense forests.

Wildlife Tourism in Java, Sumatra and Borneo : The wildlife in Indonesia is rich in varieties and species. Java, Sumatra and Borneo are known as the bio-diversity hot spots in the South East Asia. The rich biodiversity require a quick maintenance of National Parks and open Reserve Forests. The clouded tiger of Sumatra is known worldwide. Besides the primates of various species the orangutans are known to the tourists and explorers of the world. Java, Sumatra and Borneo's rain forests are a great haven to the primates. For example : Chimpanzees, Orangutans, two species of gibbon and bears, wild boars and several other mammals are found in the dense forests.

Besides this, beautiful birds, reptiles, amphibians and orthopoda are found in large numbers. The rain forests are being felled by the timber companies at an alarming rate. The land clearing for farming, encroachment by local communities is posing a threat to the orangutans in these forests. The Gunung Leuser National Park is being destroyed by timber mafias and wood samugglers at a large scale which is threatening its wildlife.

Wildlife Tourism in Papua New Guinea : Papua New Guinea is rich in bio-diversity. World's amazing animals and plants are found here. The main backbone of the economy of Paua New Guinea is tourism, timber trade and export of largest number of parrots, wild birds, ducks, lizards butterflies and other wild animals. The wild animals and plants are exported to rich countries who love to rear wild animals and birds in farms houses for personal use. The smallest trees and more than 11,000 flowering plants are exported to plant lovers in foreign countries. In the past three decades the rain forests of this country are being exploited by some foreign nations. USA, European and other rich nations are the main importers of this wood. These rainforests have been wiped out at an alarming rate. The fauna and flora of this region may become endagered quite soon.

Wildlife Tourism in NewZealand: NewZealand is known for its rich wildlife and floral diversity. The famous hollow taxa plants are found in the wetlands of New Zealand. These taxa plants are endemic to NewZealand wetlands. The orchid and fern plants are exported in large numbers to other destinations.

NewZealand is a haven for water birds, shore birds and water fowls. The NewZealand duck has a special characteristics in the world. Among the other animals are mammals, reptiles amphibians, avies, orthopoda and small mammals of local importance. NewZealand is known for its neat and clean environment. Tasman valley is popular among the tourists of the world. The valley remains covered with snow the year round. The mountain peaks remain covered with snow while in the plains and valleys the ice melts slowly. Tasman valley is quite popular for trekking, exploration and sikiing activities. The famous Ski Resort is Mountain Cook where every year 7000 ski planes and 300 helicopters get down at the airstrips. The natural slopes are liked by all the businessmen and adventure lovers of the world. Tasman glacier is 20 km. long and 4 lakh tourists come to visit Mount Cook National Park every year. Alone through skiing New Zealand earns 70 million dollars every year.

A Parrot Kakapo (Strigops habroptilus) lives in Codfish Island and elkes its nest on land. The number of Kapapo is increasing in Codfish and Pearl Island. New Zealand forests and Bird Protection Society asked the country timber industry to join Green Furniture and stop using native timber. A long portion of NewZealand forests has been wiped out by such timber companies.

There is a great need to protect Waituta forests and Fiord land National Park in South Island, NewZealand. Now the 460 sq. km of virgin forests are under permanent protection following 20 years of debate and the constant threat of logging. The forests now known as the Watuta Conservation Area lies between 12,100 sq. km. National Park and the 2171 hectare block of ancient forests.

Wildlife Tourism in Arctic : There are some sponsored tours by some adventure loving countries to explore Antarctica for knowledge, research and recreation. Three species of Penguins, sea lions, whales, sharks and several species of fishes are found under the snow of South seas adjoining the waters of Antarctica. Antarctica has no human population of its own as it is bitter cold with a temperature –89°C. Antarctica is the fifth largest continent, with an area of 14,245000 square kilometers which is twice the size of Europe or Australia. This continent is surrounded by Atlantic ocean and Southern oceans. The mainland has high mountains and huge plateaus covered by a vast ice sheet. Nine-tenths of all ice and seven-tenths of all the freshwater on earth are held in Antarctica. It is coldest place on earth, with a temperature as low as –89°C. There are frequent blizzards and gales. There is no permanent human population, but this harsh environment is home to millions of sea animals including seals, whales, penguins, terns, gulls and more than a hundred species of fishes.

An environmental group known as Green Peace is campaigning to protect Antarctica and secure it as a wildlife sanctuary or as a world peace park. The idea of making Antarctica a world peace park is supported by many governments, and conservationists. The park would be for the benefit of for all nations of the world. (1) Give complete protection to all wildlife and their habitats (2) Keep Antarctica as a region of scientific research and co-operation. (3) Keep Antarctica as a zone of peace no military or nuclear weapons would be allowed there. (4) Ban any extraction of minerals. (5) Ban the disposal of poisonous, redioactive or other harmful wastes there.

Wildlife Tourism in Arctic National Parks : The bio-diversity in the Arctic Natonal Parks is rich and recreative to human life. The sea lion, water birds, shore birds, polar bears and grizzly bears are a common sight. Among such park is the Gates of Arctic National Park which is in Alaska near the Arctic circle. The park is bitter cold and sometime the temperature is –85°C. It is full of peace and serenity. The people visit the park during summer when there are less blizzards, gales and snow storms. The area of Arctic National Park is amazingly beautiful where we face the wonders of a beautiful snowland and the island surrounded by the ocean covered with white blanket of snow. The adventure lovers all over the world visit the Gates of Arctic National Park and face the harsh climate there. It becomes one of the most wonderful experience of life to visit these isolated places of snowlands where a different world of nature exists.

Wildlife Tourism in Zapovedniks and Altai Mountain Ranges : Kazakhstan : The Zapovedniks are the state reserve forests in Russia which are most popular among the tourists and explorers of the world. Lack of maintenance and conservation is ruining them. The Altai Mountains Zapovedniks, Katunsky Zapovednik, Telekoye Lake Beluka mountains and Ukok Highlands are the wonders of natural panorama. UNESCO has declared them the World Natural Heritage Site. These beautiful mountains, scenic forestlands and grasslands have become immense attractions among the trekkers, explorers and camplovers from world over. If these forests are polluted, ruined or gone the wonders of Russia are certainly gone. So, there is a great need to preserve them with great care of conservation sense and allow sustainable tourism there. Some rare birds, preybirds and raptors of Russia are on the verge of decline. If the natural sites are not cared properly, the wildlife faces a big crisis. A breeding centre for the endangered raptors is established at the Galichya Gora Zapovednik (Lipetak oblast). This centre is working on the protection and breeding of raptors in the wild in the vicinity of the middle on River through the reintroduction of birds bred in the captivity. Zapovedniks are well known for their rich biodiversity and scenic mountains.

Wildlife Tourism in Srilanka : The wildlife Tourism in Srilanka is on the rise. This beautiful island nation has become a heaven for tourists, particularly in Southern Srilanka where there are most beautiful sea beaches, coral reefs, rainforests and a rich combination of bio-diversity. Srilanka is known for its tourist places from the period of Lord Budhdha. The statues of Lord Budhdha and his disciples are scattered all over the Srilanka's dense forests and these make a very wonderful sites amidst the forests. There are some beautiful things in Srilanka to encourage the tourists (1) Wonderful beaches, hotels and restaurants (2) Rich wild life amidst the rain forests (3) Lord Buddha's statues amidst the forests where a large number of Buddhist tourists from foreign countries come to visit (4) Wonders of natural beauty (5) The pattern of agriculatural fields i.e. sugarcane and paddy fields create a spectrum of beauty. Sri Lanka is making a sharp development through tourism and export. Tea gardens and banana orchards present a beautiful spectrum.

Wildlife Tourism in Spain : Spain is a country of various festivals and fairs. Every festival and fair is seen with national interest and given a commercial colour just to attract tourists from world wide. The beautiful island parks, natural beauty, sea beaches, wild lands are a great attractions in spain. Besides, historical places and museums, spain is a lands of natural wonders. The population of spain is 40 million and every year 50 million people visit spain through airports, sea routes and cross international borders by buses or cars. Tourism has become a backbone of spain and in the last 40 years tourism has passed through most advanced phase of development in the country. People are leading very happy and nice life as they have their own employment. Through tourism i.e. hotels, restaurants, travel agencies and several other services and jobs related to tourism are a part of tourism business. Tourism has helped overcoming the global crisis of spain in 2009 and 2010.

Wildlife Tourism is Indonesia : The Indonesian Parks are a heaven of rainforests and rich bio-diversity. Some of the National Parks are quite popular among the tourists from far and near.

The Suaq Balimbing Research Station in Gunug (Indonesia) is doing well in the survey and research work on primates, birds, bears, tigers, wild pigs and several other species of wild animals.

The Gunung Leuser National Park is being logged illegally by the timber companies despite the repeated request from the staff of research station. This rain forestland is unique one and has a rich bio-diversity. It has also a very high density of orang-utans (man of forests) Pongo pygmaeus albus. There are four species of monkeys also which are endemic to these forests. These forests are an ideal habitats for the primates. These are Macaca fascicularis, Macaca nemestrina, Presbytis thowmasii and Presbytis cristata are found in the dense forests of Gunung. Two species of gibbons : Hylobetes lar and Hylobetes syndactylus are found with their ideal habitats in the forests. The Sumatran tiger : Panthera tigris, Sumatran bears, Helarctos malayensis and wild pigs : Babyrousa babiroussa are found in these forests. The rain forests are being felled regularly at a greater speed as a result wildlife is vanishing away.

Wildlife Tourism in Small Pastures, Wetlands and Natural Areas : The ancient forests in developing countries have been wiped out at the larger scale. These have bear replaced by new growth of small forests erected in the last 50 years. The wildlife tourism and nature watching camps can be encouraged in small forests.

The Ghora Dhungee Pastures : The Ghora Dhungee pastures are a heaven for bird fauna in Uttaranchal, India. This is a place where skylark, bulbul, mousebird, turtle dove, forest crow, chakore, teetar, wild fowl, kaljeenth (black magpie) blue magpie (Karaoon); Saraoon (Red magpie), tailor bird, redfinch, black finch, bush finch, parots, kaffoo, koel, Hilaansh and several other birds are found in the wild. It is one of the best sites for bird watching. Ghora Dhungee is known for orchids, ferns, Ghanya and lily flowers. This beautiful pasture is known for more than 150 wild flowers, ferns, orchids, roots and several other medicinal plants useful to human being. For example : The edible ferns (lingad).

Kanghee (orchid), Samoya (Sweet smelling plant), Vanasha (Viola serpens). Snake lily, varbascum longifoliam, Lilium himalayensis, chiaraita, lisimachia, punctata, berginia ciliata and urginea indica are found abundantly in the wild of Ghora Dhungee. It is an ideal place for camplife.

Thandaa Paanee : Thandaa Paanee is the most beautiful wildland where a sweet, coldwater source provides solace to the people coming from far and near. Thandaa Paanee is a natural pure water source popular among the local people trekkers. During summer days, the people from the villages come here and take cold bath and collect this medicinal water for home. The surrounding wildlands and the nearby rivulets create a beautiful scene for the Thandaa Paanee surroundings. The whole barren valley which is almost a heathland and a birds's paradise. A small passing river and marshy river banks breed a lot of water animals and orthophoda in the river bed and produce enough food for birds and reptiles. The small thorny bushes produce fruits during summer and this is the nesting season for birds. They breed in the open environment in the wild and create a lot of noise while hiding in the bushes.

Katraa Siyaaraa : Katraa Siyaaraa is a beautiful wildland and an agricultural land. A small river passes through the corners of this agricultural land making a most fascinating view of the agricultural fields and the wild land turning into a mountain slope. There are some fascinating birds here i..e turtle dove, skylark, mousebird, bulbul, redfinch, tailorbird, Dhainchoo (kaljeenth or black magpie), teeter, chakore, wild fowls, water fowls and several other beautiful birds are found in the wild of Katraa Siyaara.

The large magpie like Blue magpie and Red magpie of karaoon family are also found in this valley which is nature's peaceful paradise. The place is most popular among trekkers and explorers.

The Forests of Gwaadh and Ginthaalee : The beautiful forests of Gwaadh and Ginthaalee are the typical temperatre and semitemperate forests in Pauri Hills. These forests are deep into the valley of Pabau River which flows through Jwaalpaa Devi temple resorts and create a beautiful scene throughout the wildlands and slopes of the river banks. All the moisture loving plants, trees and fruit tree are found in this valley. The most important thing is that there are several trees and plants in the forms of creepers, like maaloo, phedoo, khainna, wild cucumber and several other plants of human importance are found here. The nearby flowing water provides enough moisture to the plants and trees in the slopes and make them grow fast in the wild. The Gwaadh forests are so densely populated that even the wild animals face difficulties to pass through them. The wild animals which breed and exist in these forests are : marsh deers, mountain deers, wild boars, various species of langoors and monkies, tigers, rabbits, weasels, wild cats, foxes, bears and other animals breed and play freely in the wild of Gwaadh forests. Secondly, these forests provide enough food to the herbivores in the wild. There are several beries, solid fruits, tubers, wild grapes and several other species of wild plants and trees which provide enough food to wild animals. When tigers do not find enough food in the forests, they attack domestic animals of the villagers in the nearby forests.

The Bird's Paradise: All the semitemperate and temperate climate forests and valleys are a heaven for birds and pheasants. The pheasants are found in the dense forests of Gwaadh.

Giant Lizard (Gauloo), small lizards green, red and slate colour lizards are common here. The small black lizards are also found in the wild. The snakes cobra, python, and common green, red black and yellow snakes are found here. The bush snake, white skin and black dots are also found here in the wild. The green leaves plants are found in abundance and the herbivores find the place quite auspicious for food, fodder and reproduction. It is an ideal breeding grounds for the deers, bears, monkeys and wild birds.

During the months of spring the whole Gwaadh-Ginthraalee forests are full of green buds and flowers. Several species of birds arrive here and chirp very sweet-songs. The whole environment is pleasant and full of the music of song birds. There is enough food, insects, fruits for them and in the breeding season, when the baby chicks are grown up, they fly away from the Gwaadh forests to the higher forests to explore a new world of their own. The Gwaadh forests are now an endangered entity as there is no enough water in Pabau river and the forests are disappearing in large numbers.

Conservation Efforts : These are unique forests in the Garhwal Himalayas and need proper conservation efforts. Although, these are not Rain forests as they are not in tropical region, but their nature resembles with rain forests. The forest valley is moisturous because of the river flowing down to it. During summer the valley is exceptionally warm and during winter it is colder. But during winter it has some warmth in it and there are not chilling wild winds at all. The forests in the mountain regions are of alpine nature but in the Shivalik hills these are of temperate and semitemperate nature. The river valleys are warm and have enough moisture to grow forests and vegetables some forests have the nature of rain forests in the valleys. In the past one century two thirds of the original forests in the Shivalik Hills and Western Himalyas have been felled at a greater speed and most of the felled land still remain barren. The reforestation activities started only from 1971 and 1980s. But the growth of new trees is scanty and remnant.

Tourism, Employment and Economic Benefits : The wildlife tourism is growing up all over the world with a greater speed. This has become economic backbone in some countries. For example Canada, Colombia, Venzuela, Peru, Brazil Amazon, Atacama Desert, Patagonia Desert and South Africa have become an ideal place for wildlife exploration and nature tourism. The Krugar Natonal Park in South Africa is doing well in the areas of wildlife tourism. British Columbia, is earning 9.55 billion dollars annually and providing employment to 1,17000 citizens. There were some 21,000 indirect jobs also.

The parks surrounding with small hotels, restaurants, resthouses, swimming pools, museums, libraries and some sports court for the recreation and enjoyment of tourists coming from all over the world, have boosted the tourism in a multipurpose way.

In India, Delhi Zoo is gathering 40 lakhs tourists every year. There are 70 percent domestic visitors coming to the park. Besides this, the Rajaji National Park, Kaziranga National Park, Ranthambhour Tiger Sanctuary have attracted more visitors in the country annually.

The wildlife tourism creates employment year round and brings about a social and economic change to the local people. There is quick economic development in a nation where there are best wild life parks and they are maintained in the broader perspectives. These brings quick economic benefits to a nation. There should be modern way of recreation and amenities near the wildlife parks. Such things are quite helpful in boosting up the wildlife tourism at a larger scale.

14

Wilderness Tourism in the World

Wilderness tourism in modern times has become more popular adventure sport among the international tourists. In some countries, wilderness tourism has taken a new shape of modern tourism and has become the backbone of their economy. The wilderness exploration, trekking and camping in the wild have become more popular activities in the world.

What is a wilderness : A wilderness is a vast wild area or barrenland which never has been developed because of its rough or uneven terrain or it was difficult to live there. For example : The Amazonia wilderness are the largest wilderness in the world. The Antarctica is the last great wilderness in the world. These wilderness are the tourists paradise and there is not construction or any kind of development inside the wildland. The desert wilderness of Sahara is most dangerous one to cross it. The Patagonia wilderness is an amazing wildland and desert in the world which attrats millions of tourists every year.

Patagonia is a hostile desert. The harsh environment of this wilderness is quite popular among the adventure lovers of the world. Argentica is earning a lot of revenue from the explorers and campers of this beautiful desertland.

Barazil is earning a great amount of revenue through largest wilderness of Amazonia. Amazonia wilderness contains two third of rain forests of the world.

In Canada, British Columbia is quite popular among the nature lovers worldwide. This multi-spectrum wilderness is the world leader in wilderness tourism. This state is known for its most amazing wildlands and rich bio-diversity.

Patagonia is a vast wilderness and desert in the South Argentina and is spread in a 480,000 km^2 area. This dry desert always faces the storms with 200 km. per hour. The tourists, trekkers, explorers and camp lovers go to visit there in large numbers. There are vast areas of rain forests, wilderness, the desert land and the cold desert wilderness in this planet. There is not any human population, road or any development work in these vast wild lands, are known as wilderness.

Importance of Wilderness : The wilderness are a heaven for explores, campers and hikers of wildland. These vast wild lands have great importance in human life as they are a separate ecosystems on this planet which provide a rich bio-diversity. The Amazon wilderness contains one fifth of world's bird species, large mammals, reptiles, primates and a vast world of orthopoda. World's two third of rain forests exist in Amazonia wilderness. These wilderness have a great importance to human being as they absorb CO_2 from the atmosphere and release oxygen in large quantity just to create a good balance of CO_2 and oxygen over this earth. These rain forests are rightly called the "Lungs of Earth". They can affect our life anywhere in the world, even the place where we are sitting and talking. If the rain forests of Amazon are cleared in large numbers, this is going to affect our life. There will be an increase in global warming and several animal species of primates will be vanished away within a few years. These forests are a lifeline for the mammals, reptiles, primates, birds and orthopoda which are alive today because of the surviving rainforests.

Unfortunately, these rainforests which are two thirds of the rain forests in the world are being felled at a greater speed. At present, 16 lakh square kilometers of rain forests have been cleared for creating a grazing land for cattles; agricultural expansion, farm houses and ranches. A large area of land have been cleared for housing, roads and timber trade. The Amazon forests are providing shelter to a large world of wild animals and plants. A large number of plant species from Amazonia are used in extracting herbal medicines.

Wilderness Tourism : In the last three decades, wilderness tourism has gained momentum in some countries as it has helped in earning enough foreign exchange. The exploration activities are more recreative and a cumulative to physical fitness.

The countries who have done their best in wilderness tourism are British Columbia (Canada), Yellow Stone Natioanl Park (USA), Peru and Colombia, Andes-mountain ranges, Amazon wilderness (Brazil), Pantanal Wetland (Brazil), Ghana, Gabon, Cameroun, Congo and Zimbabwe in (Africa), Kruger National Park (South Africa), and Kakadoo National Park in Australia. The countries like Java, Sumatra and Borneo are doing well in wilderness tourism.

The tourists always prefer to visit pristine wildlands to observe wildlife and natural wonders there. Trekking, mountaineering, exploration and camping activities in the wild have given them a new experience of life. It was more romantic and adventuresome for the wilderness lovers and explorers.

Wilderness Tourism in British Columbia : British Columbia is a heaven for wilderness tourism and at present it is the world leader in wilderness tourism. 30 percent international tourists and 60 precent domestic tourists are visiting British Columbia every year. The number of international tourists some time is more than 40%. The Reasons of successful wilderness tourism in B.C. : (1) The Amazing wildlife (2) The most beautiful grasslands, meadows and wild flower pastures (3) Super, natural parks and amazing wilderness are the main attractions to a large number of tourists. (4) The amazing snowlands, glaciers, polar bears and grizzly bears are a great recreation among tourists. The other carnivores or herbivores are found here roaming into a vast territory of park and protected areas.

Wilderness tourism in British Columbia is on the increase. It is a fastest growing sector now. In the year 2001 wilderness tourism gathered $ 900 million in direct revenues. Indirect revenue from nature based tourism was US $ 2 billion. There were 21,000 part-time jobs in 2001 in 2004. There was direct revenue of US $ 9.5 billion with 117,500 full time jobs.

Here, St Elias Mountain Glacier System, covers 3,885 km^2. The Columbia icefield covers 375 km^2 and is the largest icefield in North America outside the Arctic spans the continental Divide. Its glaciers feed the headwaters of three major river systems. Columbia, Athabasca and North Saskatchewan, which flow into three oceans. The Pacific, Arctic and (via Hudsan Bay) and the Atlantic. Glacial meltwater also fills many of the lakes with which Canadian Rockies are so richly manifested. Three fifths of the British Columbia is covered with productive forests. Forestry is principal industry.

The Dougless firs are among the tallest trees 76 feet in height. Some species of humming birds are also found here. Moose and beaver are found along the valley bed. The elk, white-tailed deer and mule deer are found in the meadows. The mountain goat, bighorn sheep, hoory marmot and pica are the fauna of higher alpine pastures. Carnivores include grizzly bears and black bears, couger, lynx and volverine are found in the open forests.

Wilderness Tourism in Manu National Park : Manu National Park is a typical forest area in the Peruvian side. This wilderness is still unspoilt forest areas on the eastern side of Peruvian Andes. This wilderness is the only part of Amazon region which have escaped exploitation. The pristine natural beauty, rich bio-diversity and different habitats make it biologically richest than any other park of the Latin America.

Manu Park lies in the Selva, the great tropical forests region of the Amazon basin., The park have virgin forests and the tree with 30 meters height are found here. Peru's selva animals have been continuously hunted for meet and skins. Nearly 200 mammal species have been recorded in the Manu National Park which are more than half of Peru's original mammals. These species are intermingiling with the species of North American origin such as dears and bears with ancient South American forms; marsupials-opossums (the only marsupials to be found outside Australia and edentates (armadillos, sloths and anteaters). Manu's five species of opossums include the rare black-shouldered opossum. Known from only six species. The edentates are represented by three species of at anteaters. The giant anteaters, the tamandurs or lesser anteater, or the dwarf or the silky anteater are found here. Two species of sloths : the three toed or two toed sloths and atleast two species of armadillos, the rare giant armadillo and the common nine banded armadillo are thriving in this park. There are 13 species of primates, one among them is woolly monkey and emperor tamarin. Other endangered species include a giant otter, jaguar, ocelot, bush dog, North Andan Huemul and several species of Manu's birds. There are 1500 bird species in Peru of which 800 bird species are recorded in Manu. They range Andean condor, harpy eagle, hoatizin, 18 species of parrots, two species of endangered reptiles also occur in Manu. The black caiman, spectacled caiman, both are being hunted for meat and skins.

There are some small groups of nomadic forest Indians which live in the park and maintain their cultural activities. These include shifting cultivation, hunting, fishing and collecting turtle eggs. The world of these Indians should not be disturbed at all.

There is a great danger of burning and slashing in the forests of the park; grazing, construction of roads, drilling for goldmine have posed a great danger to the eco-system of Manu National Park.

Wilderness Tourism in Amazon : The Amazonian Wilderness are the largest wilderness in the world. They contain two third of the world's rain forests. These forests are called the lungs of earth as they absorb CO_2 from the atmosphere and release oxygen for us. This process balances the volume of CO_2 and oxygen in the environment.

At present, Amazon forests have richest biodiversity and plant species in the world. There are twenty international travel and tour companins of USA, Canada and Brazil which sponsor wilderness tours and camplife activities in the wild of Amazonia. These companies are making huge profits as a large proportion of international tourists visit them regularly.

The Amazon basin, Amazon delta and Amazon National Park are a great combination of bio-diverstiy and rich plant life. The ferns, orchids, and 200 species of medicinal plants are of immense importance to human being. The Amazon region includes 64.8 million hectare of forest areas.

Mostly, the tourists and explorers come to visity this vast wilderness to observe the wildlife here. The trekkers, explorers, camp lovers, and wild life observers flock here every year in great numbers. This has made Amazon rainforests popular among the nature lovers, bird watchers and camp lovers of the world.

Several species of snakes are found in Amazon forests including Anaconda, boatree snakes, cobra, python, green and poisonous snakes. The black darter snakes are quite popular among the snake watchers.

These forests are spread upto 4 million square kilometers. Among these forests 1.6 million forests have been cleared for agriculture, housing, ranches, grazinglands and road construction. The timber companies are the main exploiter of these forests.

Wilderness Tourism in Andes : The mountains of Andes are natures shining glory. There are most beautiful mountains, rivers and lakes. It is known among the nature lovers of the world. Andes streams and springs are the habitats of torrent ducks and other water birds. There are several wild life parks in the boundary line of Andes mountains. For example Colombia, Equador, Peru, Bolivia, Chile, Argentina etc countries have their National Parks along the Andes mountains. There are several types of forests and wilderness of different ecological systems.

The people like to visit, rain forests of Colombia, Equador, Peru, Chile and Argentina. The Atlantic forests, Andes forests and a mix of tropical and Arctic forests make a great combination and distinct ecosystems in the Andes. The rain forests and Atlantic forests have their own eco-systems and characteristics. The Atlantic forests contains Brazilian pine (Araucaria angustifolia) once were spread upto 20 million hectares now they include only 2 percent of the whole forests. These are very typical forests in the world.

Wilderness Tourism in Patagonia Desert : Patagonia is the most hostile desert and wildland in the world which is spread upto 4,80,000 square kilometers. The cold winds and dangerous storms are usual in Patagonia at the speed of 200 kilometers per hour. The cold winds are the most devastating and fly away all the things which come into their way. The best way to protect oneself is to camp between the two rocks where we can protect ourselves from the hostile winds or we should lay down under the bushes in the cruel desert of Patagonia. The desert is harsh, hostile and totally unsuitable to human nature.

The trekkers, explorers and camp lovers are attracted to the hostite nature of Patagonia. At one point of Patagonia, there is a hostile but beautiful snowland. The other parts of Patagonia is a total desert with a cover of rough bushes and scanty growth of grasses over it.

The deserts of Patagonia, its wildlife, vegetation and small water springs are amazingly beautiful and explain the rough weather and harsh environment of the desertland spread into a vast wilderness.

There are 13,00 species of plants in 10,000 sq. km. In South America 400 plant species, 580 plant species in New Guinea the fynbos floristic kingdom is so great and varied that it has become one of the best wilderness national parks in the world.

Wilderness Tourism in South Africa : The wilderness and the national parks in South Africa are a boon to the wild life lovers and nature watchers. The vast chunks of wildlands in South Africa are known as wilderness which are spread to thousands of kilometers and are a haven for wildlife. The tourists from far and near come to explore these wild lands. The wilderness tourism in South Africa is quite popular.

The Wildlands : The wildlands are full of green bushes or scanty forests. These are well-maintained by park authorities or wildlands management autohrity. This Authority also helps in the protection of wildlife in the wilderness or National Parks. There is a stay point, a restaurant or rest house in the vicinity of the park. This provides a big recreation and relaxation point to the tourists from far and near.

National Parks : The National Parks in South Africa are well protected and well maintained and captive breeding is done on scientific ground. The mammals, primates, reptiles, avies and orthopoda are protected with great interest. The forestlands, remnant forests and habitats of wild animals are seen with the purpose of breeding of wild animals in natural environment. The large mammals and small mammals both are protected well. There are some captive breeding research centres in the parks.

Flowering Pastures : South Africa is a country of famous wildlands and national parks. Once a pasture is converted into a national park it remains full of wild flowers, herbs and trees. The West Coast National Park, with rich bio-diverstiy, is a glorious floral kingdom. The flowers of spring welcome all the travellers in West Coast National Park.

The Marine Parks : The Marine Parks of South Africa are spread with the coastline and make a fine combination of land and ocean. The marine parks are attracting a large number of tourists from far and near. Four new marine parks are in the country's protected coastline and this area has been expanded from 11 to 18 per cent. The four areas are : (*i*) The Aliwal shoal, a subtidal coral reef off Umkomaas which protects threatened sharks. (ii) Pondoland including 90 km. coastline near St. Johns which extends 15 km seawards making the start of "Sardine Run" (*iii*) Bird Island in Algoa Bay that includes many rare and threatened birds species : (*iv*) The Cape Peninsula that includes all coastal waters around Table Mountain National Park.

A fifth marine protected area is planned off Namaqualand spread upto 9,70,000 hectare is South Africa's largest Marine Park.

The tourists are visiting South Africa every year in larger numbers to see its rich culture and varied wildlife.

Wilderness Tourism in Uganda, Congo, Rwanda and Cameroon : There are still vast chunks of wildlands in developing countries despite the fact that most of its tropical and original endemic forests have been wiped away by the government plans on agriculture and development projects. The timber, companies have done maximum damage to the rain forests of African countries. There is extreme poverty and most of the African countries are felling and exporting of timber from rain forests just to make quick money to sustain their economy.

The local pastoral communities are also involved in the felling and clearing of forests for agriculture as well as housing purpose. Such activities have devastated two-third of the rain forests the world over.

The governments in Uganda, Congo, Rwanda and Cameroun have displayed their courage to protect the Wildlife Parks and original rain forests but the timber mafias have spread their tentacles to wipe out the remaining standing forests there. This has ruined all the ancient forests from the rain forests and wilderness. The rain forests once were spread to millions of square kilometers now have been reduced to some thousand square kilometers. This has badly damaged the ancient standing forests and the small vegetation once grew under the canopy of these forests. A large area of remaining forests have been converted into a treeless grazing land which after some years may turn into a desert.

Conservation and Tourism : Despite the fact that clearing of rain forests remains continue but the efforts of conservation have also been increased. The rich bio-diversity in the remaining wilderness have attracted a large number of tourists to these countries. This has tripled the number of tourists in the last two decades. The countries like Ghana, Kenya, Zimbabwe and Congo have maintained their wildlife tourism to an extent. The tourists from East and West visit the wildlife Parks of these countries in large numbers.

Wilderness Tourism in Nepal : Nepal is a land of beautiful mountains, forests, valleys and wilderness. It has become a heaven for tourists coming from western countries. The Mustang Trek, the Everst Trek, Kali-Gandaki Trek, Langtang Trek, Nepal's lowland birds and animals, Baralake Trek, and Makalu-Barua valleys are some of the beautiful forests and valleys where tourists visit every year with great enthusiasm.

Mountain Tourism : Nepal is a number one country in the world to collect maximum foreign exchange through mountain tourism. The adventure sports like trekking, mountaineering, rock climbing, exploration, hang gliding, para gliding, nature watching and bird watching are among the best hobbies to entertain oneself. Camplife is best in Nepal Himalayas. The prospects of mountain tourism are much more in Nepal as it is surrounded by very beautiful mountain peaks.

Wildlife Tourism: The high altitude mountain bio-diversity is the most fragile in the world. Such climatic characteristics is not witnessed in other parts of the world. The best examples of them are Chitwan National Park and Sagarmatha National Park in Nepal. There is abundant wildlife and the adventure sports like treking and mountaineering are on the increase.

The Valleys : The valleys and slopes in Nepal Himalayas are a heavenly experience to the travellers of the world. Makalu Barun valley is known for their immense natural beauty. Nepal's lowland birds and animals live in foothills and valleys. Barun valley is considered exceptionally important for wild birds and mammals. Makalu-Barun Area has been expanded to 1400 km^2. This has given the SagarMatha National Park a new lease of life. The mountain parks of Nepal are a replica of natural wonders.

National Parks : The National Parks in Nepal are quite few but they are a world of rich bio-diversity in themselves. The SagarMatha National Park is spread in 1148 km^2 upto Makalu Barun Valley. This park was declared a World Heritage Site in 1979. The Chitwan National Park and other national parks are the best examples of wildlife tourism in Nepal.

Mountain forests : The mountain forests which remain only one third now are a big asset to Nepal. A large number of foreign explorers come to visit to these mountain forests which include mostly deoder, oak, rhododendron, Kaafal (Myrica esculenta) and Himalyan pine forests.

Barren Lands : The barrenlands are a sort of heathlands which are wide open wildlands known for small song birds. These berrenlands are an ideal asset for camplife, bird watching and picnic parties.

Tourists' Paradise : Nepal is a land of Natural beauty which always attracts the tourists and trekkers from western countries into large numbers.

Wilderness Tourism in the Himalayas : The wildlands in the Himalayan Ranges create the most impressive sights. These are the green paradise on this planet. The White Himalayas (the snow covered mountain peaks above, 17,000 are known as snow Himalyas) The green belt-starts below 16,000. The travellers and trekkers can experience and enjoy the beauty of green pastures, valleys, conifer forests and dwarf bushes and scrubs.

The tourists come to visit Nepal Himalyas in large numbers. For Example the "Alpine Forests", pastures, mountain valleys, river valleys and rivers banks are always attracting a large number of tourists with their scenic beauty.

Mountain Parks : The series of mountain ranges passes through one valley to another valley and make it a parallel folding mountain system which are visible from the highest peak of the area. The snow clad peaks shine like silver mountains with white butter or milky colour. This view somewhat haunts us when we are standing amidst the snowclad mountains.

Forests and Pastures : The conifer forests of deodar, pinus, juniper, kail, "oak, rhododendron and Myrica esculenta" (Canopies) are the soul of mountain forests, valleys and pastures as at some places thay are standing in remnant forms. These forests are rich in mammals, primates, reptiles, avifauna and orthopoda.

River banks and Water falls : The river banks remain full of white sands which immensely attracts us. The flowering plants, berries, wild grasses are a beautiful thing to watch. During summer days, the banks of the rivers are a peaceful paradise.

Slopes and Valleys : The slopes and valleys are full of greenery and wild flowers. The tourists from far and near come here to visit the flower covered valleys and slopes and enjoy some days in the lap of nature. Some of the valley forests are known for their thriving bio-diversity. The camplife and picnic holidays can be organized in the valley pastures. Besides camplite the green valleys are an ideal place for exploration activities and nature study tours. Wildlife tourism is most popular among the Himalyan states where millions of people flock to see the amazing wildlife, plants, trees, ferns and orchids etc and enjoy the bio-diversity. The number of tourists is growing up every year. At present 6.5 million tourists arrive in India every year to observe its wild life and its natural beauty.

Wilderness Tourism in Cambodia, Laos and Thailand: These three countries have similar environment, river system and fertile valleys. Cambodia and Thialand have fertile Mekong basin and grow sufficient foodgrains there. The Mekong Delta has good forestland, plains of reeds, fertile valleys and vast fields and plains made by Mekong river. The basin is spread up to 6,20,000 square km. and is considered among the largest wetlands of the world.

Wilderness tourism is most enjoyable activity in Mekong delta. It has vast expanded forests which are rich in bio-diversity. Thailand, Laos, Cambodia and Vietnam come in the region of Mekong delta. There are two parts of the Mekong Delta: (1) Upper Mekong Basin and (2) Lower Mekong Basin. The Lower Mekong Basins have some excellent growth of secondary forests and a distinct ecology. There are some pristine ancient forests in Laos, Thailand, Cambodia and Vietnam where the tourists enjoy wild life amidst dense forests. The Mekong delta has an amazing bio-diversity.

Wilderness Tourism in Ursula Island : Ursula Island is a beautiful island known for its beautiful birds. It is known for its natural areas to visit. Ursula is situated at the coast of Palawan Island's Southern side. This Island is 150 nautional miles from Puerto Princess city which is a home to 26 species of migratory birds which nest and breed in the Island. This has been declared as Ursula Island Bird Sanctury. The Philippine government is paying attention to protect this bird island.

There are some reports that local fishermen kill the birds for food and eggs and this has hampered the growth of this bird in the island.

Ursula Bird Island is an excellent place for a visit and camplife. At the coasts of Ursula island the view of the ocean is quite beautiful and amazing. Here we can observe the beauty of ocean and the forests to observe the bird life: their nesting, laying eggs and producing baby bird from the eggs is most enjoyable activity. The camplife can be enjoyed inside the island where there are trees and plants. The noise of the birds is one of the best music in the air.

Wilderness Tourism in Australia : (Kakadoo), Tasmania and Queensland : The Kakadoo in Australia is among the most popular wilderness and National Park in the world. This Park is rich in bio-diversity and natural beauty. The grasslands, the forests the openlands and dwarf bushes are some of the main attraction of this National Park.

Kakadoo is spread upto thousands of square km. including beautiful pastures, grasslands and forests with most scenic views. Besides this, there are several National Parks in Australia which are known for their rich bio-diversity, natural beauty and wetlands. There are several beautiful rivers, valleys and waterfalls which promote nature tourism in Australia. The National Parks in Australia are well maintained and are used for the growth and development of Tourism.

Tasmania is an island in the south of Victoria province of Australia. Tasmania is known for its beautiful beaches, rain forests and amazing wild life in the world. The Tasmanian animals are known as the Tasmanian Devils. Among them is a Kangaroo like animal which lives on island is Koala.

The Marsupial animals : Small bearlike animals which live on the trees and eats the leaves are quite different from the wild life found in other parts of the world. The Tasmania Island is a rainforest island and an ideal place for exploration activities. During summer, the environment is pleasant and it is the bestime for camplife in the Island.

Great Australian Bight : This is the largest Sea Beachline in the world. This is the most beautiful long curve in the Australian coast which is spread from the bottom of Western Ausatralia to the South Australian sea coasts. This is called the Great Australian Bight. Infact, this the longest curved beach in the world and is quite popular among the beach lovers of the world. Here we can observe the sea, seabeach and the adjoining forests of the mainland. The people from several countries come to enjoy this sea beach. It is an amazing sight when one a observes it from the small planes. It is spread upto thousands of kilometers through the sea coast.

Wilderness Tourism in TasmanValley, New Zealand : Tasman valley is a beautiful valley in NewZealand, fully covered with snow. This is quite popular among international tourists. The valley is a heaven for the visitors coming from far and near.

Tasman Glacier : This is a 28 km. long impressive glacier. The trekkers from foreign nations come to see this glacier. Tasman glacier has a big importance for the people of New Zealand and the explorers from foreign countries.

Mount Cook National Park : Mount Cook National Park is a trekkers paradise. Every year, 300 helicopters and 700 ski planes are getting down at the base of Mount Cook National Park. Every year 3,50,000 visitors come to visit this park for skiing and trekking.

Mount Cook National Park has become a great attraction among all NewZealanders and the tourists from Australia and Western countries. This National Park provides all the snow sports. Recreation centres and stay points are near the sites of National Park and this has given them a good time for relaxation while exploring the park area.

Tasman Glaciar and Tasman Valley have added more beauty by expanding the area of the Mount Cook National

Park. The park, Tasman glacier and Tasman Valley is well maintained and managed by the New Zealand Park Authorities. The people have a great civic sense and inspiration for the cleaning activities and protection of the park. The waste is collected by the Park Service employees for which they are paid.

The elder citizens, businessmen, government authorities co-operate and support such efforts to make the park pollutionless.

Wilderness Tourism in the Alps

The Alps are the most beautiful mountains of Europe. These are Western Europe's principal mountain systems. The Alps make a barrier between Southern Germany and Northern Italy. It separates the Po valley and Northern Adriatic sea from the Baltik and the Northsea.

The scenic Alps mountains are spread in 1,65000 km^2. These extend 800 km from the French Mediterranean coast of Provence across Switzerland, France, Italy, Germany and Austria to the outskirts of Vienna and the Danube river.

There are many things to observe in the Alps of Western Europe : The mountain principally represent the Alpine Ecology. The Rhone river which runs between snow capped peaks 4,000m/13000 feet high. The peaks attain their maximum height in the west Mount Blanc (4,807m/13,000 feet. The mountain peaks lowers to 8000 ft. in the eastern side. There is always high temperature in southern Alps and winter precipitation and dry summer in Northern Alps. The European countries have some largest rivers and beautiful river valleys to visit. They are Rhine, Danube, Rhone and Po river. Mountain scenery is enhanced by some beautiful lakes. Geneva, Como, Maggiore, Lucerne, Thun and several other beautiful lakes create a scenic spectrum.

Forests: The Alpine forests include both diciducous and coniferous trees. Oak beech, and pine among them. The southern slopes of the valleys face more sun and warmth than the northern which is famous for deiduous fruits, woodland and grassland in the north. The lower slopes form a patchwork of vineyards, orchards, forests and fields, merging above the treeline into the broad alpine meadows and pastureland for grazing in spring and summer.

The Swiss National Park : This park is located in the Grison of Eastern Switzerland where it adjoins Italy's Stelvio National Park (1,482 km^2). The Swiss National Park lies at the height of 1500–3,174 meters and covers an area of 168 km^2. The park stands in a Magnificent alpine setting amidst splendid peaks. There are some scenic peaks to enjoy mountaineering and trekking. The Swiss people are born, natural climbers like the people of Uttaranchal, Himachal and Nepal. One Third of the park is forest, one third grassland and one third is bare rock and scree. Dwarf mountain pine is the dominant tree species. At lower slopes are scots pine, arolla pine, larch and Norway spruce. Wild animals are fox, brownbear, lynx, red deer, chemois and lbex. About 100 species of birds, 60 of them nest in the park, capercaillie, ptarmigan, black woodpecker, nutcracker and golden eagle are some of them. The wilderness management and exploration is one of the best recreative activity in the world.

Wilderness Trekking : The trekking through the wilderness is not only full of recreation but an activity to keep a man mentally alert and physically fit. There are most beautiful pastures and green valleys in the mountains of Himalayas. These are quite popular among tourists during summer as well as winter. The Deserts are also great wilderness in the world. The Govi Desert, The Sahara Desert. The Utah Desert, The Namib Desert, The Thar Desert and the Desert of Patagonia. The people like to visit and explore the deserts of Patagonia as it is an amazing landscape in the world. It is covering an area of 4,80,000 km^2. The storms are violent and move at the speed of 200 km. per hour.

Wilderness Camping : To camp in a vast wildland for some days it provides us an internal peace and happiness as we spend time in perfect peace and harmony. We spend some days in the company of our friends sharing our work, experience and knowlodge in the wild. Camping in a wilderness, provides us better health and energise our physical activity.

Bird Watching : Whenever we see a forestland or a valley we spend our time in watching birds. Bird watching can be enjoyed during a camplife for some days. During this period we come across many wild animal habitats, trees, bushes and rock cavities where birds make nests and lay eggs. There is a great need to learn more about natural areas, birds, their habitats and nesting in the wild. Bird watching is the best entertainment in the wilderness.

Nature Watching: The beautiful valleys, slopes, forestlands and river banks are the most impressive natural sites to observe in the wild. For example, the river valleys in European Alps and Indian Himalayas are the pristine and important sites of natural beauty. The pastures, valleys and slopes have most impressive greenery and attracts the people from far and near to camp amidst lush green vegetation in the wild. Nature watching is a most beautiful pastime hobby in the mountain valleys i.e. the Andes mountains, the Alps and the Himalayas.

Outdoor Eductaion: There are numerous adventure activities which provide professional knowledge in outdoor education. Some adventure activities provide us outdoor education in a systematic ways a some country adventure tourism has become the backbone of their economy. For example, Spain is the world leader, in nature tourism. Spain has a population of 40 million and attracts 50 million people every year. Spain is doing well in wildlife and nature tourism. It has most beautiful islands. British Columbia a State of Canada is earning 9.5 billion dollars every year because of outdoor activities. British Columbia is a world leader wilderness tourism. Amazonian wilderness in Brazil is earning billions of dollars through its sponsored outdoor tours. Some 21 travels 2 tours companies are involved in it. The countries like Colombia, Peru, Venezuela and Andes countries are doing well in wilderness tourism and wildlife parks making maximum profits.

15

Wild Birds and Tourism

The Birds are a beautiful creature which attracts our mind near homes or near the pasture land. Their sweet chirping, laughing and tweeting makes us happy and delightful. The birds: big or small always recreates our mind into a very fascinating way whether they are catching insects or taking food grains from the ground they always impresses us from their acts of moving or flying here and there on the earth.

Take the small pretty bird Sparrow (Passer Passer domestics) it has been vanished away from the villages of northern India. Three decades back every house was full of noise of sparrow songs. The people were happy enough to see the bird chirping here and there in the houses. Sometime they fly into groups to the fields of wheat or paddy. Picking up their share of first crop in the agricultural fields and then again flying away to distant villages and then returning back to see their counterparts happy and safe. The domestic birds have suffered the worst in the last three decades becuse of global warming and pollution.

In the last three decades several birds have been vanished away from the forests, pastures, valleys, wetlands and patch lands, (small scattered forest in a rural area). Some bird species here disappeared or have become endangered in the last one century in the Indian Himalayas. Particularly, the Central Himalayas and Shivalik hills the population of wild birds have disappeared continuously. Changing climate, low rainfall and continuously growing global warming, increasing pollution, receding wetlands, reduction in the area of heathlands and open barren lands have caused the extinction of beautiful birds from the Himalayan States of India.

In the desertland of Rajasthan, the desert quail had disappeared in 1889. Since then, no species of this bird has been spotted in Rajasthan and adjoining areas. This was a big loss for the bird lovers and ornithologists all over the world. It was like a world of birds is gone. The naturologists and ornithologists also believe that this bird may still exist in some parts of Rajasthan deserts. Unfortunately, nobody has noticed its presence in the deserts, forests or agriculture lands by now.

Some beautiful wildfowls and waterfowls of Gujarat have been disappeared in the last one century. The Continuous felling of forests, scratching the grass of barren lands and encroachment of mangroves have made it uneasy for some wild birds to survive in a changed environment or emigrate to some whereelse to other places.

The ornithologists in Gujarat explain into a dreary mood: "During our student days we had spotted from kingfisher and hornbill quite easily but it becomes very difficult to find out the birds like turtle dove, hupoe, bulbul and skylark. We are quite disappointed now as these creatures were our great recreation in free time."

The black preybird in the Shivalik hills is no more visible as it was spotted commonly in the valleys three decades ago. Dhainchoo, Kaljeenth or black prey bird as it is known in the Shivalik hills is quite rare now. The bifurcated tailed bird is visible only after a big effort. The valleys popular for some pheasants and small birds are quite silent and without the songs of birds. This is the most dreary situation for a bird lover who is not capable to locate the beautiful birds of his school days when he passed through scenic valleys and spotted several birds during his taking rest in the open valleys and pastures. "When we pass through these valleys it becomes quite difficult to locate the birds like turtle dove, Skylark. Karaoon, Saraoon, Kaljeenth, Bulbul, Huppoe, Tailorbird, red finch, black finch" teetar, chakore, mouse birds, Neelkanth, Peet Pakshi, Himalayan wildfowls, waterfowls, and cheer Pheasant have become quite rare. Some of the birds of the warm valleys have been migrated to the far off forests and wildlands," said Dr. K.S. Saroj, an expert on wild birds and their habitats.

"A large population of" chanchur" (fuleira birds) one large species and other small species, have been vanished away. Once, there was a heavy noise in these traditional village forests but now there are only a few to be spotted. Where have all the birds are gone," Explains a village woman whose life is spent from village to forest and forest to village just to collect fuel wood and grass for the cattles. "It is quite sad and some time, when we do not see the birds in forests, I do not feel well at all. It is quite disappointing...As far as the question is to maintain the forests, they are in good state now. The plants and trees in the valleys are in the same form and now the growth of the trees is making good progress. The berries and wild fruits have grown again... Then why the birds are not returning in these forests and valleys is quite surprising," she exclaimed.

Chakor: a bird which comes out of the bushes in moonlit nights and moves here and there in open pastures and valleys in search of food is also not visible. A very few population in the valleys is seen in the morning and evening but in a few numbers. Three decades back, there used to be 20, 15, 10 chakor in groups and used to fly from one place to another in search of food and habitation.

Skylark: Three and half decade back I was in "Ghora Dhunghee" a wildland and pasture in Simtoli: Pauri Hills in Garhwal Himalayas and noticed there a large population of skylark making nests on the rock cavities raised from the ground. It was a nice experience to face them. The colour of skylark is just like common sparrow (Passes Passer Domestics) but the tail/and head is quite long. In those days, the whole pasture was a barrenland and there was no growth of forests in the valleys and mountains. Fortunately common sparrow and skylarks both of them like the open pastures without forests and trees. Yes, they like small bushes in the open pastures. At the base of a bush skylark make their nests. Common sparrow make their nests in the traditional houses and in the walls of villages. The food habits of both are the same. In 1970-1976 the population of Skylark in Ghora Dhunghee pastures was thriving and the sparrow at villages was increasing in a large number. At that time, the mountain agriculture was also in good proportion and the farmers were happy. After 1976, there was no monsoon rain and the whole crop dried up. The farmers started to migrate to cities in search of good jobs and well being. The villages remained deserted and isolated.

After 1976 the Ghora Dhunghee pastures developed a new growth of pine trees and the whole pasture was covered with pine forests. New native plants and local bushes. As soon as the pine forest came into existence, the skylark disappeared from the pasture as it had migrated to nearby pastures and open heathlands: a barren wideland with some thorny bushes.

The habitats of skylark are always in open pastures, as they can watch their enemies i.e. snakes, small cat, fox and prey birds from the wide openlands. These animals are always harmful to skylark and its nests.

The eagle sometime penetrates into its nests and eat eggs and baby birds. Seeing the danger of prey birds, the skylarks make their nests into a narrowland wall cavity which externally remains covered with green bushes so that no animal and bird can locate the nests. In this way, skylarks is an expert in making nests. A survey was conducted on the position of land and the location of nests under the green bushes. It was noticed that Skylark makes their nests after observing safety rules of their own.

Dhainchoo (Kaljeenth): It is a beautiful black bird of the Shivalik hills and makes its nests near the river banks in bushes, trees, tall trees and sometime in the branches of bamboo trees. There are some traditional trees and bushes where we have seen its nests. The trees are Khareek (celtis....), Khinna, Sullu (Surai), Pine tree branches, Hissaloo bushes, bamboo tree, and several other trees and bushes. In terai area we have seen its nests on the branches of mango tree after a long span of time.

The bird is seen in the branches of tall trees in the valleys near river banks. It is an amazing bird which struggles very hard to fight against common crow, eagle and other birds of prey and chase, them far away to protect its nest from the invaders.

Dhainchoo has become rare and almost endangered in the Shivalik hills. The reason is clear:

1. There is continuous global warming in the last four decades. The monsoon rain is not sufficient in the hills, almost remain dry.
2. The continuous deforestation of trees and bushes. The forests remain only one third now. The traditional fruit trees, bushes of berries and mangroves have been vanished away from the river banks, wetlands and small ponds.
3. Almost all the wetlands have receded or dried up in the last four decades. The new invading plants are growing up there which are harmful to native plants and herbs.

4. **Increasing Pollution:** The Valleys, rivers and sweet water sources are being polluted by local population and tourists coming from far and away. It is a matter of great concern to all those who love these natural places and want to see them fresh and pollution free.
5. **Loss of original habitats:** It is worth to mention here that most of the habitats, traditional bushes, rock cavities, and wildlands have been developed into houses, roads and agricultural lands. This has badly disturbed the breeding areas of wild animals and birds. The habitat loss is considered the worst and most devastating for the population of wild birds.
6. **Moisture and wetness of land is gone:** In the last 40 years, there was no substantive rainfall in the Shivalik hills as a result the trees, bushes and herbs did not grow at the proper speed. The whole area was turned into a dry zone with a very few grass cover on it.
7. Small rivers, brooklets, rivulets were completely dried up and the aquatic plants and mangroves vanished away from the river banks. The native plants and grasses are being replaced by an invading species of Kala Bansha (black bush) and Lantana Bush (Lantern flower), a thorny bush has come into existence. The whole river belt is badly attacked by these plants and the native vegetation is disappearing away.
8. The river birds and animals like Pankauwa, Bagula, Kingfisher, white paradise, river crow and sand birds have either been migrated to somewhere else or vanished away completely.
9. Some species of waterfowls, wildfowl's and mountain pheasants have been disappeared in the last one century.

The ancient bird Dodo had disappeared from the earth some thousands year ago.

It is learnt that since 1600, 115 species of birds have gone extinct, mostly because of human interference in the forests or hunting them for food.

There was a largest bird on earth Dromornis stirtoni from Australia has been disappeared long ago. The bird lived between one million and 15 million years ago. Its wingspan was 3 meters and weight 500 kg.

The tallest bird was from NewZealand as Dinornus maximus, a giant moa from NewZealand wetlands. It was 3.7 meters. Another extinct bird was South America's the Giant Teraton (Argentavis magnificens) had a wingspan of 6 meters and as large as 7.5 meters.

At present the largest living bird is Ostrich (Struthio Camelus). This everpopular bird stands a magnificent 2.74 meters high and can weigh 160 kg. The heaviest flying bird is Kori Bustard of Africa (Ardeotis Kori) weight 19 kg.

The Eurasian Bustard (Otis tarda) and Mute swan both of which have been recorded at 18 kg.

The wing span is also considered an important object seeing the flying importance of the bird. Andean condor (Vultur gryphus) with wing span of 3 meters. Maribou Stork (Leptoptilus crumeniferous) with a wing span of 2.87 meters.

The birds of sea: The Royal Albatross (Diomedea epomophora) has a wingspan of 3.5 meters. However, the Wandering Albatross (Diomedea exulans) has a wing span of 3.63 meters.

There is a vast majority of bird lovers all over the world. The Royal Society For the Protection of Birds (RSPB) has more than 1.5 million members. The number is increasing every year. The National Audubon Society of America (USA) has 55,000 members worldwide. The Wild Bird Society of Japan has a great numbers of bird lovers in Japan.

There are 9703 species of birds in the world divided into 23 orders, 142 families and 2057 genera (Sibley and Monroe

1992). Birds can be found in every part of the world. From desert to snowland the birds are a great source of human recreation.

The Sudanese Red Cliff Swallow (Hirundo perdita) was last seen in 1984 and the orange-Necked Partridge (Arborophila davidi) was last seen in 1927.

The Mauritius Kestrel (Falco puntatus) once were left 4 last seen in nature but the number now has reached to 300. In the same way the Californian Condor (Gymnogyps california nus) was left 9 to 27 individuals in nature. Now, this has reached to 150. The captive breeding for such birds and animals is quite fruitful. Even a large number of Ostrich birds are being breeded in Captivity and are left in the forests of Africa, Australia, Newzeland and Northern and Southern American forests and deserts.

In many countries, the tigers, lions, eagles, vultures and birds of paradise are being captive breeded just to increase their population in the wild. After the session of their captive breedings is over they are taught natural instincts of hunting and left in the wild forever.

The corn crakes is the most threatened bird globally. In UK, it became extinct one century ago. It was mainly because of intensive farming. Just to make it alive and rejuvenate in nature. The Royal Society for the Protection of Birds, Zoological Society of London and English Nature are combinedly launching project to re-establish corncrake population in England.

Nearly 100 corncrakes had been released in 2005 by The RSPB, Nonewashes resevere in Cambindgeshire eastern England, and the scheme received a boost when a family of corncrake chicks were seen at the reserve.

Unfortunately, there is continuous hunting of common Quail (Coturnix coturnix) and turtle dove (Streptopelia turtur) in the name of organized hunting tourism in Serbia and Montenegro.

Under the Serbian law, these species can be hunted from August to 30 September. Most of the species are declining in most of Europe and are being offered as game birds to visiting foreign hunters, particularly from Italy. There is widespread use of illegal methods of killing, such as the use of pump action guns which allow a single hunter to kill 300 quails in a morning. These are wide spread methods in the northern Vojvodina province and there in concern that protected species such as corncrakes are also falling victim to hunters.

The Bird Protection and Study Society of Vojvodina and League of Ornithologists Action on Serbia and Montenegro have proposed a permanent ban on hunting two target species as well as their removal from the country's game birds list and inclusion on the list of Natural Rarities.

It was more interesting to learn that 20 red kites were released near the Gateshead of northern England as part of the Northern Kites initiative in 2005. The fourth and final phase of the English Red Kite Reintroduction Programme. The birds have not been recorded from Northern England in the last 150 years. This is thought to be the first attempt to introduce the redkite into a semi-urban environment.

The birds have their own freedom to sing in the pastures, forests and valleys. But their songs are affected by habitat fragmentation.

This has been proved by analysis of the song of the nearly threatened Dupont's lark (Cherophilus dupontii. It has revealed that neighbouring larks in fragment at habitats mimic each others songs more closely than in non fragmented habitats. Song mimicry is a common occurrence among birds appears to act as a threat signal between males. It is thought that male larks in fragmented habitats only perceive close neighbours with which they engage in counter singing as rivals.

The Bald Ibis is found in Northern Africa, Turky, Jordan and neighboring countries. This wonder bird is on the verge of extinction because of global warming, climate change and increasing pollution near its habitats. The wetland and marshes where it is found are disappearing away gradually.

The bird is critically endangered. Bald ibis (Geronticus eremita) was the subject of an exhibition of photograph in the old town of Damascas in February 2006. It was seen as an attempt to create mass awareness to promote conservation of this species. It is believed that there are only 20-50 birds surviving in this peculiar environment of the world.

The Indian vultures are on the verge of extinction. The main reason of the declining of Indian vulture species is the use of various insecticides by the farmers for their crops. Some insecticides are responsible for the deaths of vulture community.

The experiments on captive vultures have shown that the non steroidal anti-inflamatory (NSAID) drug Meloxicam has no side effects on the birds unlike the NSAID Diclofenac. The Meloxicam was tested in a number of vulture species and found that it has no side effects at all.

The discovery of 70 white shouldered Ibis (Pseudibis davisoni) at Cambodias Western Siem Pang IBA in November 2005 is an exciting experience. Now the population of this critically endangered bird has reached to 250. The previous highest count was 33 birds in November 2004.

The Ibis decline has been linked to habitat loss, mainly through logging and drainage of wetlands for agriculture. Western Siem Pang IBA is one of the most important sites for birds in Cambodia.

It is also a matter of fact that the ocean wanderers are killing millions of birds every year. According to a satellite tracking data 16 species of albatrosses and three species of petrel are all time threatened by commercial and private long time fishing.

In the waters of NewZealand, Southeast Australia , the South West Indian ocean, South Atlantic and North Pacific, more than 3,00,000 seabirds including 100,000 albatrosses die is bycatch from long time fleets every year.

In the year of 2006, Bird of Paradise (Berlepsch six wired bird) was found in the Foya mountain forests of Western New Guinea.

The Raptors of Estonia: A study in Estonia has found that forest dwelling raptors prefer to nest in natural forests as opposed to managed forests.

It was seen that the ratpors mostly made their nests on the tall trees of ancient forests. In Lebanon, two reserve areas has been established in the area of high biodiversity. Ebel es Saqui, a potential bird area and raptor flying bottleneck and the Kfarzabad Marshlands.

The research on rainforests of South West Sri Lanka has revealed that endemic forest dwelling birds and small mammals find it harder to adjust to modified landscapes other than taxa.

In several studies, it has been noticed that the endemic animal species are none detrimental rather than non-endemic species. Because most of the natural landscapes and eco system is modified according to the needs and nature of the endemic species.

The Western Hemisphere Shorebird Reserve Network, a partnership of organization working to protect shorebirds and their habitats the rough Network across the Americas. The Panama Bay IBA has joined the network to protect its shorebirds and their habitats.

Every year the Upper Panama is visited by 2 million shore birds travelling between North and South America via the Isthmus of Panama. Counts of shorebirds along Panama coast at times exceed 10,000 per km. The site is used by more than 30 percent of the world female population of Western Sand piper (Calidris mauri) and is globally important for atleast six Shorebird species.

The Saker falkons area highly prized birds are traded for falconery in former Russian block countries and Arabia. A large number of such birds are smuggled from the wild of these countries on high prices. These are the prey birds and are used in hunting of wild fowls, rabbits and other birds. In the Arabia, the birds are used for hunting wild birds and hares for food from the very ancient time.

From time to time, Sri Lankan birds have been described with great importance. The last new bird was added was in 1868. A new bird Serendipscopsow (otusthilo hoffmanni was recently described from the island. About this owl was first heard in 1995 but it was until February 2001 that the first picture were obtained. The species was captured and released in August 2001 and a voucher specimen was obtained in November 2002. In a survey in 2004, it was noticed that there are 45 individuals in the lowland rainforests of Kitugala; Kannelia and Eratna Gilimale in the South West of Island.

In the Island of Calayan in the northern most part of Philippines, a new species of bird has been discovered. In May 2004, a new species of "flightless rail" named Calayan Rail (Gallirallus Calayanensis). Its closest relatives is Okinawa rail (Gallirallus okinawae) in the Ryukyu Archipelago off Japan, 100 km, of North.

The new species appears to be almost flightless and restricted to forests on coralline limestone areas, which probably make up more than 50% of the islands surface.

A liquid natural gas company Chevron—Texaco has received authorisation from Mexican Secretary of the Environment and Natural Resources to build, natural gas importation plant off the coast of Tijuana in the lee of the Los Coronados Islands.

The plant will threaten at least 10 sea bird species that nest on islands. The main concern is Xantus murrelet an endemic species that is found only on far Islands.

There is a vast world of birds existing in Arctic, Antarctic, deserts, islands, lakes and in the river banks. In colour, varieties, shape and size these are amazing and are a great source of recreation.

The climatic influence, ecological variations, adaptable ecosystem and the types of forests also make a sense in a variety of bio-diversity. The ecological variations in Tibetan Plateaus, the Western Himalaya, Central Himalaya and Eastern Himalayas has a great difference in the growth and evolution of wildlife. These geographical parts have a different rain fall, snowfall and their typical ecosystems. In true geographical sense, climate varies from place to place.

For example, Sahara desert, Indian Thar desert, Govi desert, Namib desert, Atacama and Patagonia deserts have different geographical formation as well as ecological variations.

The Western Palearctic Zoo-geographical region includes whole of Europe, North Africa Southwards to the central Sahara including the Hoggar and Tibesti, the Middle East wards to the border of Iran (but excluding most of the Arabian Peninsula the Azores, Madeira, the Canary Islands, the Islands of Banc d' Arguin off Mauritania and the Cape Verde Islands. This is the sky way of the sea birds and shore birds who migrate during winter.

Almost, there are some 900 species recorded from Western Palaearctic region. The Western Palaerctic is more natural faunal unit than Europe alone. Since, it is the Sahara and Arabian deserts, not the mediterrenean, that are the true Southern boundaries of Europe. To the east the Ural's and the Caspian form a geographically convenient boundary (but one largely recognised by birds) between the western and eastern Sub-divisions of the vast Palaerctic region that extends to the east across the whole of Asia north of the Himalayas and the mountains of Central China.

The Western Palaearctic Region is important one for the migration of birds during snowfall or winter. This is the traditional Sky fly way of migrating birds.

1. Bank d' Arguin
2. Netherlands
3. Belgium
4. Luxembourg
5. Switzerland
6. Austria
7. Czech Republic
8. Slovakia
9. Hungary
10. Moldova
11. Slovenia
12. Croatia
13. Bosnia Herzegovina
14. Serbia Montenegro
15. Macedonia
16. Albania
17. Balearic Islands
18. Corsica
19. Sardinia
20. Sicily
21. Crete
22. Cyprus
23. Lebanon
24. Israel
25. Jordan
26. Kuwait
27. Georgia
28. Armenia
29. Azerbaijan

The coastal nations of Medeterranean are a heaven for seabirds and shore birds and the coastal wetlands are the largest breeding centres of migrating birds from Europe and Central Asia.

Some of the birds of the World are shown here with their families and some of them are on the verge of extinction. Some of the birds have been left in the wild after captive breeding. Such birds are increasing their population in the wetlands and the moisturous forests.

The birds are:

1. Ostrich	Struthionidac
2. Divers or (loons)	Gavial
3. Grebs	Podicipedidae

4.	Albatrosses	Diomedsidae
5.	Petrels or Shear waters:	Procellaridae
6.	Storm Petrels	Hydrobatidec
7.	Tropic birds	Phacthan Tidac
8.	Gannets and Boobies	Subdac
9.	Cormorants	Phalacrocoracidac
10.	Darters	Anhingidae
11.	Pelicans	Pelecanidae
12.	Frigate birds	Fregatidae
13.	Herons and Egrets	Ardeidae
14.	Storks	Ciconiidae
15.	Ibises and Spoonbills	Threskiornithidae
16.	Flamingos	Phoemicopteridae
17.	Wildflowl (or waterfowl)	Anatidae
18.	Hawks and Eagles	Accipitridae
19.	Osprey	Pandionidae
20.	Falcons	Falconidae
21.	Grouse	Tetraonidac
22.	Pheasants & Partridges	Phasianidae
23.	Goinea fowl	Numididae
24.	Button Quails	Turnicidae
25.	Rails:	Rallidae
26.	Cranes:	Gruidae
27.	Bustards	Otididae
28.	Painted snipes	Rostratulidae
29.	Oyster Catchers	Haematopodidae
30.	Stilts and Avocets	Recurvirostridac
31.	Crab-Plover	Dromadidae

32.	Thick-Knees	Burhinidae
33.	Coursers Pratincoles	Glareolidae
34.	Plovers	Charadriidae
35.	Sand pipers	Scolopacidae
36.	Skuas	Stercorariidae
37.	Gulls	Laridae
38.	Terns	Stermidae
39.	Skimmers	Rynchopidae
40.	Auks (or Alicids)	Alcidae
41.	Sand grouse	Petroclididae
42.	Pigeons and Doves	Columbidae
43.	Parrots	Psittacidae
44.	Cuckoos	Cuculidae
45.	Owls	Tytonidae and Strigidae
46.	Nightjars	Caprimulgidae
47.	Swifts	Apodidae
48.	Kingfisher	Alcedinidae
49.	Bee-eaters	Meropidae
50.	Rollers	Coraciidae
51.	Hoopoes	Upupidae
52.	Wood peckers	Picidae
53.	Tyrant flycatchers	Tyrannidae
54.	Larks	Alaudidae
55.	Swallows and Martins	Hirundinidae
56.	Pipits and Wagtails:	Motacillidae
57.	Bulbuls:	Pycnonotidae
58.	Waxwings and Hypocoliys	Bombay cillidae
59.	Dippers	Cinclidae

60. Wrens	Troglodytidae
61. Mocking birds and Thrashers	Mimidae
62. Accentors:	Prunellidae
63. Thrushes & chats:	Turdidae
64. Warblers:	Sylviidae
65. Fly Catchers:	Muscicipadae
66. Babblers:	Timaliidae
67. Longtailed tits	Aegithalidae
68. Tits:	Paridae
69. Nuthatches:	Sittidae
70. Wallcreepers:	Tichodromadidae
71. Tree creepers:	Certhiidae
72. Penduline tits	Remizidae
73. Sunbirds	Nectarimidae
74. Orioles	Oriolidae
75. Shrikes	Laniidae
76. Crows:	Corvidae
77. Starlings:	Sturnidae
78. Sparrows:	Passeridae
79. Weavers:	Ploceridae
80. Woxbills:	Esterildidae
81. Vireos:	Vireonidae
82. Finches:	Fringillidae
83. American Wood Warblers:	Parulidae
84. Tanagers:	Thraupidae
85. Buntings:	Emberizidae
86. American Orioles and Blackbirds:	Icteridac

The Protection of Wild birds:

The Hinduism and Buddhism are called the religion of protection and conservation in the world. The enlightened and benevolent attitudes towards wildlife conservation helped in the conservation of wildlife in Indian Subcontinent and Sri Lanka. The birds are facing many threats all over the world.

1. The Main Threats:
2. Deforestation Activities:
3. Receding Wetlands
4. Grasslands
5. Deserts
6. Agricultural Habitats:
7. Other Threats:

Main Conservation organizations are supporting the protection of birds:

1. Wild Bird Society of India:
2. Wild Bird Society of Japan.
3. Birdlife International, UK
4. Royal Society for the Protection of Birds, UK
5. Wetlands International—Asia Pacific
6. World Pheasant Association South Asia
7. Worldwide Fund For Nature
8. World Wide Fund For Nepal
9. World Wide Fund For Bhutan
10. Oriental Bird Club, UK
11. Mountain Research Foundation, Dehradun, India
12. Fauna & Flora International, UK
13. Wild Fowl And Wild Land Trust, UK

14. Wild Bird Trust, UK
15. National Society For Clean Air and Environment Protection, UK
16. National Association for Outdoor Education, UK
17. National Association For Environmental Education, UK
18. Marine Conservation Society, UK
19. Living Earth, UK
20. International Centre For Conservation Education, UK
21. Institute For Earth Education, UK
22. Friends of Earth, UK
23. Green Peace, UK
24. Environmental Council UK
25. Council for Environmental Education, UK
26. The Asiatic Society, Bombay
27. Institute of Wildlife Study
28. Peoples Initiative for Environment, Himachal, India
29. Hornbill Research Foundation, Thailand
30. Scottish Natural Heritage, UK
31. Bird Protection & Study Society of Vojvodina
32. League for Ornithological Action, Serbia & Montenegro
33. The Hans Foundation, India : Environment, education and lifestyle, health, hygiene and peoples action.
34. The Hans Foundation: Environmental Awareness, Conservation, Reforestation, Wetlands conservation, wildlife and Eco-tourism studies
35. Vulture conservation and Breeding Centre, Pinjore, Haryana
36. Ostrich Research Centre, Australia

37. Wildlife Captive Breeding Centre, Kruger National Park, South Africa
38. International Society for Mountains Study and Research, Dehradun, India.
39. Orangutan Research Centre, Borneo.
40. Milky Stock Research Centre, Philippines
41. Tsomoriri Conservation Trust, Leh, Ladakh, India

Acronyms

ATP	Asian Tiger Project
AEP	Asian Elephant Project
AACL	Association of Alpine Clubs of India
AOS	American Orchid Society
AWA	American Wilderness Alliance
AWF	African Wildlife Foundation,
IPA	Important Plant Areas
IBA	Important Bird Areas
ISGVI	International Society For Global Villages of India
ISWFAP	International Society For Wildflowers and Alpine Plants, India
IWA	International Wilderness Association India
IDS	Institute of Development Studies, UK
IWL	International Wilderness Leadership, USA
FFI	Fauna and Flora International, UK
ACIAR	Australian Council for International Agricultural Research
ACORD	Agency Cooperation Research and Development
ADRAO	Association de Development du d' Afrique Quest (WARDA)
AERDD	Agricultural Extension and Rural Development Department (UK)

AGRITEX	Government of Zimbabwe Agricultural Extension Service
ASARECA	Association for Strengthening Agricultural Research in Eastern and Central Africa
AWF	African Wildlife Foundation
BAIF	Bharatiya Agro-Industries Foundation
BIRD	BAIF Institute for Rural Development (India)
BRAC	Bangladesh Rural Advencement Committee
CABI	Commonwealth Agricultural Research and Development Institute
CABUNGO	Capacity Building Unit for NGOs
CARDI	Caribbean Agricultural Research and Development Institute
CATIE	Research and Training Center for Tropical Agronomy (Costa Rica)
CAZRI	Central Arid Zone Research Institute
CECAT	China-EU Centre for Agricultural Technology
CDRN	Community Development Resource Network (Uganda)
CIAT	International Center for Tropical Agriculture
CIKARD	Center for Indigenous Knowledge for Agricultural and Rural Development (USA)
CIMMYT	International Center for the Improvement of Maize and Wheat
CIRAD	Center for International Cooperation in Agricultural Development Research (France)
CTA	Technical Center For Agricultural and Rural Corporation (The Netherlands)
DANIDA	Danish International Development Assistance
DARSHN	Development Action Through Self Help Network (India)

DFID	Department for International Development (UK)
DRN	Development Researchers' Network
DSE	Development Researchers Network
ECDPM	European Center for Development Policy Management
ETC	Educational Training Consultants
FADO	Finnish Organisation for Assistance in Development
FAO	United Nations Food and Agriculture Organisation
FCO	Foreign and Commonwealth Office (UK)
FINNIDA	Finnish Development Agency
GRET	Group for Technological Research (France)
GTZ	German Agency for Technical Cooperation
IARI	Indian Agricultural Research Institute
ICAFDA	International Centre for Agricultural Research in Dry Areas
ICIMOD	International Center for Integrated Mountain Development
ICLARM	International Center for Living Aquatic Resources Management (Philippines)
GHF	Greenland Heritage Foundation
TWS	The Wilderness Society USA
NCWFR	National Commission For Wild Flower Research
NEWFS	New England Wildflower Society
NWFRC	New England Wildflower Research Center
PCA	Predator Conservation Alliance
WAW	Wild Alabama Wilderness
ICRAF	International Center for Research in Agroforestry

ECRISAT	International Center for Research in the Semi-Arid Tropics
IDES	Interface Development Interventions
IDPM	Institute Development Policy and Management (UK)
IDRC	International Development Research Council (Canada)
IGADD	Inter Governmental Authority on Drought and Development
IGFRI	Indian Grassland and Fodder Research Institute
IIED	International Institute for Environment and Development (UK)
IIEE	International Institute for Environment Education (Sri Lanka)
IIRR	International Institute of Rural Reconstruction (Philippines)
IITA	International Institute of Tropical Agriculture (Nigeria)
ILEIA	Information Center for Low External Input Agriculture (The Netherlands)
ILRI	International Livestock Research Institute
INRA	National Institute for Agronomic Research (France)
IRMA	Institute of Rural Management
IRRI	International Rice Research Institute
ISNAR	International Center for Low external Input Agriculture (The Netherlands)
ITDG	Intermediate Technology Development Group (UK)
IUCN	World Conservation Union
JIVC	Japan International Volunteer Center

KIT	Royal Tropical Institute (The Netherlands)
KRIBHCO	Krishak Bharati Cooperative Ltd. (India)
MARDI	Malaysian Research and Development Institute
NARO	National Agricultural Research Organisation (Uganda)
NCAP	National Center for Agricultural Economy and Policy Research
NORAGRIC	Norwegian Center of International Agricultural Development
NRI	Natural Resources Institute (UK)
ODI	Overseas Development Institute (UK)
RIMISP	International Network for Methodology and research Production Systems (Chile)
SIDA	Swedish International Development Cooperation Agency
UNDP	United Nations Development Programme
USAID	United States Agency for International Development
WARDA	West Africa Rice Development Association
WARF	West Africa Rural Foundation
WWF	World Wide Fund of Nature
WFPS	Wild Flowers Preservation Society. USA
WEA	Wilderness Education Association USA
FOW	Friends of Wilderness
IWL	International Wilderness Leadership
WSL	Wilderness Survival League
WTY	Wilderness Trek for Youth
WUEA	Wilderness Use Education Association
WIW	Women in the Wilderness
WHC	Wild Heritage Campaign

WTU	Wild Things Unlimited
UNEP	United Nations Environment Programme, New Delhi
UNU	United Nations University, Tokyo, Japan
ECDO	Eco System Development Organisation, Nigeria
WPRPL	Woodville Palace Resorts Private Limited, Shimla, India
WAO	Woodville Apple Orchards, Nerwa, HP, India
IOS	International Orchid Society, Dehradun
IFS	International Fern Society, Dehradun
IOC	International Orchid Club, Dehradun
IFC	International Fern Club, Dehradun
IFC	International Field Council, UK

References

1. Wildlife and Eco-Tourism, Taj Rawat, Paryavaran Magazine, Ministry of Environment and Forestry.
2. American Herbal News Bulletin USA.
3. The Botanical Market Place, Robert D'McCaleb, USA.
4. The Wilderness Society Bulletin, USA.
5. Journal of Non-Timber Forest products, Taj Rawat
6. Ethnobotanical Studies, Indian Journal of Forestry
7. Glimpes of Indian Ethnobotany, S.K. Jain, IBH
8. Evolution of Crop Plants, Simmonds, NW, Longman
9. Environment of The Himalayas, Taj Rawat
10. Eco Forum, Nairobi, Kenya.
11. Wilderness Management in the Mountains, Taj Rawat
12. The Beauty of Orchids, Taj Rawat, Hindustan Times, April 28, 96.
13. Japanese Journal of Himalayan Botany, Univ. of Tokyo.
14. Herb Products, American Herbs Association, CA, USA.
15. The Orchids, American Orchid Society Fl, USA.
16. Fauna and Flora International Cambridge, UK.
17. Pahari-Kheti Bari-Medicinal Plants, G.B.P. University
18. The Valley of Gods and Goddesses Taj Rawat, (Press)
19. Exploring the High Mountain Pastures Taj Rawat, (Press)

20. Lindleyana, American Orchid Society 1997.
21. The Ecologist, UK.
18. Flora: New Threat, Raj Chengappa, India Today, May 31, 1993.
19. Conservation of Orchid Forests of Dehradun, National Herald 1996, Taj Rawat.
20. Lindleyana, American Orchid Society 1997.
21. The Ecologist, UK.
22. Science, AAAS. USA.
23. Nature Resources, UNESCO, Paris France.
24. Environment Conservation, Univ, New Castle, U.K.
25. Indian Journal of Botany, ICSR, New Delhi.
26. Medicinal Plants of the Garhwal Hills, Taj Rawat (Press)
27. Farm Radio Bulletins, Developing Countries Farm Radio Network, Canada.
28. The Great American Wilderness, WWF-1997.
29. Hamara Paryavaran, Taj Rawat Takshshila Publishing
30. Mountain Tourism and Range Land Management, ICIMOD, Kathmandu, Nepal.
31. Oryx, Fauna and Flora International, U.K.
32. The Importance of Tibetan Plateau, Environment of the Himalayas by Taj Rawat, New Delhi.
33. Wild life Habitat Enhancement Council, Silver Springs, MD, USA.
34. Wilderness Medical Society, CA, USA.
35. Wildernes Watch, WI, USA.
36. Wildernes Education Association, New York, USA.
37. Rocky Mountain Center for Botanical Studies, Boulder Co., USA.
38. Adventure Education, U.K.
39. Wilderness Society, Washington DC, USA.

40. Wildlife Harvest Magazine, Gooselake, IA, USA.
41. Natural History Magazine, NY, USA.
42. International Wilderness Association, Woodville Resorts, Shimla.
43. Grassland Heritage Foundtion, USA.
44. The Wild Foundation, CA, USA.
45. International Society For Mountain Studies and Research, New Delhi.
46. International Society For Global Village of India, New Delhi.
47. The Mountaineers, WA, USA.
48. Falcon Publishing Inc. MT, USA.
49. Nomad Mountain Publications UK.
50. The Wilderness Society, USA.
51. The Woodville Palace Resorts Pvt. Ltd., Shimla, H.P.
52. The Woodville Orchards, Nerwa, H.P., India
53. Geography of Tourism and Recreation Michael Hill Stephen J. Page Routledge, UK.
54. Encyclopedia of Eco-Tourism, Weaver, Cabi-UK.
55. Managing Environment For Leisure And Recreation, Broad Hurst, UK
56. Eco-Tourism in Less Development World, Weaver, Cabi, UK.
57. Tourism in Western Europe, Cabi, UK
58. Wilderness Management and Eco-Tourism: Taj Rawat, Sunshine, New Delhi.
59. Exploring The High Mountain Wilderness: Taj Rawat, (Press) New Delhi.
60. Vishwa Paryavaran: Ek Adhyayan, Taj Rawat, Praveen Prakashan New Delhi.
61. Paryavaran Paryatan Evam Lok Sanskriti, Taj Rawat, New Academic Publishers.

62. Paryatan Bazar, Sanchar Evan Vigyapan Prabandhan, Taj Rawat.
63. Paryaravan Paryatan Evam Prabandhan, Taj Rawat, Takshshila.
64. Progressing Tourism Research Bill Faulkner-Viva Books.
65. Shopping Tourism: Daldon Timothy-Viva
66. Recreational Tourism: ChisRyan-Viva Books
67. Natural Areas Tourism: Newsome: Moare and Douling
68. Tourism and Employment: Sharplley Telfer
69. Tourism and Employment: Riley, Ladkin, Szivas
70. Tourism, Globalization and Cultural Change, Donald Mcleod.
71. Tourism Marketing: Fyall and Garrod
72. Tourism, Recreation and Climate Change. Hall and Higham
73. Sport Tourism: Ritchei and Adain
74. Sport Tourism Development. Hinch and Higham
75. Tourism Mobility and Second Home: Hall and Muller
76. Tourism Development: Issues for Vulnerable Industry.
77. Nature based Tourism in Peripheral Areas. Hall and Boyd
78. Holidays and Celebration: Mathen Denni
79. Encyclopaedia of Earth Science
80. Encyclopaedia of Environmental Studies. Ashworth/Lihle
81. Encyclopaedia of World Geography. RM Mccou
82. Encyclopaedia of Biology. Rithner and Mcabe
83. Encyclopaedia of Blizzards: Michael Alkmby
84. Sustainable Tourism. Lasly France: Earthscan
85. The Global Environment: Vig and Axelord
86. Global Action for Bio-diversity: Twnethy Swanson

87. Global Environment; Outlook, UNEP
88. The Root Causes of Biodiversity loss: Wood and Mary Earthen.
89. The Basis of Rural Tourism: International Perspectives. J. Page D. Getz.
90. Community, Ecology and Environment VK Prabhakar.
91. Across the Peaks and Passes in Garhwal Himalaya: H. Kapadia.
92. Across The Himalayan Gap: An Indian Quest for Understanding China/Tan Chung.
93. Agricultural Modernisation in Eastern Himalayas: MC Behra.
94. Alpine Plants of Western Himalayas C.M. Sharma.
95. Altai Himalaya: Travel Diary: N. Roerich
96. Bio-diversity and Environment A. Kumar
97. Bio-diversity social and Ecological Perspective.
98. Bio-diversity and its Conservation in India: S.S. Negi
99. British Kumaon Garhwal: R.S. Tolia.
100. Central Asia and Tibet : Seven Hedin
101. Central Asia and Kashmir Himalaya : P. Kachroo
102. Aspects of Geology and Environment of the Himalaya: Charu Pant, Arun Sharma
103. Comprehensive Ecological Botanical Survey of the Grasses : A.B. Chaudhuri.
104. Citadel of Ice Dakshin Gangotri: The First Indian Wintering in Antarctica: Satya S. Sharma.
105. Chamba Himalaya: Amazing land, Unique Culture: R. Bharati.
106. Ecological Crisis is the Himalayas S.K. Chadha.
107. Ecological Impact of Apple Cultivation in the Himalaya Vir Singh.

108. Himalayan Biodiversity : Conservation Strategies: U. Dhar.

109. Himalayan Desert : (Tibet, Ladakh, Lahaul, Spiti, Mustang. Nina Rao

110. High Pasturelands of Ladakh Himalaya, Prem Singh Jeena.

111. Himalaya : Environment, Resources and Development NK Shah.

112. Himalayan Kingdom: Roof of the World: Jon Burbank.

113. Himalayan Mysteries: Ganesh Saili.

114. Trekking in the Himalaya: Harshpat Singh.

115. TransHimalaya Discoveries and Adventures : Sven Hedin.

116. Flora of Corbett National Park: P.C. Pant, Botanical Survey

117. Plant Wealth of Nanda Devi Biosphere Reserve: Bipin Balodi, P.K. Hajra, Botanical Survey of India

118. Forest Ecology and Conservation: Adrian C. Newton, Oxford University Press

119. High Altitude Wetlands of Ladakh: WWF India: 2002

120. Flora of Great Himalayan National Park: S.K. Singh, G.S. Rawat: Bishan-Mahendra, Dehradun

121. Ungulates of India: Wildlife Institute of India, Dehradun

122. Wellands: National Research Council, USA

123. Indian Wetlands Birds and Conservation: Arun Kumar, JP sati.

124. Bio-diversity in India: J.P. Rao, National Botanical Research Institute

125. Bio-diversity Action Plan Bhutan: 2002

126. Field Days. AJT John Singh: Wildlife Institutes of India.

Index

C

U

W

Y

Z